5 ingredient COOKBOOK

Taste of Home BOOKS

RDA ENTHUSIAST BRANDS, LLC
MILWAUKEE, WI

Taste of Home. Reader's digest

EDITORIAL

Editor-in-Chief: Catherine Cassidy
Creative Director: Howard Greenberg
Editorial Operations Director: Kerri Balliet

Managing Editor, Print & Digital Books: Mark Hagen
Associate Creative Director: Edwin Robles Jr.

Editor: Christine Rukavena
Art Director: Jessie Sharon
Layout Designer: Courtney Lovetere
Editorial Production Manager: Dena Ahlers
Copy Chief: Deb Warlaumont Mulvey
Copy Editors: Mary-Liz Shaw, Dulcie Shoener
Contributing Copy Editor: Steph Kilen

Content Operations Manager: Colleen King
Content Operations Assistant: Shannon Stroud
Editorial Services Administrator: Marie Brannon

Food Editors: James Schend; Peggy Woodward, RD
Recipe Editors: Mary King; Jenni Sharp, RD; Irene Yeh

Test Kitchen & Food Styling Manager: Sarah Thompson
Test Cooks: Nicholas Iverson (lead), Matthew Hass,
Lauren Knoelke
Food Stylists: Kathryn Conrad (senior), Leah Rekau,
Shannon Roum
Prep Cooks: Megumi Garcia, Melissa Hansen,
Bethany Van Jacobson, Sara Wirtz

Photography Director: Stephanie Marchese
Photographers: Dan Roberts, Jim Wieland
Photographer/Set Stylist: Grace Natoli Sheldon
Set Stylists: Stacey Genaw, Melissa Haberman, Dee Dee Jacq
Photo Studio Assistant: Ester Robards

Editorial Business Manager: Kristy Martin
Editorial Business Associate: Samantha Lea Stoeger

BUSINESS

General Manager, Taste of Home Cooking School:
Erin Puariea
Executive Producer, Taste of Home Online Cooking School:
Karen Berner

THE READER'S DIGEST ASSOCIATION, INC.

President and Chief Executive Officer: Bonnie Kintzer
Chief Financial Officer: Colette Chestnut
Vice President, Chief Operating Officer, North America:
Howard Halligan
Vice President, Enthusiast Brands, Books & Retail:
Harold Clarke
Chief Marketing Officer: Leslie Dukker Doty
Senior Vice President, Global HR & Communications:
Phyllis E. Gebhardt, SPHR
Vice President, Brand Marketing: Beth Gorry
Vice President, Chief Technology Officer: Aneel Tejwaney
Vice President, Consumer Marketing Planning: Jim Woods

For other *Taste of Home* books and products, visit us at
tasteofhome.com.

For more Reader's Digest products and information,
visit **rd.com** (in the United States) or **rd.ca** (in Canada).

International Standard Book Number: 978-1-61765-408-4
Library of Congress Control Number: 2014957259

Pictured on front cover:
Easy Stuffed Shells, page 78; Fudgy Mint Cookies, page 238;
Shrimp Pasta Alfredo, page 137; Roasted Turkey with Maple
Cranberry Glaze, page 120; Strawberry Cake, page 206.

Pictured on back cover: S'Moreos, page 236; Chicken &
Vegetable Kabobs, page 113; Burger Americana, page 64.

Pictured on spine: Cranberry-Apricot Pork Tenderloins,
page 100.

Printed in China.
1 3 5 7 9 10 8 6 4 2

Contents

MINISTER'S DELIGHT, 227

MARMALADE FRENCH TOAST SANDWICHES, 15

ZESTY CHICKEN SOFT TACOS, 111

SPINACH-ARTICHOKE RIGATONI, 145

Breakfast 6
Appetizers & Beverages 24
Soups & Sandwiches 48
Beef 70
Pork 88
Poultry 106
Fish & Seafood 124
Meatless 140
Salads & Salad Dressings . . . 150
Sides & Condiments 162
Breads & Rolls 188
Cakes, Pies & Desserts 202
Cookies, Bars & Candies 228
Indexes 246

SLOW COOKER BEEF AU JUS, 75

 LIKE US
facebook.com/tasteofhome

 **TWEET US**
@tasteofhome

 FOLLOW US
pinterest.com/taste_of_home

SHOP WITH US
shoptasteofhome.com

SHARE A RECIPE
tasteofhome.com/submit

Take5

CRISPY BAKED CHICKEN, 112

IT'S TRUE! Delicious homemade dinners are just minutes away with the **427 incredibly easy recipes** you'll find inside. Best of all, each dish in this collection uses just **5 ingredients or less!** Save time and money with these simple family favorites from smart home cooks. (Recipes may also call for salt, pepper, water, and canola or olive oil.)

Inside, you'll find:

- More than **11 dozen easy dinners** that conveniently make the most of your kitchen time
- **Sides, salads and other dishes** to round out meals: **75 in all**
- **77 tantalizing sweets** so there's always time for dessert
- Dozens of **in-a-flash breads, snacks, breakfasts** and more

Look for these **handy icons** throughout the book.

FAST FIX

Eat great on even your busiest days. Discover 200+ recipes table-ready in 30 minutes or less!

SLOW COOKER

Savor slow-cooked entrees, side dishes, sandwiches, soups and more. Simmer up these 23 delicious dishes while you're on the go!

5 Success Tips for Busy Cooks!

1 *Start with ingredients that pile on the flavor.* Jarred sauces, packaged mixes and canned soups offer simple, tasty jumpstarts to mealtime. **Dawn Bartholomew's** Spinach Pizza uses pizza crust mix, jarred Alfredo sauce and a packaged blend of cheeses. *page 147*

2 *Use mixes in surprising new ways.* Cookies and bars made from cake mix can be just the beginning! For example, biscuit mix is the shortcut to Sour Cream Blueberry Muffins from **Tory Ross** of Cincinnati, Ohio. *page 198*

3 *Fake your way to homemade with easy add-ins to convenience products.* Chopped fresh apple, celery and onion quickly dress up boxed stuffing mix in **Terri McKitrick's** winning recipe for Apple Stuffing. Enjoy it with pork chops, chicken or turkey. *page 181*

4 *Get back to basics with wholesome dishes that let the ingredients shine.* Savor the simple joys of classic dishes such as homemade yeast bread, creme brulee custard and more. **Joan Churchill's** Scallops in Sage Cream recipe highlights the seafood's delicate flavor with fresh sage and a simply elegant shallot cream sauce. *page 126*

5 *Feel free to experiment and make the recipe your own.* Whip up **Taste of Home's** signature homemade pesto using a blend of basil, cilantro, parsley...whatever you have on hand. Use it in any of the eight dishes that feature pesto, which you'll find in the recipe index. Or come up with your own way to serve your creation! *page 184*

**TENA KROPP'S LOADED
BREAKFAST POTATOES**
PAGE 17

Breakfast

**CHRISTEEN PRZEPIOSKI'S
BANANA CHIP PANCAKES**
PAGE 12

**TRUDIE HAGEN'S MAPLE-GLAZED
SAUSAGES** *PAGE 14*

**FRANCES PIETSCH'S NUTTY
WAFFLE SANDWICHES**
PAGE 22

Scrambled Egg Poppers

These handy grab-and-go breakfast buns are ideal for weekday mornings. They're sure to be a favorite with the kids.

—**KATIE WILLIAMS** BLACK CREEK, WI

PREP: 15 MIN. • **BAKE:** 25 MIN. •**MAKES:** 8 SERVINGS

- 2 loaves (1 pound each) frozen whole wheat bread dough, thawed
- 8 eggs
- ½ cup fat-free milk
- ¼ teaspoon salt
- ¼ teaspoon pepper
- ½ cup bacon bits, divided
- ½ cup shredded cheddar cheese

1. Preheat oven to 350°. Divide each loaf into eight pieces. Roll into balls. Place in muffin cups coated with cooking spray. Bake 20-25 minutes or until golden brown.

2. Meanwhile, in a large bowl, whisk eggs, milk, salt and pepper; stir in ¼ cup bacon bits. Coat a large nonstick skillet with cooking spray and place over medium heat. Add egg mixture to skillet (mixture should set immediately at edges).

3. As eggs set, push cooked edges toward the center, letting uncooked portion flow underneath. When the eggs are set, remove from the heat.

4. Using a melon baller, scoop out the center of each roll, leaving a ¼-in. shell (discard removed bread or save for another use). Spoon 3 tablespoons cooked egg mixture into each roll. Top with remaining bacon bits and sprinkle with cheese. Bake 2-3 minutes longer or until cheese is melted.

SCRAMBLED EGG POPPERS

Pull-Apart Caramel Coffee Cake

The first time I made this delightful treat for a brunch party, it was a huge hit. Now I get requests every time family or friends do anything around the breakfast hour! I always keep the four simple ingredients on hand.

—**JAIME KEELING** KEIZER, OR

PREP: 10 MIN. • **BAKE:** 25 MIN. • **MAKES:** 12 SERVINGS

- 2 tubes (12 ounces each) refrigerated flaky buttermilk biscuits
- 1 cup packed brown sugar
- ½ cup heavy whipping cream
- 1 teaspoon ground cinnamon

1. Preheat oven to 350°. Cut each biscuit into four pieces; arrange evenly in a 10-in. fluted tube pan coated with cooking spray. Combine brown sugar, cream and cinnamon; pour over biscuits.

2. Bake 25-30 minutes or until golden brown. Cool coffee cake 5 minutes before inverting onto a serving platter.

DID YOU KNOW?

Dark brown sugar contains more molasses than light or golden brown sugar. The types are generally interchangeable in recipes. But if you prefer a bolder flavor, choose dark brown sugar.

MEAL IN A
MUFFIN PAN

Meal in a Muffin Pan

This meal-in-a-pan breakfast is ideal for busy weekday mornings. I just add fresh fruit and beverages.
—**MICHELLE PLUMB** MONTROSE, CO

PREP: 20 MIN. • **BAKE:** 15 MIN. • **MAKES:** 4-6 SERVINGS

- 1 can (15 ounces) corned beef hash
- 6 eggs
   Salt and pepper to taste
- 1 package (8½ ounces) corn bread/muffin mix

1. Preheat oven to 400°. Grease a 12-cup muffin pan. Divide hash into six of the cups; press onto the bottom and up the sides to form a shell. Break an egg into each shell; season with salt and pepper. Mix muffins according to package directions. Spoon batter into the other six cups.
2. Bake 15-20 minutes or until muffins are golden brown and eggs are set.

FAST FIX
Creamy Peaches

High in protein and virtually fat-free, this creamy fruit dish can double as a healthy dessert.
—**DON PROKIDANSKY** NEW PORT RICHEY, FL

START TO FINISH: 10 MIN. • **MAKES:** 4 SERVINGS

- 1 can (15 ounces) sliced peaches in extra-light syrup, drained
- 1½ cups (12 ounces) fat-free cottage cheese
- 4 ounces fat-free cream cheese, cubed
   Sugar substitute equivalent to 1 tablespoon sugar

1. Thinly slice four peach slices; set aside for garnish. Place remaining peaches in a food processor; add cottage cheese. Cover and process until blended. Add cream cheese and sugar substitute; cover and process until blended.
2. Spoon into four serving dishes. Top with reserved peaches. Refrigerate until serving.
NOTE *This recipe was tested with Splenda no-calorie sweetener.*

JAM 'N' CREAM
FRENCH TOAST

Jam 'n' Cream French Toast

My grandmother used to make this for me when I was a child. You can experiment with other flavors of jam and bread.

—**B. MACKINNON** KODAK, TN

START TO FINISH: 10 MIN. • **MAKES:** 1 SERVING

- 2 **tablespoons cream cheese, softened**
- 2 **thick slices cinnamon-raisin bread**
- 2 **tablespoons strawberry jam**
- 1 **egg**
- 1 **tablespoon butter**
  Maple syrup, optional

1. Spread cream cheese on one slice of bread. Spread jam on the other slice; place jam side down over the cream cheese. In a shallow bowl, beat egg. Dip both sides of bread into egg.
2. In a small skillet, melt butter; toast bread for 3-4 minutes on each side or until golden brown. Serve with syrup if desired.

FAST FIX

Sausage Cheese Biscuits

These biscuits are a brunch-time favorite. I love that they don't require any special ingredients.

—**MARLENE NEIDEIGH** MYRTLE POINT, OR

START TO FINISH: 30 MIN. • **MAKES:** 10 SERVINGS

- 1 **tube (12 ounces) refrigerated buttermilk biscuits**
- 1 **package (8 ounces) frozen fully cooked breakfast sausage links, thawed**
- 2 **eggs, beaten**
- ½ **cup shredded cheddar cheese**
- 3 **tablespoons chopped green onions**

1. Preheat oven to 400°. Roll out each biscuit into a 5-in. circle; place each in an ungreased muffin cup. Cut sausages into fourths; brown in a skillet. Drain. Divide sausages among cups.
2. In a small bowl, combine eggs, cheese and onions; spoon into cups. Bake 13-15 minutes or until browned.

Cherry Yogurt

Top this thick, rich yogurt with wholesome granola for a quick breakfast. Or layer it in a parfait glass with granola and fruit for something special. It will keep in the refrigerator for a week. Look for 100% cherry juice at the store; the cocktail blends have added sugar.

—**TASTE OF HOME TEST KITCHEN**

PREP: 10 MIN. + CHILLING • **MAKES:** 3 CUPS

- 4 **cups (32 ounces) reduced-fat plain yogurt**
- 1 **cup frozen pitted dark sweet cherries, thawed and quartered**
- ½ **cup cherry juice**
- 3 **tablespoons confectioners' sugar**
- 1½ **teaspoons vanilla extract**

1. Line a strainer with four layers of cheesecloth or one coffee filter and place over a bowl. Place yogurt in prepared strainer; cover yogurt with edges of cheesecloth. Refrigerate for 8 hours or overnight.
2. Remove yogurt from cheesecloth and discard liquid from bowl. Place yogurt in a small bowl; stir in the remaining ingredients. Cover and refrigerate until serving.

APPLE SAUSAGE PUFFS

FAST FIX

Apple Sausage Puffs

I love serving these tender little puffs when I entertain during the holiday season. I need just four basic ingredients to prepare them, and no one is able to resist.
—VERONICA JOHNSON JEFFERSON CITY, MO

START TO FINISH: 25 MIN. • **MAKES:** 2 DOZEN

- 1 **pound bulk pork sausage**
- 1 **medium apple, finely chopped**
- 3 **ounces cream cheese, softened**
- 3 **tubes (8 ounces each) refrigerated crescent rolls**

1. Preheat oven to 375°. In a large skillet, cook sausage and apple over medium heat until meat is no longer pink; drain. Stir in cream cheese.
2. Unroll one tube of crescent dough; separate into eight triangles. Place 1 tablespoon filling on the long side of each triangle. Roll up, starting with the long side; pinch seams to seal.
3. Place point side down 2 in. apart on a greased baking sheet. Repeat with remaining crescent dough and filling. Bake 10-12 minutes or until golden brown. Serve warm.

FAST FIX

Banana Chip Pancakes

Perfect for weekends or a special birthday-morning treat, these fluffy pancakes can be customized to your heart's content! One of my kids eats the plain banana pancakes, another likes just chocolate chips added, and a third one goes for the works.
—CHRISTEEN PRZEPIOSKI NEWARK, CA

START TO FINISH: 30 MIN. • **MAKES:** 12 PANCAKES

- 2 **cups biscuit/baking mix**
- 1 **egg**
- 1 **cup milk**
- 1 **cup mashed ripe bananas**
- ¾ **cup swirled milk chocolate and peanut butter chips**
  Maple syrup and additional swirled milk chocolate and peanut butter chips, optional

1. Place biscuit mix in a large bowl. Whisk the egg, milk and bananas; stir into biscuit mix just until moistened. Stir in chips.
2. Pour batter by ¼ cupfuls onto a greased hot griddle; turn when bubbles form on top. Cook until the second side is golden brown. Serve with syrup and additional chips if desired.

SAUSAGE HASH SKILLET

Green 'n' Gold Egg Bake

This dish has a delicious spinach flavor that's welcome for breakfast or as a light lunch.
—**MURIEL PACELEO** MONTGOMERY, NY

PREP: 15 MIN. • **BAKE:** 45 MIN. • **MAKES:** 9 SERVINGS

- 1 cup seasoned bread crumbs, divided
- 2 packages (10 ounces each) frozen chopped spinach, thawed and squeezed dry
- 3 cups (24 ounces) 4% cottage cheese
- ½ cup grated Romano or Parmesan cheese
- 5 eggs

1. Preheat oven to 350°. Sprinkle ¼ cup bread crumbs into a greased 8-in.-square baking dish. Bake 3-5 minutes or until golden brown.
2. Meanwhile, in a large bowl, combine spinach, cottage cheese, Romano cheese, three eggs and remaining crumbs. Spread over the baked crumbs. Beat remaining eggs; pour over spinach mixture.
3. Bake, uncovered, at 350° 45 minutes or until a knife inserted near the center comes out clean. Let stand 5-10 minutes before serving.

FAST FIX ▶
Sausage Hash Skillet

I created this recipe working only with what I had in the refrigerator. It's a terrific way to use up leftover potatoes from last night's dinner. Skin-on red potatoes are terrific here.
—**KARI KELLEY** PLAINS, MT

START TO FINISH: 30 MIN. • **MAKES:** 2 SERVINGS

- ½ pound bulk pork sausage
- 2½ cups cubed cooked potatoes
- 1 cup thinly sliced sweet onion
- 1 cup sliced fresh mushrooms
- 2 tablespoons butter
- ¼ teaspoon salt
- ¼ teaspoon pepper

1. In a large heavy skillet over medium heat, cook sausage until no longer pink; drain and set aside.
2. In the same skillet, cook and stir the potatoes, onion and mushrooms in butter until potatoes are lightly browned. Stir in the sausage, salt and pepper; heat through.

GREEN 'N' GOLD EGG BAKE

WEEKEND BREAKFAST BAKE

Weekend Breakfast Bake

My family really enjoys this rich, satisfying breakfast casserole on weekends and holidays. I love that it's so quick to prepare.

—MELISSA BALL PEARISBURG, VA

PREP: 15 MIN. • **BAKE:** 30 MIN.
MAKES: 8 SERVINGS

- 1 **pound bulk pork sausage**
- ⅓ **cup chopped onion**
- 4 **cups (16 ounces) shredded Monterey Jack or cheddar cheese**
- 8 **eggs**
- 1 **can (10¾ ounces) condensed cream of mushroom soup, undiluted**

1. Preheat oven to 400°. In a large skillet, cook sausage and onion over medium heat until meat is no longer pink; drain. Transfer to a greased 13x9-in. baking dish. Sprinkle with cheese. Whisk eggs and soup; pour over cheese.

2. Bake casserole, uncovered, 30-35 minutes or until a knife inserted near the center comes out clean. Let stand 5 minutes before cutting.

FAST FIX

Maple-Glazed Sausages

These sugar-and-spice sausages are my first choice when I want to round out a morning menu of French toast and fruit compote.

—TRUDIE HAGEN ROGGEN, CO

START TO FINISH: 20 MIN.
MAKES: 10 SERVINGS

- 2 **packages (6.4 ounces each) frozen fully cooked breakfast sausage links**
- 1 **cup maple syrup**
- ½ **cup packed brown sugar**
- 1 **teaspoon ground cinnamon**

In a large skillet, brown sausage links. In a small bowl, combine the syrup, brown sugar and cinnamon; pour over sausages. Bring to a boil. Reduce heat; simmer, uncovered, until sausages are glazed.

FAST FIX

Peanut Butter Banana Oatmeal

The classic flavors of peanut butter and bananas come together in this kid- and adult-friendly oatmeal. We have eaten it many a morning.

—DEBORAH PURDUE WESTLAND, MI

START TO FINISH: 15 MIN.
MAKES: 4 SERVINGS

- 3 **cups milk or water**
- ¼ **teaspoon salt**
- 1½ **cups quick-cooking oats**
- 2 **large bananas, sliced**
- 2 **tablespoons peanut butter**
- ½ **teaspoon vanilla extract**

In a large saucepan, bring the milk and salt to a boil. Stir in oats; cook for 1-2 minutes or until thickened, stirring occasionally. Remove from the heat. Stir in the bananas, peanut butter and vanilla.

MAPLE-GLAZED SAUSAGES

Marmalade French Toast Sandwiches

I will make these toasty sandwiches with sweet or savory jellies, depending on my mood. Try hot pepper jelly when you want a little sizzle in the morning.

—DANIELLE LORING LEWISTON, ME

START TO FINISH: 25 MIN.
MAKES: 6 SERVINGS

- 1 **container (8 ounces) whipped cream cheese**
- 12 **slices sourdough bread**
- ¾ **cup orange marmalade**
- 4 **eggs**
- 2 **tablespoons 2% milk**
  Maple syrup, optional

1. Spread the cream cheese over six slices of bread; top with the marmalade and remaining bread. In a shallow bowl, whisk the eggs and milk.

2. Lightly grease a griddle; heat over medium heat. Dip both sides of sandwiches into egg mixture. Place sandwiches on griddle; toast 2-3 minutes on each side or until golden brown. If desired, serve with syrup.

DID YOU KNOW?

Sourdough bread gets its rising action and distinctive flavor from a sourdough starter. The starter is a living organism of wild yeasts that must be "fed" periodically with flour and water to keep it alive. Starters develop more complex flavors as they age, and some are well over 100 years old.

MARMALADE FRENCH
TOAST SANDWICHES

FAST FIX

Cappuccino Chip Muffins

I use a muffin mix, white chips and instant coffee granules to make these coffeehouse treats.
—**KRIS PRESLEY** SUMMERVILLE, SC

START TO FINISH: 30 MIN. • **MAKES:** 1 DOZEN

- 1 **package (18¼ ounces) double chocolate muffin mix**
- 1 **cup water**
- 1 **egg**
- 2 **tablespoons instant coffee granules**
- 1 **teaspoon ground cinnamon**
- ½ **cup white baking chips**

1. Preheat oven to 425°. In a large bowl, combine muffin mix, water, egg, coffee granules and cinnamon just until moistened. Fold in chips. Fill greased muffin cups three-fourths full.
2. Bake 18-21 minutes or until a toothpick inserted in center comes out clean. Cool 5 minutes before removing from pan to a wire rack.

FAST FIX

Ham 'n' Swiss Rolls

I've always preferred no-fuss recipes in planning breakfasts. Our children were big fans of ham and cheese when they were growing up. So these rolls are perfect; they're great for families on the go.
—**MARJORIE CAREY** ALAMOSA, CO

START TO FINISH: 20 MIN.
MAKES: 4 SERVINGS

- 1 **tube (8 ounces) refrigerated crescent rolls**
- 1 **cup diced fully cooked ham**
- ¾ **cup finely shredded Swiss cheese**
- 1½ **teaspoons prepared mustard**
- 1 **teaspoon finely chopped onion**

1. Preheat oven to 375°. Separate crescent rolls into eight triangles. In a small bowl, combine ham, cheese, mustard and onion; place 2 tablespoons mixture in the center of each triangle.
2. Fold points toward center and pinch edges to seal. Place on a lightly greased baking sheet. Bake 11-13 minutes or until lightly browned.

CHEDDAR BROCCOLI QUICHE

Cheddar Broccoli Quiche

This savory quiche is a snap to make with canned broccoli cheese soup. Pair it with fresh fruit at breakfast.
—**BARBARA CUSIMANO** MANCHESTER, CT

PREP: 25 MIN. + CHILLING • **BAKE:** 35 MIN.
MAKES: 6-8 SERVINGS

- 1 **sheet refrigerated pie pastry**
- 1 **cup (4 ounces) shredded cheddar cheese, divided**
- 6 **eggs, lightly beaten**
- 1 **can (10¾ ounces) condensed cream of broccoli and cheese soup, undiluted**
- ⅔ **cup milk**

1. Unroll pastry sheet into a 9-in. pie plate; flute edge. Refrigerate 30 minutes. Preheat oven to 400°.
2. Line unpricked pastry with a double thickness of foil. Fill with pie weights, dried beans or uncooked rice. Bake on a lower oven rack 10-15 minutes or until edges are golden brown. Remove foil and weights; bake 3-6 minutes longer or until bottom is golden brown. Cool on a wire rack.
3. Reduce oven setting to 350°. Sprinkle pastry shell with ½ cup cheese. In a large bowl, combine eggs, soup and milk. Pour into crust. Cover edges loosely with foil.
4. Bake 30 minutes. Sprinkle with remaining cheese; bake 5-10 minutes longer or until a knife inserted near the center comes out clean. Let stand 5 minutes before cutting.

LOADED BREAKFAST POTATOES

FAST FIX
Loaded Breakfast Potatoes

My kids love loaded potatoes in restaurants, so I modified them to make at home. Using the microwave for the potatoes will save you about 10 minutes. I also use thin-skinned red potatoes instead of russets to save on peeling time.

—TENA KROPP AURORA, IL

START TO FINISH: 30 MIN. • **MAKES:** 6 SERVINGS

- 1½ **pounds red potatoes, cubed**
- ¼ **pound bacon strips, chopped**
- ¾ **cup cubed fully cooked ham**
- 1 **cup (4 ounces) shredded cheddar cheese**
- ½ **teaspoon salt**
- ¼ **teaspoon pepper**
  Sour cream

1. Place potatoes in a microwave-safe dish and cover with water. Cover and microwave on high for 4-5 minutes or until tender.
2. Meanwhile, in a large skillet, cook bacon over medium heat until crisp. Remove to paper towels with a slotted spoon. Drain potatoes; saute in drippings until lightly browned. Add the ham, cheese, salt, pepper and bacon. Cook and stir over medium heat until cheese is melted. Serve with sour cream.

FAST FIX
Spicy Sausage Patties

Jazz up any breakfast with these subtly spiced sausage patties. They're sure to perk up your taste buds and get your motor running! Plus, they only take about 20 minutes to make!

—ATHENA RUSSELL FLORENCE, SC

START TO FINISH: 20 MIN. • **MAKES:** 4 SERVINGS

- ¾ **pound ground pork**
- ½ **teaspoon salt**
- ½ **teaspoon dried sage leaves**
- ¼ **teaspoon ground coriander**
- ¼ **teaspoon pepper**
- ⅛ **to ¼ teaspoon crushed red pepper flakes**

1. Crumble pork into a large bowl. Sprinkle with seasonings; mix well. Shape into four 3-in. patties.
2. In a large skillet, cook patties over medium heat for 5-6 minutes on each side or until a thermometer reads 160°. Drain on paper towels.
FREEZE OPTION *Wrap each patty in plastic wrap; transfer to a resealable plastic freezer bag. Freeze up to 3 months. To use, preheat oven to 350°. Unwrap patties and place on a baking sheet coated with cooking spray. Bake 15 minutes on each side or until heated through.*

GLAZED BACON

Kids' Favorite Blueberry Muffins

FAST FIX

My daughter, Cayla, had just gotten out of bed when we threw together these great muffins. I love cooking with my little girl!

—**LISA ALLEN** JOPPA, AL

START TO FINISH: 30 MIN.
MAKES: 1 DOZEN

- 2½ cups pancake mix
- ½ cup sugar
- 1 egg
- ⅔ cup water
- ¼ cup canola oil
- 1½ cups fresh or frozen blueberries

1. Preheat oven to 400°. In a large bowl, combine pancake mix and sugar. In another bowl, whisk egg, water and oil. Stir into dry ingredients just until moistened. Fold in blueberries.
2. Fill paper-lined muffin cups two-thirds full. Bake muffins for 14-16 minutes or until a toothpick inserted in center comes out clean. Cool 5 minutes before removing from pan to a wire rack.
NOTE *If using frozen blueberries, use without thawing to avoid discoloring the batter.*

KIDS' FAVORITE BLUEBERRY MUFFINS

Glazed Bacon

Brown sugar, mustard and wine make bacon a little more special in this recipe. It's easy to prepare while working on the rest of the meal.

—**JUDITH DOBSON** BURLINGTON, WI

PREP: 10 MIN. • **BAKE:** 30 MIN.
MAKES: 8 SERVINGS

- 1 pound sliced bacon
- 1 cup packed brown sugar
- ¼ cup white wine or unsweetened apple juice
- 2 tablespoons Dijon mustard

1. Preheat oven to 350°. Place bacon on a rack in an ungreased 15x10x1-in. baking pan. Bake for 10 minutes; drain.
2. Combine the brown sugar, wine and mustard; drizzle half over bacon. Bake 10 minutes. Turn bacon over; drizzle with the remaining glaze. Bake for 10 minutes or until golden brown. Place bacon on waxed paper until set. Serve warm.

Blueberry Oatmeal

FAST FIX

We love homemade oatmeal, and this delicious recipe tastes like dessert. Best of all, it's good for you.

—**LESLEY ROBESON** CASPER, WY

START TO FINISH: 10 MIN.
MAKES: 2 SERVINGS

- 1¾ cups 2% milk
- 1 cup quick-cooking oats
- ⅛ teaspoon salt
- ⅓ cup packed brown sugar
- ½ teaspoon ground cinnamon
- ¾ cup fresh or frozen blueberries, thawed

1. In a small saucepan, bring milk to a boil.
2. Stir in oats and salt. Cook over medium heat for 1-2 minutes or until oatmeal is thickened, stirring occasionally. Stir in brown sugar and cinnamon.
3. Divide between two serving bowls; top with blueberries.

Chocolate-Orange Scones

Pancake mix is the quick secret to these fluffy, tender scones. They're great with a cup of coffee, herbal tea or milk.

—MARGARET WILSON SUN CITY, CA

START TO FINISH: 25 MIN.
MAKES: 8 SCONES

- 1½ cups complete buttermilk pancake mix
- ¾ cup heavy whipping cream
- 2 to 3 teaspoons grated orange peel
- 2 milk chocolate candy bars (1.55 ounces each), chopped

1. Preheat oven to 400°. In a small bowl, combine pancake mix, cream and orange peel.

Turn onto a lightly floured surface; knead 6 times. Knead in chocolate.
2. Pat into a 9-in. circle. Cut into eight wedges. Separate wedges and place on a greased baking sheet. Bake 9-11 minutes or until lightly browned. Serve warm.

Spanish Omelets

Wake up your taste buds with yummy Mexican-flavored omelets that feature warm refried beans, salsa and shredded cheese. Whip up this satisfying hot breakfast in 15 minutes flat; spice it up with a hot salsa or add sizzling cooked bacon for a smoky twist.

—TERESA GUNNELL LOVETTSVILLE, VA

START TO FINISH: 15 MIN.
MAKES: 2 SERVINGS

- 6 eggs
- ¼ cup water

CHOCOLATE-ORANGE SCONES

SPANISH OMELET

- 1 cup refried beans, warmed
- ¼ cup chopped red onion
- ½ cup shredded Mexican cheese blend, divided
- ¼ cup salsa

1. Heat a 10-in. nonstick skillet coated with cooking spray over medium heat. Whisk eggs and water. Add half of the egg mixture to skillet (mixture should set immediately at edges).
2. As eggs set, push cooked edges toward the center, letting uncooked portion flow underneath. When the eggs are set, spoon half of the beans and half of the onion on one side and sprinkle with 2 tablespoons cheese; fold other side over filling. Slide omelet onto a plate. Repeat. Garnish with salsa and remaining cheese.

TOP TIP

Beans pack a nutritional one-two punch of protein and fiber, which helps you feel fuller longer. They're a green, economical protein source.

CHEESE SOUFFLES

Cheese Souffles

Great for brunch, a light late-night supper for two or as a versatile side dish, these melt-in-your-mouth souffles are flavorful, fluffy and fun.

—LYNN MCALLISTER MT. ULLA, NC

PREP: 15 MIN. • **BAKE:** 20 MIN. • **MAKES:** 2 SERVINGS

- 4½ teaspoons butter
- 4½ teaspoons all-purpose flour
- ½ cup 2% milk
- ½ cup shredded cheddar cheese
- 2 eggs, separated

1. In a large saucepan, melt butter. Whisk in flour until smooth; gradually add milk. Bring to a boil over medium heat; cook and stir for 1-2 minutes or until thickened. Reduce heat; stir in cheese until melted. Remove from the heat. Beat egg yolks. Stir a small amount of hot mixture into yolks; return all to the pan, stirring constantly. Cool slightly.
2. Preheat oven to 350°. In a small bowl, beat egg whites until stiff peaks form. Fold into egg yolk mixture. Pour into two ungreased 8-oz. ramekins or custard cups.
3. Bake for 20-25 minutes or until tops are puffed and centers appear set. Serve immediately.

Corned Beef 'n' Cheese Strata

If you like Reuben sandwiches, you'll love the flavor of this easy strata that works for any meal of the day.

—ANITA BUKOWSKI GREENDALE, WI

PREP: 15 MIN. + CHILLING • **BAKE:** 50 MIN.
MAKES: 9-12 SERVINGS

- 10 slices rye bread, cut into ¾-inch cubes
- 1½ pounds cooked corned beef, shredded
- 2½ cups (10 ounces each) shredded Swiss cheese
- 6 eggs
- 3 cups milk
- ¼ teaspoon pepper

1. Place bread cubes in a greased 13x9-in. baking dish. Sprinkle with the corned beef and cheese. Whisk the eggs, milk and pepper; pour over the top. Cover and refrigerate overnight.
2. Preheat oven to 350°. Remove strata from the refrigerator 30 minutes before baking. Cover and bake 40 minutes. Uncover; bake 10 minutes longer or until a thermometer reads 160°. Let stand 5-10 minutes before cutting.

FAST FIX
Apple Yogurt Parfaits

Start the morning right with this super-simple parfait. For easy variations, try preparing it with flavored applesauces.

—REBEKAH RADEWAHN WAUWATOSA, WI

START TO FINISH: 10 MIN. • **MAKES:** 4 SERVINGS

- 1 cup sweetened applesauce
  Dash ground nutmeg
- ½ cup granola with raisins
- 1⅓ cups vanilla yogurt

In a small bowl, combine applesauce and nutmeg. Spoon 1 tablespoon granola into each of four parfait glasses. Layer each with ⅓ cup yogurt and ¼ cup applesauce; sprinkle with remaining granola. Serve immediately.

CORNED BEEF 'N' CHEESE STRATA

NUTTY WAFFLE
SANDWICHES

FAST FIX
Nutty Waffle Sandwiches

You can't go wrong with peanut butter and Nutella, but the secret here is using really juicy strawberries. Never tried Nutella? Look for the hazelnut-flavored spread near the peanut butter at the grocery store.

—**FRANCES PIETSCH** FLOWER MOUND, TX

START TO FINISH: 15 MIN. • **MAKES:** 4 SERVINGS

- 8 **frozen multigrain waffles**
- ½ **cup Nutella**
- 2 **medium bananas, sliced**
- 1 **cup sliced fresh strawberries**
- ½ **cup peanut butter**

Toast waffles according to package directions. Spread four waffles with Nutella. Layer with bananas and strawberries. Spread remaining waffles with peanut butter; place over top.

FAST FIX
Fluffy Biscuit Muffins

These biscuits are simple and have a wonderful aroma when baking. This is one of my husband's favorites.

—**VIRGINIA FOSTER** PADUCAH, KY

START TO FINISH: 20 MIN. • **MAKES:** 4 BISCUITS

- 1 **cup self-rising flour**
- 2 **tablespoons mayonnaise**
- ½ **cup milk**

Preheat oven to 425°. In a bowl, cut flour and mayonnaise together until mixture resembles coarse crumbs. Add milk; stir just until mixed. Spoon into four greased muffin cups. Bake for 14-16 minutes or until lightly browned.

NOTE *As a substitute for 1 cup of self-rising flour, place 1½ teaspoons baking powder and ½ teaspoon salt in a measuring cup. Add all-purpose flour to measure 1 cup.*

Breakfast Bread Bowls

These are so creative and convenient, you'll wonder why you haven't been making them for years. The best part is that you can customize the fillings to your liking as well as play with different combinations of seasonings.

—**PATRICK LAVIN, JR.** BIRDSBORO, PA

PREP: 20 MIN. • **BAKE:** 20 MIN. • **MAKES:** 4 SERVINGS

- ½ cup chopped pancetta
- 4 crusty hard rolls (4 inches wide)
- ½ cup finely chopped fresh mushrooms
- 4 eggs
- ⅛ teaspoon salt
- ⅛ teaspoon pepper
- ¼ cup shredded Gruyere or fontina cheese

1. Preheat oven to 350°. In a small skillet, cook pancetta over medium heat until browned, stirring occasionally. Remove with a slotted spoon; drain on paper towels.

2. Meanwhile, cut a thin slice off the top of each roll. Hollow out the bottom, leaving a ½-in.-thick shell (save removed bread for another use); place shells on an ungreased baking sheet.

3. Add mushrooms and pancetta to bread shells. Carefully break an egg into each; sprinkle eggs with salt and pepper. Sprinkle with cheese. Bake 18-22 minutes or until egg whites are completely set and yolks begin to thicken but are not hard.

FAST FIX

Berry Yogurt Cups

Blueberries and strawberries jazz up plain yogurt in this perfect-for-summer easy dessert or light breakfast. Try other fruit combinations, such as banana and kiwi.

—**SHANNON MINK** COLUMBUS, OH

START TO FINISH: 10 MIN. • **MAKES:** 4 SERVINGS

- 1½ cups sliced fresh strawberries
- 1½ cups fresh blueberries
- ¾ cup (6 ounces) vanilla yogurt
- 1 teaspoon sugar
- ⅛ to ¼ teaspoon ground cinnamon

Divide strawberries and blueberries among four individual serving dishes. In a small bowl, combine the yogurt, sugar and cinnamon; spoon over fruit.

BERRY
YOGURT
CUPS

AMY GRIM'S GARLIC TOAST PIZZAS
PAGE 46

Appetizers & Beverages

VIKKI SPENGLER'S GREEK DELI KABOBS *PAGE 40*

BONNIE HAWKINS' LEMONY COOLER *PAGE 28*

NANETTE HILTON'S HOMEMADE GUACAMOLE *PAGE 38*

Chocolate-Covered Bacon

A hit at state fairs everywhere, this salty-sweet concoction is easy to make at home. Some say bacon can't get any better, but we think chocolate makes everything better!

—*TASTE OF HOME* TEST KITCHEN

PREP: 20 MIN. • **BAKE:** 20 MIN. • **MAKES:** 1 DOZEN

- 12 thick-sliced bacon strips (about 1 pound)
- 12 wooden skewers (12 inches)
- 6 ounces white candy coating, chopped
- 1 cup semisweet chocolate chips
- 1 tablespoon shortening
  Optional toppings: chopped dried apple chips, apricots and crystallized ginger, finely chopped pecans and pistachios, toasted coconut, kosher salt, brown sugar, cayenne pepper and coarsely ground black pepper

1. Thread each bacon strip onto a wooden skewer. Place on a rack in a large baking pan. Bake at 400° for 20-25 minutes or until crisp. Cool completely.
2. In a microwave, melt candy coating; stir until smooth. Combine chocolate chips and shortening; melt in a microwave and stir until smooth.
3. With pastry brushes, coat bacon on both sides with melted coatings. Top each strip as desired. Place on waxed paper-lined baking sheets. Refrigerate until firm. Store in the refrigerator.

CHOCOLATE-COVERED BACON

AFTER-DINNER WHITE CHOCOLATE MOCHA

FAST FIX
After-Dinner White Chocolate Mocha

Here, a childhood favorite gets a grown-up makeover. If you're serving this drink to children, just leave out the coffee granules.

—**SCARLETT ELROD** NEWNAN, GA

START TO FINISH: 15 MIN. • **MAKES:** 2 SERVINGS

- 1½ cups 2% milk
- 3 ounces white baking chocolate, chopped
- 2 tablespoons instant coffee granules
- 1 teaspoon vanilla extract
  Optional toppings: whipped cream and baking cocoa

1. In a small saucepan, heat milk over medium heat until bubbles form around sides of pan (do not boil).
2. Place the remaining ingredients in a blender. Add hot milk; cover and process until frothy. Serve in mugs. Top mocha with whipped cream and cocoa if desired.

LEMON GARLIC
HUMMUS

FAST FIX ►
Lemon Garlic Hummus

Whipping up this smooth and creamy bean dip requires just five ingredients. It's a delicious part of our family's Christmas Eve party every year.

—KRIS CAPENER OGDEN, UT

START TO FINISH: 10 MIN. • **MAKES:** 1½ CUPS

- ¾ **cup canola oil**
- 2 **cups canned garbanzo beans or chickpeas, rinsed and drained**
- 3 **tablespoons lemon juice**
- 2 **teaspoons minced garlic**
- ½ **teaspoon salt**
  Pita bread, cut into wedges

In a food processor, combine the oil, beans, lemon juice, garlic and salt; cover and process mixture until smooth. Transfer to a small bowl. Serve with pita wedges.

FAST FIX ►
Baked Crab Rangoon

Check out how easy these creamy crab wonton cups are to make. Baking the appetizers instead of deep-frying them not only saves time, it reduces the mess.

—SUE BENNETT SHELBURN, IN

START TO FINISH: 30 MIN. • **MAKES:** 1 DOZEN

- 12 **wonton wrappers**
- 4 **ounces cream cheese, softened**
- ¼ **cup mayonnaise**
- 1 **can (6 ounces) crabmeat, drained, flaked and cartilage removed**
- ¼ **cup thinly sliced green onions**

1. Press wonton wrappers into greased miniature muffin cups. Bake at 350° for 6-7 minutes or until lightly browned.
2. Meanwhile, in a small bowl, beat cream cheese and mayonnaise until smooth. Stir in the crab and onions; spoon into wonton cups. Bake for 10-12 minutes or until heated through. Serve warm.

Lemony Cooler

Everyone thinks I've gone to a lot of trouble to make this refreshing summer drink, but it's so easy! I also like to make my own pretty ice cubes by adding ½ cup lemon juice and the leaves from a mint sprig to 4 cups of water.

—**BONNIE HAWKINS** ELKHORN, WI

PREP: 15 MIN. + CHILLING
MAKES: 8 SERVINGS (2 QUARTS)

- 3 **cups white grape juice**
- ½ **cup sugar**
- ½ **cup lemon juice**
- 1 **bottle (1 liter) club soda, chilled**
  Ice cubes
  Assorted fresh fruit, optional

1. In a pitcher, combine the grape juice, sugar and lemon juice; stir until sugar is dissolved. Refrigerate until chilled.

2. Just before serving, stir in club soda. Serve over ice. Garnish with fruit if desired.

DID YOU KNOW?

Club soda is carbonated water with a small addition of sodium bicarbonate (baking soda), potassium derivatives or other mineral-like substances. It tastes similar to seltzer water, which is simply carbonated water without the addition of minerals. Club soda may have more of a mineral flavor than seltzer, but the two are interchangeable in recipes.

LEMONY COOLER

Italian Meatball Buns

One of the greatest gifts I love to share with my six grandchildren is making special recipes just for them. The meatballs inside these rolls are a savory surprise.

—TRINA LINDER-MOBLEY CLOVER, SC

PREP: 30 MIN. + RISING
BAKE: 15 MIN.
MAKES: 2 DOZEN

- **12 frozen bread dough dinner rolls**
- **1 package (12 ounces) frozen fully cooked Italian meatballs, thawed**
- **2 tablespoons olive oil**
- **¼ cup grated Parmesan cheese**
- **¼ cup minced fresh basil**
- **1½ cups marinara sauce, warmed**

1. Let dough stand at room temperature 25-30 minutes or until softened.
2. Cut each roll in half. Wrap each portion around a meatball, enclosing meatball completely; pinch dough firmly to seal. Place on greased baking sheets, seam side down. Cover with kitchen towels; let rise in a warm place until almost doubled, about 1½ to 2 hours.
3. Preheat oven to 350°. Bake buns 12-15 minutes or until golden brown. Brush tops with oil; sprinkle with cheese and basil. Serve with marinara sauce.

CARAMEL APPLE AND BRIE SKEWERS

FAST FIX ▶
Caramel Apple and Brie Skewers

I'm a caterer, and this is one of my best-selling appetizers. The shortcut of using prepared caramel makes these little gems a snap to prepare.

—CAMILLE ELLIS TAMPA, FL

START TO FINISH: 10 MIN.
MAKES: 6 SKEWERS

- **2 medium apples, cubed**
- **1 log (6 ounces) Brie cheese, cubed**
- **½ cup hot caramel ice cream topping**
- **½ cup finely chopped macadamia nuts**
- **2 tablespoons dried cranberries**

1. On each of six wooden appetizer skewers, alternately thread apple and cheese cubes; place on a serving tray.
2. Drizzle with caramel topping; sprinkle with macadamia nuts and cranberries.

ITALIAN MEATBALL BUNS

MINI PHYLLO TACOS

Mini Phyllo Tacos

For a winning appetizer, serve crispy phyllo cups filled with taco-seasoned ground beef and zesty shredded cheese. The handheld munchies will be a popular item on any menu.

—ROSEANN WESTON PHILIPSBURG, PA

PREP: 30 MIN. • **BAKE:** 10 MIN. • **MAKES:** 2½ DOZEN

- 1 **pound lean ground beef (90% lean)**
- ½ **cup finely chopped onion**
- 1 **envelope taco seasoning**
- ¾ **cup water**
- 1¼ **cups shredded Mexican cheese blend, divided**
- 2 **packages (1.9 ounces each) frozen miniature phyllo tart shells**

1. Preheat oven to 350°. In a small skillet, cook beef and onion over medium heat until meat is no longer pink; drain. Stir in taco seasoning and water. Bring to a boil. Reduce heat; simmer, uncovered, for 5 minutes. Remove from heat; stir in ½ cup of cheese blend.

2. Place tart shells in an ungreased 15x10x1-in. baking pan. Fill with taco mixture.

3. Bake 6 minutes. Sprinkle with remaining cheese blend; bake 2-3 minutes longer or until cheese is melted.

FREEZE OPTION *Freeze cooled pastries in a freezer container, separating layers with waxed paper. To use, reheat pastries on a baking sheet in a preheated 350° oven until crisp and heated through.*

FAST FIX ▶
Chutney-Topped Brie

You'll need only four ingredients for this easy, elegant appetizer. Just about any flavor of chutney will work for this toasty melt-in-your-mouth delight.

—REBECCA IRONS LUBBOCK, TX

START TO FINISH: 15 MIN. • **MAKES:** 8 SERVINGS

- 1 **round (8 ounces) Brie cheese**
- ¼ **cup chutney**
- 2 **tablespoons bacon bits**
  Assorted crackers

Place the cheese in an ungreased ovenproof serving dish. Top with chutney and bacon. Bake, uncovered, at 400° for 10-12 minutes or until the cheese is softened. Serve with crackers.

MOZZARELLA STICKS

Broccoli Cheddar Spread

People assume this spread is prepared with spinach and are surprised when I tell them it's broccoli. The trick is to chop the broccoli into small bits so it's conducive to dipping.

—BETH PARKER GRAYSVILLE, AL

PREP: 15 MIN. • **BAKE:** 20 MIN. • **MAKES:** 3 CUPS

- 4 **cups chopped fresh broccoli**
- 1 **tablespoon water**
- 2 **cups (16 ounces) reduced-fat sour cream**
- ½ **cup plus 1 tablespoon shredded reduced-fat cheddar cheese, divided**
- 1 **envelope vegetable recipe mix (Knorr)**
  Pita chips or reduced-fat crackers

1. Preheat oven to 350°. Place broccoli and water in a 1½-qt. microwave-safe dish. Cover and microwave on high 3-4 minutes or until the broccoli is crisp-tender; drain. In a large bowl, combine sour cream, ½ cup cheese and recipe mix. Gently stir in broccoli.
2. Transfer to an ungreased shallow 1-qt. baking dish. Sprinkle with the remaining cheese. Bake, uncovered, 20-25 minutes or until heated through. Serve with pita chips or crackers.

FAST FIX
Mozzarella Sticks

You won't believe something this easy could taste so fantastic! Crunchy on the outside, gooey on the inside... this is a treat that all ages will love. Kids could help wrap them, too.

—SHIRLEY WARREN THIENSVILLE, WI

START TO FINISH: 20 MIN. • **MAKES:** 1 DOZEN

- 12 **pieces string cheese**
- 12 **egg roll wrappers**
  Oil for deep-fat frying
  Marinara or spaghetti sauce

1. Place a piece of string cheese near the bottom corner of one egg roll wrapper (keep remaining wrappers covered with a damp paper towel until ready to use). Fold bottom corner over cheese. Roll up halfway; fold sides toward center over cheese. Moisten remaining corner with water; roll up tightly to seal. Repeat with the remaining wrappers and cheese.
2. In an electric skillet, heat ½ in. of oil to 375°. Fry sticks, a few at a time, for 30-60 seconds on each side or until golden brown. Drain on paper towels. Serve with marinara sauce.

FAST FIX
Dunked Strawberries

Dressed-up strawberries give any meal an elegant finish. With brown sugar and a hint of lime, they're sweet, tangy and so tasty, you'll want more!

—JENNIFER REID FARMINGTON, ME

START TO FINISH: 5 MIN. • **MAKES:** 4 SERVINGS

- ½ **cup sour cream**
- ½ **teaspoon grated lime peel**
- ½ **cup packed brown sugar**
- 12 **fresh strawberries**

In a small bowl, combine sour cream and lime peel. Place brown sugar in another small bowl. Dip the strawberries in sour cream mixture, then coat with brown sugar. Serve immediately.

AMARETTO-PEACH CHEESE SPREAD

Cheese Straws

Transform just a few ingredients into crispy cracker sticks. These snacks make for easy mingling at parties.
—**ELIZABETH ROBINSON** CONROE, TX

PREP: 20 MIN. • **BAKE:** 15 MIN. + COOLING
MAKES: 2½ DOZEN

- ½ cup butter, softened
- 2 cups (8 ounces) shredded sharp cheddar cheese
- 1¼ cups all-purpose flour
- ½ teaspoon salt
- ¼ teaspoon cayenne pepper

1. Preheat oven to 350°. In a large bowl, beat butter until light and fluffy. Beat in cheese until blended. Combine flour, salt and cayenne; stir into cheese mixture until a dough forms. Roll into a 15x6-in. rectangle. Cut into thirty 6-in. strips. Gently place strips 1 in. apart on ungreased baking sheets.
2. Bake 15-20 minutes or until lightly browned. Cool 5 minutes before removing from pans to wire racks to cool completely. Store cheese straws in an airtight container.

FAST FIX

Amaretto-Peach Cheese Spread

During the Christmas season, we have an appetizer dinner with two other couples. This super-simple item is one we've served. You can use it for either an appetizer or dessert.
—**JUDY WILSON** SUN CITY WEST, AZ

START TO FINISH: 10 MIN. • **MAKES:** 16 SERVINGS

- 2 packages (8 ounces each) cream cheese, softened
- 1 jar (18 ounces) peach preserves
- 1 cup finely chopped pecans
- 2 tablespoons Amaretto
  Gingersnap cookies

Place the cream cheese on a serving plate. In a small bowl, combine the preserves, pecans and Amaretto; spoon over the cream cheese. Serve with gingersnap cookies.

FAST FIX

Pina Colada Fruit Dip

A taste of the tropics is always welcome and refreshing. This cool and creamy appetizer dip is also terrific to munch on with fruit or pound cake after dinner.
—**SHELLY BEVINGTON** HERMISTON, OR

START TO FINISH: 15 MIN. • **MAKES:** 2½ CUPS

- 1 package (8 ounces) cream cheese, softened
- 1 jar (7 ounces) marshmallow creme
- 1 can (8 ounces) crushed pineapple, drained
- ½ cup flaked coconut
  Assorted fresh fruit or cubed pound cake

In a small bowl, beat the cream cheese and marshmallow creme until fluffy. Fold in pineapple and coconut. Cover and chill until serving. Serve with fruit or pound cake.

Sweet & Salty Popcorn

There's nothing like making memories with grandchildren in the kitchen and seeing their excited, happy faces while they help.

—**DIANE SMITH** PINE MOUNTAIN, GA

START TO FINISH: 25 MIN.
MAKES: 4 QUARTS

- 10 **cups popped popcorn**
- 1 **cup broken miniature pretzels**
- 1 **cup candies of your choice, such as Almond Joy pieces or milk chocolate M&M's**
- 1 **cup chopped dried pineapple**
- 10 **ounces white candy coating, coarsely chopped**

1. In a large bowl, combine popcorn, pretzels, candies and pineapple. In a microwave, melt candy coating; stir until smooth. Pour over popcorn mixture; toss to coat.

2. Immediately spread onto waxed paper; let stand until set. Break into pieces. Store in airtight containers.

TOP TIP

Easily dress up a holiday gift tin by including a recipe card for the sweet treats the recipient will find inside. Secure the recipe card to the lid with a festive magnet.

SWEET & SALTY POPCORN

DEEP-FRIED
CHEESE BITES

Deep-Fried Cheese Bites

These beer-battered cheese curds are the ultimate in delicious comfort food. Try serving them with ranch dressing alongside for dipping.

—**KATIE ROSE** PEWAUKEE, WI

PREP: 10 MIN. • **COOK:** 5 MIN./BATCH
MAKES: 12 SERVINGS

- 1¼ cups all-purpose flour, divided
- 1 pound cheese curds or cubed cheddar cheese
- 1 cup beer
  Oil for deep-fat frying

1. Place ¼ cup flour in a large resealable plastic bag. Add cheese curds, a few pieces at a time, and shake to coat.
2. In an electric skillet or deep fryer, heat oil to 375°. Meanwhile, in a large bowl, whisk beer and remaining flour. Dip cheese curds, a few at a time, into batter and fry for 2-3 minutes on each side or until golden brown. Drain on paper towels.

DID YOU KNOW?

Cheese curds are freshly made cheese that has not yet had the excess moisture pressed out. Very fresh curds have a characteristic squeak when eaten. Cheddar curds are the most popular type.

Luscious Lime Slush

People love this sweet-tart refresher any time of year. You can also do a lemon version, swapping in lemonade concentrate for the limeade.

—**BONNIE JOST** MANITOWOC, WI

PREP: 20 MIN. + FREEZING
MAKES: 28 SERVINGS (¾ CUP EACH)

- 9 cups water
- 4 individual green tea bags
- 2 cans (12 ounces each) frozen limeade concentrate, thawed
- 2 cups sugar
- 2 cups lemon rum or rum
- 7 cups lemon-lime soda, chilled

1. In a Dutch oven, bring water to a boil. Remove from the heat; add tea bags. Cover and steep for 3-5 minutes. Discard tea bags. Stir in the limeade concentrate, sugar and rum.
2. Transfer to a 4-qt. freezer container; cool. Cover and freeze for 6 hours or overnight.
TO USE FROZEN LIMEADE MIXTURE *Combine the limeade mixture and soda in a 4-qt. pitcher. Or for one serving, combine ½ cup limeade mixture and ¼ cup soda in a glass. Serve immediately.*

FAST FIX

Pepper Shooters

Pop one of these savory peppers into your mouth for a tantalizing array of flavors. It's like an antipasto platter all in one bite.

—*TASTE OF HOME* TEST KITCHEN

START TO FINISH: 30 MIN. • **MAKES:** 2 DOZEN

- 24 pickled sweet cherry peppers
- 4 ounces fresh mozzarella cheese, finely chopped
- 2¾ ounces thinly sliced hard salami, finely chopped
- 3 tablespoons prepared pesto
- 2 tablespoons olive oil

Cut tops off peppers and remove seeds; set aside. In a small bowl, combine the cheese, salami and pesto; spoon into peppers. Drizzle with oil. Chill until serving.

Cheese-Stuffed Meatball Sliders

You can make these ahead of time and warm them up at the game on the grill. They're easy and oh so good!

—**HILARY BREINHOLT** GLENWOOD, UT

PREP: 15 MIN. • **BAKE:** 25 MIN. • **MAKES:** 16 SERVINGS

- 1½ pounds bulk Italian sausage
- 16 cubes part-skim mozzarella cheese
- 1 jar (24 ounces) spaghetti sauce
- 1 jar (8.1 ounces) prepared pesto
- 16 dinner rolls, split and toasted

1. Divide sausage into 16 portions. Shape each portion around a cube of cheese. Place on a greased rack in a shallow baking pan. Bake at 350° for 25-30 minutes or until meat is no longer pink. Remove to paper towels to drain.

2. In a large saucepan, combine spaghetti sauce and pesto; bring just to a boil over medium heat, stirring occasionally. Add meatballs; heat through, stirring gently. Serve on rolls.

FAST FIX

Green Onion Bagel Dip

Forty years ago, I used to make this dip. It was always the most popular item at parties. It's still one of the top dips on the table; my family loves it!

—**JOY PASBY** SONORA, CA

START TO FINISH: 10 MIN. • **MAKES:** 2⅓ CUPS

- 1 teaspoon chicken bouillon granules
- 2 tablespoons hot water
- 1 package (8 ounces) cream cheese, softened
- 1 cup mayonnaise
- 6 green onions, chopped
- 4 to 5 bagels, split and cut into bite-size pieces

In a small bowl, dissolve bouillon in water; cool slightly. In a small bowl, beat cream cheese and mayonnaise until smooth. Add bouillon mixture and beat until blended. Stir in onions. Serve with bagel pieces.

BALSAMIC-GLAZED CHICKEN WINGS

3. Meanwhile, combine brown sugar and reserved marinade in a small saucepan. Bring to a boil; cook until liquid is reduced by half.

4. Place wings in a large bowl. Pour glaze over wings and toss to coat.

NOTE *Uncooked chicken wing sections (wingettes) may be substituted for whole chicken wings.*

FREEZE OPTION *Cover and freeze cooled wings in freezer containers. To use, partially thaw in refrigerator overnight. Reheat wings in a foil-lined 15x10x1-in. baking pan in a preheated 325° oven until heated through, covering if necessary to prevent excess browning.*

FAST FIX

Foolproof Mushrooms

These simple bites pack a lot of zingy flavor. Try adding chopped artichoke hearts for an extra-special touch.
—**GAIL LUCAS** OLIVE BRANCH, MS

START TO FINISH: 25 MIN. • **MAKES:** 2½ DOZEN

- 1 **package (6½ ounces) garlic-herb spreadable cheese**
- 3 **tablespoons grated Parmesan cheese, divided**
- 30 **small fresh mushrooms, stems removed**
  Thinly sliced fresh basil, optional

1. Preheat oven to 400°. In a small bowl, combine spreadable cheese and 2 tablespoons Parmesan cheese; spoon into mushroom caps.

2. Transfer to a foil-lined baking sheet; sprinkle with the remaining Parmesan cheese. Bake for 10-12 minutes or until lightly browned. Garnish with basil if desired.

Balsamic-Glazed Chicken Wings

Tired of the same old buffalo and BBQ sauces? Try spreading your wings with a new balsamic-brown sugar glaze. Sweet and mildly tangy, these have a taste that'll appeal to any crowd.
—**GRETCHEN WHELAN** SAN FRANCISCO, CA

PREP: 20 MIN. + MARINATING • **BAKE:** 25 MIN.
MAKES: ABOUT 1½ DOZEN

- 2 **pounds chicken wings**
- 1½ **cups balsamic vinegar**
- 2 **garlic cloves, minced**
- 2 **teaspoons minced fresh rosemary or**
  ½ teaspoon dried rosemary, crushed
- ¼ **teaspoon salt**
- ¼ **teaspoon pepper**
- ¼ **cup packed brown sugar**

1. Cut chicken wings into three sections; discard wing tip sections. In a small bowl, combine the vinegar, garlic, rosemary, salt and pepper. Pour ½ cup marinade into a large resealable plastic bag. Add the chicken; seal bag and turn to coat. Refrigerate for 1 hour. Cover and refrigerate remaining marinade.

2. Drain chicken and discard marinade; place in a greased 15x10x1-in. baking pan. Bake at 375° for 25-30 minutes or until no longer pink, turning every 10 minutes.

FOOLPROOF MUSHROOMS

BERRY BERRY LEMONADE

Berry Berry Lemonade

We serve this tea daily on our U-pick organic blueberry farm and get many requests for the recipe. You can strain the tea or leave in the tasty bits of blueberry.

—**DELORES GREEN** MONTICELLO, FL

PREP: 20 MIN. + CHILLING
MAKES: 8 SERVINGS (1 CUP EACH)

- 7 **individual tea bags**
- 3 **cups boiling water**
- ½ **cup fresh or frozen blueberries**
- ½ **cup sugar**
- 4 **cups cold water**
- ¾ **cup thawed raspberry lemonade concentrate**
- 1 **medium lemon, sliced**
  Ice cubes

1. Place tea bags in a 4-cup glass measuring cup. Add boiling water; steep 3-5 minutes according to taste. Discard tea bags. Cool tea slightly.
2. Place blueberries in a small food processor; process until pureed.

3. In a pitcher, combine tea and sugar, stirring to dissolve sugar. Stir in cold water, lemonade concentrate, lemon slices and blueberry puree. Refrigerate until chilled. Serve over ice.

Candied Pecans

I like to pack these crispy pecans in jars, tied with pretty ribbon, for family and friends. My granddaughter gave some to a doctor at the hospital where she works, and he said they were too good to be true!

—**OPAL TURNER** HUGHES SPRINGS, TX

PREP: 25 MIN. • **BAKE:** 30 MIN. • **MAKES:** ABOUT 1 POUND

- 2¾ **cups pecan halves**
- 2 **tablespoons butter, softened, divided**
- 1 **cup sugar**
- ½ **cup water**
- ½ **teaspoon salt**
- ½ **teaspoon ground cinnamon**
- 1 **teaspoon vanilla extract**

1. Place pecan halves in a shallow baking pan in a 250° oven for 10 minutes or until warmed. Grease a 15x10x1-in. baking pan with 1 tablespoon butter and set aside.
2. Grease the sides of a large heavy saucepan with the remaining butter; add sugar, water, salt and cinnamon. Bring to a boil, stirring constantly to dissolve sugar. Cover; cook 2 minutes to dissolve any sugar crystals that may form on sides of pan.
3. Cook, without stirring, until a candy thermometer reads 236° (soft-ball stage). Remove from the heat; add vanilla. Stir in warm pecans until evenly coated.
4. Spread onto prepared baking pan. Bake at 250° for 30 minutes, stirring every 10 minutes. Spread on a waxed paper-lined baking sheet to cool.
NOTE *We recommend that you test your candy thermometer before each use by bringing water to a boil; the thermometer should read 212°. Adjust your recipe temperature up or down based on your test.*

MOM'S TANGERINE ICED TEA

Mom's Tangerine Iced Tea

Take a sip of this sweet tea with a citrus twist. You'll love it.

—MARY MILLER POPLARVILLE, MS

PREP: 10 MIN.
COOK: 5 MIN. + CHILLING
MAKES: 4 SERVINGS

- 2¾ cups water, divided
- 4 individual black tea bags
- ⅔ cup sugar
- 2 cups fresh tangerine juice (about 12 tangerines)
  Ice cubes
  Tangerine slices and mint sprigs, optional

1. In a small saucepan, bring 2 cups water to a boil. Remove from the heat; add tea bags. Steep for 3-5 minutes. Discard tea bags; cool tea slightly.
2. In another saucepan, combine remaining water and sugar; bring to a boil. Cook and stir until sugar is dissolved. Remove from the heat; cool slightly.
3. Transfer tea and sugar syrup to a pitcher; stir in tangerine juice. Refrigerate until chilled.
4. Serve over ice; add tangerine slices and mint if desired.

FAST FIX
Homemade Guacamole

My daughters sometimes call this "five-finger" guacamole to help them remember it's made with only five ingredients. It's so simple!

—NANETTE HILTON LAS VEGAS, NV

START TO FINISH: 10 MIN.
MAKES: 2 CUPS

- 3 medium ripe avocados, peeled and cubed
- ¼ cup finely chopped onion
- ¼ cup minced fresh cilantro
- 2 tablespoons lime juice
- ⅛ teaspoon salt
  Tortilla chips

In a small bowl, mash avocados with a fork. Stir in onion, cilantro, lime juice and salt. Serve with tortilla chips.

HOW TO

REMOVE AN AVOCADO PIT

❶ Wash avocado. Cut in half lengthwise, cutting around the pit. Twist halves in opposite directions to separate.

❷ Slip a tablespoon under the pit to loosen it from the fruit. Then slip the spoon between flesh and peel to scoop out the flesh. Slice as desired.

HOMEMADE GUACAMOLE

SLOW COOKER
Marmalade Meatballs

I brought this snappy recipe to work for a potluck. I started cooking the meatballs in the morning, and by lunchtime they were ready. They disappeared fast!
—**JEANNE KISS** GREENSBURG, PA

PREP: 10 MIN. • **COOK:** 4 HOURS
MAKES: ABOUT 5 DOZEN

- 1   bottle (16 ounces) Catalina salad dressing
- 1   cup orange marmalade
- 3   tablespoons Worcestershire sauce
- ½   teaspoon crushed red pepper flakes
- 1   package (32 ounces) frozen fully cooked homestyle meatballs, thawed

In a 3-qt. slow cooker, combine the salad dressing, marmalade, Worcestershire sauce and pepper flakes. Stir in meatballs. Cover and cook on low for 4-5 hours or until heated through.
FREEZE OPTION *Freeze cooled meatball mixture in freezer containers. To use, partially thaw in refrigerator overnight. Microwave, covered, on high in a microwave-safe dish until heated through, gently stirring and adding a little water if necessary.*

FAST FIX
Easy Black Bean Salsa

This salsa is a staple at my house. I can make it in just a few minutes, so it's great for quick meals or snacks.
—**BETTY LAKE** SCOTTSDALE, AZ

START TO FINISH: 10 MIN. • **MAKES:** ABOUT 4 CUPS

- 1   can (14½ ounces) Mexican stewed tomatoes
- 1   can (15 ounces) black beans, rinsed and drained
- 1   can (4 ounces) chopped green chilies, undrained
- ½   cup chopped onion
- ¼   cup minced fresh cilantro
- ½   teaspoon salt
- 1   can (2¼ ounces) sliced ripe olives, drained, optional

1. Drain the tomatoes, reserving juice. Cut up tomatoes; place in a large bowl. AAdd juice, beans, chilies, onion, cilantro, salt and, if desired, olives; stir until combined.
2. Cover and store in the refrigerator. Serve with tortilla chips or Mexican food.

GREEK DELI KABOBS

Greek Deli Kabobs

These pretty skewers combine marinated cheese, veggies and meat into a fun and fresh appetizer that's a snap to make.

—VIKKI SPENGLER OCALA, FL

PREP: 30 MIN. + MARINATING • **MAKES:** 2 DOZEN

- 2 jars (7½ ounces each) roasted sweet red peppers, drained
- 1 pound part-skim mozzarella cheese, cut into ½-inch cubes
- 24 fresh broccoli florets
- 24 slices hard salami
- ½ cup Greek vinaigrette

1. Cut red peppers into 24 strips; place in a large resealable plastic bag. Add remaining ingredients. Seal bag and turn to coat; refrigerate for 4 hours or overnight.

2. Drain and discard the marinade. Thread the cheese, vegetables and meat onto frilled toothpicks or short skewers.

TOP TIP

You can roast your own peppers by broiling them close to the heat until blackened on all sides. Place in a bowl and cover tightly for 15 minutes or until skins are easy to remove. Seed peppers and slice as desired.

FAST FIX

Grilled Shrimp with Spicy-Sweet Sauce

These finger-lickin' shrimp practically fly off the platter at my get-togethers. Play with the amount of Sriracha to get the spice level just the way you like it.

—SUSAN HARRISON LAUREL, MD

START TO FINISH: 30 MIN.
MAKES: 15 SERVINGS (⅓ CUP SAUCE)

- 3 tablespoons reduced-fat mayonnaise
- 2 tablespoons sweet chili sauce
- 1 green onion, thinly sliced
- ¾ teaspoon Sriracha Asian hot chili sauce or ½ teaspoon hot pepper sauce
- 45 uncooked large shrimp (about 1½ pounds), peeled and deveined
- ¼ teaspoon salt
- ¼ teaspoon pepper

1. In a small bowl, mix mayonnaise, chili sauce, green onion and Sriracha. Sprinkle shrimp with salt and pepper. Thread three shrimp onto each of 15 metal or soaked wooden skewers.

2. Moisten a paper towel with cooking oil; using long-handled tongs, rub on grill rack to coat lightly. Grill shrimp, covered, over medium heat or broil 4 in. from heat 3-4 minutes on each side or until shrimp turn pink. Serve with sauce.

FAST FIX

Honey Cinnamon Milk

You can use this warm, comforting milk to help you on your way to dreamland.

—LEONY SANTOSO WINCHESTER, VA

START TO FINISH: 10 MIN. • **MAKES:** 1 SERVING

- 1 cup fat-free milk
- 1 cinnamon stick (3 inches)
  Dash ground nutmeg
  Dash ground allspice
- 1½ teaspoons honey

In a small saucepan, combine milk, cinnamon stick, nutmeg and allspice. Cook and stir mixture over medium heat until heated through; whisk in honey. Serve warm in a mug; garnish with cinnamon stick.

GRILLED SHRIMP WITH SPICY-SWEET SAUCE

WHITE CHOCOLATE
BRIE CUPS

FAST FIX
Effortless Egg Rolls

Egg rolls are such a cinch with this recipe, you'll wonder why you haven't been making them all along! Find a good dipping sauce in the Asian aisle of the supermarket.
—**ANGEL RANDOL** APPLE VALLEY, CA

START TO FINISH: 30 MIN. • **MAKES:** 10 EGG ROLLS

- ½ **pound bulk pork sausage**
- 2½ **cups frozen stir-fry vegetable blend, thawed and chopped**
- 1 **tablespoon teriyaki sauce**
- 10 **egg roll wrappers**
  Oil for frying

1. In a large skillet, cook sausage and vegetables over medium heat until meat is no longer pink; drain. Stir in teriyaki sauce.
2. Place 3 tablespoons of sausage mixture in the center of one egg roll wrapper. (Keep remaining wrappers covered with a damp paper towel until ready to use.) Fold bottom corner over filling. Fold sides toward center over filling. Moisten remaining corner with water; roll up tightly to seal. Repeat.
3. In an electric skillet, heat 1 in. of oil to 375°. Fry egg rolls in batches for 3-4 minutes on each side or until golden brown. Drain on paper towels.

EFFORTLESS
EGG ROLLS

FAST FIX
White Chocolate Brie Cups

Try these unique little tarts as an appetizer before a special meal, or save them for a surprisingly different dinner finale. They're sweet, creamy and crunchy—and very addictive!
—**ANGELA VITALE** DELAWARE, OH

START TO FINISH: 25 MIN. • **MAKES:** 15 APPETIZERS

- 1 **package (1.9 ounces) frozen miniature phyllo tart shells**
- 1½ **ounces white baking chocolate, chopped**
- 2 **ounces Brie cheese, chopped**
- ⅓ **cup orange marmalade**
  Kumquat slices, optional

1. Preheat oven to 350°. Fill each tart shell with chocolate, then cheese. Place on an ungreased baking sheet. Top with marmalade.
2. Bake 6-8 minutes or until golden brown. Serve warm. If desired, top with kumquat.

Peanut Butter Chocolate Pretzels

Chocolate and peanut butter, sweet and salty, crunchy and smooth—what's not to love about these dipped and drizzled pretzels? They're sure to garner smiles from party guests.

—MARCIA PORCH WINTER PARK, FL

PREP: 30 MIN. + STANDING • **MAKES:** ABOUT 3 DOZEN

- 2 **cups (12 ounces) semisweet chocolate chips**
- 4 **teaspoons canola oil, divided**
- 35 to 40 **pretzels**
- ½ **cup peanut butter chips**

1. In a microwave, melt the chocolate chips and 3 teaspoons oil; stir until smooth. Dip pretzels in chocolate; allow excess to drip off. Place on waxed paper-lined baking sheets to set.
2. Melt the peanut butter chips and remaining oil; transfer to a small resealable plastic bag. Cut a small hole in a corner of bag; drizzle over pretzels. Allow to set. Store in airtight containers.

PEANUT BUTTER CHOCOLATE PRETZELS

STRAWBERRY LEMONADE SMOOTHIE

FAST FIX ▶

Strawberry Lemonade Smoothie

My family loves the perfect blend of sweet and tart in this refreshing citrus smoothie. It's so easy to throw together, I often find myself whipping up a batch for a midday snack.

—JAMIE KING DULUTH, MN

START TO FINISH: 5 MIN. • **MAKES:** 4 SERVINGS

- 2 **cups lemonade**
- ¾ **cup (6 ounces) lemon yogurt**
- ½ **teaspoon vanilla extract**
- 2 **cups frozen unsweetened strawberries**

Place all ingredients in a blender; cover and process 15 seconds or until blended. Serve immediately.

POLENTA PARMIGIANA

FAST FIX

Polenta Parmigiana

This warm Italian-flavored appetizer can also double as a light lunch. I prefer this veggie version, but my kids like to add pepperoni or sausage to create mini pizzas.

—CAROLYN KUMPE EL DORADO, CA

START TO FINISH: 30 MIN.
MAKES: 16 APPETIZERS

- 1 tube (1 pound) polenta, cut into 16 slices
- ¼ cup olive oil
- 1 cup tomato basil pasta sauce, warmed
- ½ pound fresh mozzarella cheese, cut into 16 slices
- ¼ cup grated Parmesan cheese
- ½ teaspoon salt
- ⅛ teaspoon pepper
  Fresh basil leaves, optional

1. Preheat oven to 425°. Place polenta in a greased 15x10x1-in. baking pan; brush with olive oil. Bake for 15-20 minutes or until edges are golden brown.
2. Spoon the pasta sauce over polenta slices. Top each with a mozzarella cheese slice; sprinkle with Parmesan cheese, salt and pepper. Bake 3-5 minutes longer or until cheese is melted. Garnish with basil if desired.

FAST FIX

Chocolate Mint Apple Fondue

This recipe is simple to make and kids go crazy for it! You can dip just about any fruit, bread or cookie that would taste good with chocolate.

—DEB DANNER DAYTON, OH

START TO FINISH: 10 MIN.
MAKES: 2½ CUPS

- 1 can (14 ounces) sweetened condensed milk
- 1 cup (6 ounces) semisweet chocolate chips
- 10 chocolate-covered peppermint patties, chopped
  Sliced apples

In a small saucepan, combine milk, chocolate chips and the peppermint patties. Cook and stir over medium-low heat until smooth. Serve warm with apples.

FAST FIX

Fun-on-the-Run Snack Mix

My children love this snack mix and have no idea they're eating cranberries. It's a great healthy snack for car rides, hikes or picnics.

—CARRIE HUBBARD BUENA VISTA, CO

START TO FINISH: 5 MIN.
MAKES: 8 CUPS

- 2 cups Wheat Chex
- 2 cups miniature fish-shaped crackers
- 2 cups pretzel sticks
- 1 cup salted peanuts
- 1 cup dried cranberries

In a large bowl, combine cereal, crackers, pretzels, peanuts and cranberries. Store mixture in an airtight container.

CHOCOLATE MINT APPLE FONDUE

Raspberry-Swirled Lemon Milk Shakes

Ice cream, sorbet and raspberry puree combine to creates a standout shake in minutes. Pour this blend into your prettiest glasses and enjoy its cool comfort.

—**LISA SPEER** PALM BEACH, FL

START TO FINISH: 15 MIN.
MAKES: 4 SERVINGS

- 2 **cups fresh or frozen raspberries, thawed**
- ¼ **cup confectioners' sugar**
- 1 **tablespoon raspberry liqueur, optional**
- ½ **cup 2% milk**
- 2 **cups vanilla ice cream, softened**
- 1 **cup lemon sorbet, softened**
- ¾ **cup crushed ice**
  Optional garnishes: whipped cream, fresh raspberries and mint sprigs

1. Place the raspberries, confectioners' sugar and liqueur, if desired, in a blender; cover and process until blended. Strain and discard seeds.

2. In a clean blender, combine the milk, ice cream, sorbet and ice; cover and process 30 seconds or until smooth. Layer raspberry puree and ice cream mixture into four serving glasses. Garnish with whipped cream, berries and mint if desired.

RASPBERRY-SWIRLED
LEMON MILK SHAKES

FAST FIX

Garlic Toast Pizzas

Between working full time, going to school and raising three children, finding time-saving recipes that my family actually enjoys is one of my biggest challenges. These quick little pizzas pack a huge amount of flavor.

—AMY GRIM CHILLICOTHE, OH

START TO FINISH: 15 MIN.
MAKES: 8 SLICES

- 1 **package (11¼ ounces) frozen garlic Texas toast**
- ½ **cup pizza sauce**
- 1 **package (3½ ounces) sliced regular or turkey pepperoni**
- 2 **cups (8 ounces) shredded part-skim mozzarella cheese**

1. Preheat oven to 425°. Place Texas toast in a 15x10x1-in. baking pan. Bake 5 minutes.
2. Spread toast with pizza sauce; top with pepperoni and cheese. Bake 4-5 minutes longer or until cheese is melted.

TOP TIP

Great way to let kids help make dinner. Works well on the grill, too, so you don't have to turn on the oven in the summer.

—CHICKLUVS2COOK
TASTEOFHOME.COM

GARLIC TOAST PIZZAS

PARTY PRETZELS

Party Pretzels

Turn ordinary pretzels into instant party food with a garlicky dill seasoning. This could also be done with pretzel sticks and makes a popular after-school snack.

—**CARRIE SHAUB** MOUNT JOY, PA

START TO FINISH: 25 MIN. • **MAKES:** 12 CUPS

- 1 package (16 ounces) fat-free miniature pretzels
- ¼ cup canola oil
- 3 teaspoons garlic powder
- 1 teaspoon dill weed
- ½ teaspoon lemon-pepper seasoning

1. Preheat oven to 350°. Place the pretzels in an ungreased 15x10x1-in. baking pan. Combine oil, garlic powder, dill and lemon-pepper; drizzle over pretzels and toss to coat.

2. Bake 12 minutes, stirring twice. Cool on a wire rack. Store in an airtight container.

Ham & Pickle Wraps

I decided to try this recipe with my card club, and they loved it. The ingredients can be swapped out and the recipe changed in so many different ways, and it always turns out. What an easy, great-tasting centerpiece over a hand of cards.

—**DETRA LITTLE** MOULTRIE, GA

PREP: 10 MIN. + CHILLING • **MAKES:** 1 DOZEN

- 2 ounces cream cheese, softened
- 1½ teaspoons spicy ranch salad dressing mix
- 2 slices deli ham
- 2 whole dill pickles

In a small bowl, combine the cream cheese and dressing mix. Spread over ham slices. Place a pickle on each ham slice. Roll up tightly; wrap in plastic wrap. Refrigerate for at least 1 hour or until firm. Cut each wrap into six slices.

Savory Stuffed Figs

I turn to this three-ingredient recipe whenever I want a fancy appetizer that's simple to make. It can be prepped ahead for convenience, and it's nice for both elegant and casual parties.

—**TECKLA MISAELIDIS** ANCHORAGE, AK

PREP: 30 MIN. • **GRILL:** 5 MIN. • **MAKES:** 2 DOZEN

- 12 bacon strips
- 24 dried figs
- 24 pecan halves

1. Cut bacon strips in half widthwise. In a large skillet, cook bacon over medium heat until partially cooked but not crisp. Remove to paper towels to drain; keep warm.

2. Cut a lengthwise slit down the center of each fig; fill with a pecan half. Wrap each with a piece of bacon.

3. Grill, covered, over medium heat or broil 4 in. from the heat for 5-8 minutes or until bacon is crisp, turning once.

**KATHERINE WHITE'S
TEX-MEX SHREDDED BEEF
SANDWICHES** *PAGE 66*

Soups & Sandwiches

HEATHER ROREX'S SPICY PUMPKIN & CORN SOUP *PAGE 60*

JENNIFER MOORE'S ORANGE TURKEY CROISSANTS *PAGE 55*

SUE WEST'S SIMPLE CHICKEN SOUP *PAGE 57*

SPRINGTIME
STRAWBERRY
SOUP

Springtime Strawberry Soup

Laden with strawberries, this chilled soup is certain to become a new hot-weather favorite.
—**VERNA BOLLIN** POWELL, TN

PREP: 15 MIN. + CHILLING • **MAKES:** 6 SERVINGS

- 2 **cups vanilla yogurt**
- ½ **cup orange juice**
- 2 **pounds fresh strawberries, halved (8 cups)**
- ½ **cup sugar**
   Additional vanilla yogurt and fresh mint leaves, optional

1. In a blender, combine the yogurt, orange juice, strawberries and sugar in batches; cover and process until blended. Refrigerate for at least 2 hours.
2. Garnish with additional yogurt and mint leaves if desired.

SLOW COOKER
Spicy French Dip

If I'm cooking for a party or family get-together, I can put this beef in the slow cooker in the morning and then concentrate on other preparations. It's a great time-saver and it never fails to get rave reviews.
—**GINNY KOEPPEN** WINNFIELD, LA

PREP: 10 MIN. • **COOK:** 8 HOURS • **MAKES:** 12 SERVINGS

- 1 **beef sirloin tip roast (3 pounds), cut in half**
- ½ **cup water**
- 1 **can (4 ounces) diced jalapeno peppers, drained**
- 1 **envelope Italian salad dressing mix**
- 12 **crusty rolls (5 inches)**

1. Place beef in a 5-qt. slow cooker. In a small bowl, combine the water, jalapenos and dressing mix; pour over beef. Cover and cook on low for 8-10 hours or until meat is tender.
2. Remove beef and shred using two forks. Skim fat from cooking juices. Serve beef on rolls with the juice.

Louisiana-Style Taco Soup

This is one of my family's favorite quick and easy soups on a cold winter's day. With just a few ingredients and your favorite garnish, it's ready in no time.
—**JULIE WHITLOW** ALEXANDRIA, IN

PREP: 5 MIN. • **COOK:** 35 MIN.
MAKES: 13 SERVINGS (ABOUT 3 QUARTS)

- 1 **package (8 ounces) red beans and rice mix**
- 1 **package (9 ounces) tortilla soup mix**
- 1 **pound ground beef**
- 1 **cup salsa**
- ¼ **cup sour cream**

Prepare mixes according to package directions. Meanwhile, in a Dutch oven, cook beef over medium heat until no longer pink; drain. Stir in the salsa, prepared rice and soup. Cook, uncovered, for 5 minutes or until heated through. Garnish with sour cream.
NOTE *This recipe was prepared with Zatarain's New Orleans-Style Red Beans and Rice and Bear Creek Tortilla Soup mix.*

TURKEY & APRICOT WRAPS

FAST FIX
Turkey & Apricot Wraps

For these wraps, I combined the traditional Southern appetizer of jam and cream cheese on crackers with the turkey sandwiches we ate at my bridal luncheon. I like to sneak fresh baby spinach into all sorts of recipes because it has such a nice crunch and fresh flavor.

—**KIM BEAVERS** NORTH AUGUSTA, SC

START TO FINISH: 15 MIN. • **MAKES:** 4 SERVINGS

- ½ cup reduced-fat cream cheese
- 3 tablespoons apricot preserves
- 4 whole wheat tortillas (8 inches), room temperature
- ½ pound sliced reduced-sodium deli turkey
- 2 cups fresh baby spinach or arugula

In a small bowl, mix cream cheese and preserves. Spread about 2 tablespoons over each tortilla to within ½ in. of edges. Layer with turkey and spinach. Roll up tightly; wrap in plastic wrap. Refrigerate until serving.

FAST FIX
Asian Shrimp Soup

My mother passed her delicious Asian soup recipe along to me. A package of store-bought ramen noodles speeds up the preparation of this zesty broth with shrimp and carrots.

—**DONNA HELLINGER** LORAIN, OH

START TO FINISH: 15 MIN. • **MAKES:** 4 SERVINGS

- 3½ cups water
- 1 package (3 ounces) Oriental ramen noodles
- 1 cup cooked small shrimp, peeled and deveined
- ½ cup chopped green onions
- 1 medium carrot, julienned
- 2 tablespoons soy sauce

1. In a large saucepan, bring water to a boil. Set aside seasoning packet from noodles. Add ramen noodles to the boiling water; cook and stir for 3 minutes.
2. Add the shrimp, onions, carrot, soy sauce and contents of seasoning packet. Cook 3-4 minutes longer or until heated through.

GRILLED
SEASONED
BRATWURST

FAST FIX

Grilled Seasoned Bratwurst

Whether you're hosting a picnic at home or at a park, cook the bratwurst on the stovetop first. Then you can quickly brown them on the grill.

—*TASTE OF HOME* TEST KITCHEN

START TO FINISH: 25 MIN.
MAKES: 8 SERVINGS

- 8 uncooked bratwurst links
- 3 cans (12 ounces each) beer or nonalcoholic beer
- 1 large onion, halved and sliced
- 2 tablespoons fennel seed
- 8 bratwurst sandwich buns, split

1. Place the bratwurst in a Dutch oven; add the beer, onion and fennel. Bring to a boil. Reduce heat; cover and simmer for 8-10 minutes or until meat is no longer pink. Drain and discard beer mixture.

2. Grill the bratwurst, covered, over indirect medium heat for 7-8 minutes or until browned, turning occasionally. Serve on buns.

TOP TIP

Fennel seed has a slightly sweet and licorice-like flavor. It's frequently used in baked goods, sausage, and pork and seafood dishes, as well as German, Italian, Indian and Middle Eastern cuisines.

GRILLED SEASONED BRATWURST

RAMEN BROCCOLI SOUP

Mushroom Swiss Burgers

These skillet burgers are perfect cold-weather fare. Heaping with mushrooms and the wonderful flavor of Swiss cheese, they really deliver. Your family will request this recipe often.

—**JAMES BOWLES** IRONTON, OH

START TO FINISH: 30 MIN.
MAKES: 6 SERVINGS

- 1½ **pounds ground beef**
- 1 **pound sliced fresh mushrooms**
- 1 **can (10¾ ounces) condensed cream of mushroom soup, undiluted**
- 1 **cup water**
- 6 **slices Swiss cheese**
- 6 **hamburger buns, split**

1. Shape beef into six patties. In a large skillet, cook over medium-high heat for 5-7 minutes on each side or until a thermometer reads 160° and juices run clear.
2. Remove to paper towels; drain, reserving 2 tablespoons drippings. Saute mushrooms in drippings until tender.
3. Meanwhile, in a microwave-safe bowl, combine soup and water. Cover and microwave on high for 2½ to 3½ minutes or until heated through.
4. Return patties to the skillet. Stir in soup mixture. Bring to a boil. Reduce heat; simmer, uncovered, for 3 minutes.
5. Top each patty with a slice of cheese. Remove from the heat; cover and let stand until cheese is melted. Serve on buns topped with mushrooms.

FAST FIX ▶
Ramen Broccoli Soup

Cheese and garlic powder are the secret to this heartwarming and tasty soup. Loaded with noodles and broccoli, it hits the spot on cool winter days.

—**LUELLA DIRKS** EMELLE, AL

START TO FINISH: 20 MIN.
MAKES: 7 SERVINGS

- 5 **cups water**
- 1 **package (16 ounces) frozen broccoli cuts**
- 2 **packages (3 ounces each) chicken ramen noodles**
- ¼ **teaspoon garlic powder**
- 3 **slices process American cheese, cut into strips**

1. In a large saucepan, bring water to a boil. Add broccoli; return to a boil. Reduce heat; cover and simmer for 3 minutes. Return to a boil. Break noodles into small pieces; add to water. Cook for 3 minutes longer, stirring occasionally.
2. Remove soup from the heat. Add the garlic powder, cheese and contents of the seasoning packets from the ramen noodles; stir soup until cheese is melted. Serve immediately.

SPINACH SAUSAGE SOUP

Chicken Parmesan Patty Melts

I came up with this dish to re-create the comforting flavors of a restaurant-style sandwich. Now it's my husband's favorite dinner.

—**DEBORAH BIGGS** OMAHA, NE

START TO FINISH: 30 MIN. • **MAKES:** 4 SERVINGS

- 5 tablespoons grated Parmesan cheese, divided
- 1 cup marinara sauce, divided
- ¼ teaspoon pepper
- ⅛ teaspoon salt
- 1 pound lean ground chicken
- 2 ounces fresh mozzarella cheese, thinly sliced
- 2 ciabatta rolls, split and toasted

1. In a large bowl, combine 3 tablespoons Parmesan cheese, 2 tablespoons marinara sauce, pepper and salt. Crumble chicken over mixture and mix well. Shape into four patties.

2. Place on a baking sheet coated with cooking spray. Broil 4 in. from the heat for 4-6 minutes on each side or until a thermometer reads 165° and juices run clear.

3. Top with remaining marinara, the mozzarella and remaining Parmesan. Broil 1-2 minutes longer or until cheeses are melted. Top each roll half with a patty.

FAST FIX

Spinach Sausage Soup

Chock-full of potatoes, Italian sausage and spinach, this rich soup is sure to disappear fast. Not only is it delicious and quick, but it also freezes well. Adjust the amount of broth to suit your family's preference.

—**BONITA KRUGLER** ANDERSON, IN

START TO FINISH: 30 MIN.
MAKES: 10 SERVINGS (2½ QUARTS)

- 1 pound bulk Italian sausage
- 4 cans (14½ ounces each) chicken broth
- 8 small red potatoes, quartered and thinly sliced
- 1 envelope Italian salad dressing mix
- 2 cups fresh spinach or frozen chopped spinach

1. In a large skillet, brown sausage over medium heat until no longer pink. Meanwhile, in a Dutch oven, combine the broth, potatoes and salad dressing mix. Bring to a boil; cover and simmer for 10 minutes or until potatoes are tender.

2. Drain sausage. Add sausage and spinach to broth mixture; heat through.

CHICKEN PARMESAN PATTY MELTS

ORANGE TURKEY CROISSANTS

FAST FIX

Smoky Gouda & Chicken Sandwiches

Here's a hearty, hot, delectable sandwich to take along on a picnic or to enjoy for a low-key dinner. Ready-to-eat rotisserie chicken makes it quick to prepare.

—**NANCY MOCK** COLCHESTER, VERMONT

START TO FINISH: 20 MIN. • **MAKES:** 4 SERVINGS

- ¼ cup garlic-herb mayonnaise, divided
- 8 slices country white bread (½ inch thick), toasted
- 2 cups shredded rotisserie chicken
- ¼ teaspoon salt
- ⅛ teaspoon pepper
- 2 small peaches or medium plums, thinly sliced
- 4 slices smoked Gouda cheese

1. Preheat broiler. Spread 2 tablespoons mayonnaise over four slices toast; place on a foil-lined baking sheet. Arrange chicken over top; sprinkle with salt and pepper. Layer with peaches and cheese.

2. Broil 3-4 in. from heat 2-3 minutes or until cheese is melted. Spread remaining mayonnaise over remaining toast; place over tops.

FAST FIX

Orange Turkey Croissants

Sweet and tangy orange marmalade and crunchy pecans make this easy, amazing sandwich truly delicious and special.

—**JENNIFER MOORE** CENTERVILLE, IA

START TO FINISH: 10 MIN. • **MAKES:** 6 SERVINGS

- 6 tablespoons spreadable cream cheese
- 6 tablespoons orange marmalade
- 6 croissants, split
- ½ cup chopped pecans
- 1 pound thinly sliced deli turkey

Spread cream cheese and marmalade onto croissant bottoms. Sprinkle with pecans. Top with turkey; replace croissant tops.

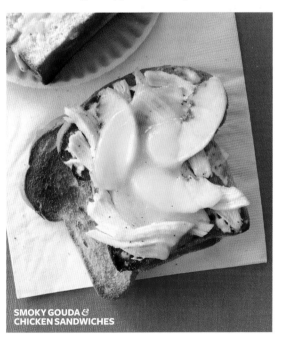

SMOKY GOUDA & CHICKEN SANDWICHES

SHREDDED TURKEY SANDWICHES

SLOW COOKER 🍲
Shredded Turkey Sandwiches

This slow-cooked sandwich gets its zesty flavor from onion soup mix and beer. You can feed a crowd with minimal effort!

—**JACKI KNUTH** OWATONNA, MN

PREP: 15 MIN. • **COOK:** 7 HOURS • **MAKES:** 24 SERVINGS

- 2 boneless skinless turkey breast halves (2 to 3 pounds each)
- 1 bottle (12 ounces) beer or nonalcoholic beer
- ½ cup butter, cubed
- 1 envelope onion soup mix
- 24 French rolls, split

Place turkey in a 5-qt. slow cooker. Combine the beer, butter and soup mix; pour over meat. Cover and cook on low for 7-9 hours or until meat is tender. Shred meat and return to slow cooker; heat through. Serve on rolls.

💬 **TOP TIP**

It was a big hit so we will be making it again. Dill pickles, BBQ sauce and maybe Miracle Whip on the side if folks want. Much better than the turkey sandwiches from most street fair vendors.

—**SANDCRAB57** TASTEOFHOME.COM

SLOW COOKER 🍲
Potato Chowder

One of the ladies in our church quilting group brought this potato soup to a meeting, and everyone loved how rich it was. Assemble the chowder in the morning and let it simmer on its own all day.

—**ANNA MAYER** FORT BRANCH, IN

PREP: 15 MIN. • **COOK:** 8 HOURS
MAKES: 12 SERVINGS (3 QUARTS)

- 8 cups diced potatoes
- 3 cans (14½ ounces each) chicken broth
- 1 can (10¾ ounces) condensed cream of chicken soup, undiluted
- ⅓ cup chopped onion
- ¼ teaspoon pepper
- 1 package (8 ounces) cream cheese, cubed
- ½ pound sliced bacon, cooked and crumbled, optional
  Minced chives, optional

1. In a 5-qt. slow cooker, combine the first five ingredients. Cover and cook on low for 8-10 hours or until potatoes are tender.
2. Add cream cheese; stir until blended. Garnish with bacon and chives if desired.

FAST FIX ▶
Gumbo in a Jiffy

This gumbo recipe could not be any easier to make. Try it on a busy weeknight with crusty bread for dipping!
—**AMY FLACK** HOMER CITY, PA

START TO FINISH: 20 MIN. • **MAKES:** 6 SERVINGS

- 3 Italian turkey sausage links, sliced
- 1 can (14½ ounces) diced tomatoes with green peppers and onions, undrained
- 1 can (14½ ounces) reduced-sodium chicken broth
- ½ cup water
- 1 cup uncooked instant rice
- 1 can (7 ounces) whole kernel corn, drained

In a large saucepan, cook sausage until no longer pink; drain. Stir in the tomatoes, broth and water; bring to a boil. Stir in rice and corn; cover and remove from the heat. Let stand for 5 minutes before serving.

SIMPLE CHICKEN SOUP

Mozzarella Ham Stromboli

The original recipe for this savory bread called for salami, but I use ham instead. People are always amazed that it takes only about 15 minutes to assemble. I usually serve it with tomato soup.

—**JANICE BRIGHTWELL**
JEFFERSONVILLE, IN

PREP: 15 MIN. • **BAKE:** 20 MIN.
MAKES: 6 SERVINGS

- 1 **tube (11 ounces) refrigerated crusty French loaf**
- 2 **cups (8 ounces) shredded part-skim mozzarella cheese**
- ¼ **pound thinly sliced deli ham**
- 1 **tablespoon butter, melted**
- 1 **tablespoon grated Parmesan cheese**

1. Preheat oven to 375°. On a lightly floured surface, unroll dough. Pat dough into a 14x12-in. rectangle. Sprinkle mozzarella cheese over dough to within ½ in. of edges. Top with a single layer of ham.
2. Roll up tightly from a short side; pinch seam to seal. Place seam side down on an ungreased baking sheet. Brush top of loaf with butter; sprinkle with Parmesan cheese.
3. Bake 20-25 minutes or until golden brown. Cool on a wire rack 5 minutes. Cut with a serrated knife.

FAST FIX
Simple Chicken Soup

I revised a recipe that my family loved so it would be lighter and easier to make. It's a hearty and healthy meal served with a green salad and fresh bread.

—**SUE WEST** ALVORD, TX

START TO FINISH: 20 MIN.
MAKES: 6 SERVINGS

- 2 **cans (14½ ounces each) reduced-sodium chicken broth**
- 1 **tablespoon dried minced onion**
- 1 **package (16 ounces) frozen mixed vegetables**
- 2 **cups cubed cooked chicken breast**
- 2 **cans (10¾ ounces each) reduced-fat reduced-sodium condensed cream of chicken soup, undiluted**

In a large saucepan, bring broth and onion to a boil. Reduce heat. Add the vegetables; cover and cook for 6-8 minutes or until crisp-tender. Stir in chicken and soup; heat through.

TOMATO & AVOCADO
SANDWICHES

Tomato & Avocado Sandwiches

I'm a vegetarian, and this is a tasty, quick and healthy lunch that I could eat for every meal. At my house, we call these sandwiches HATS: hummus, avocado, tomato and shallots. They're all ingredients I almost always have on hand.

—**SARAH JARAHA** MOORESTOWN, NJ

START TO FINISH: 10 MIN. • **MAKES:** 2 SERVINGS

- ½ medium ripe avocado, peeled and mashed
- 4 slices whole wheat bread, toasted
- 1 medium tomato, sliced
- 2 tablespoons finely chopped shallot
- ¼ cup hummus

Spread avocado over two slices of toast. Top with tomato and shallot. Spread hummus over remaining toast; place over tops.

Root Beer Pulled Pork Sandwiches

My sister shared this simple recipe with me. My husband is a huge fan of pulled pork sandwiches, and this one works well for potlucks or family dinners.

—**CAROLYN PALM** WALTON, NY

PREP: 20 MIN. • **COOK:** 8½ HOURS • **MAKES:** 12 SERVINGS

- 1 boneless pork shoulder butt roast (3 to 4 pounds)
- 1 can (12 ounces) root beer or cola
- 1 bottle (18 ounces) barbecue sauce
- 12 kaiser rolls, split

1. Place roast in a 4- or 5-qt. slow cooker. Add root beer; cook, covered, on low 8-10 hours or until meat is tender.
2. Remove roast; cool slightly. Discard cooking juices. Shred pork with two forks; return to slow cooker. Stir in barbecue sauce. Cook, covered, until heated through, about 30 minutes. Serve on rolls.

HAM AND SWISS
STROMBOLI

Ham and Swiss Stromboli

This pretty swirled sandwich loaf is fast and versatile. Fill it with anything your family likes. Try sliced pepperoni and provolone cheese, or anchovies and olives if you're feeling adventurous.

—**PAT RAPORT** GAINESVILLE, FL

PREP: 20 MIN. • **BAKE:** 30 MIN. • **MAKES:** 8 SERVINGS

- 1 tube (11 ounces) refrigerated crusty French loaf
- 6 ounces thinly sliced deli ham
- 6 green onions, sliced
- 8 bacon strips, cooked and crumbled
- 1½ cups (6 ounces) shredded Swiss cheese

1. Preheat oven to 350°. Unroll dough into a rectangle on a greased baking sheet. Place ham over dough to within ½ in. of edges; sprinkle with onions, bacon and cheese. Roll up jelly-roll style, starting with a long side. Pinch seam to seal and tuck ends under. Place seam side down on baking sheet.
2. With a sharp knife, cut several ¼-in.-deep slits on top of loaf. Bake 26-30 minutes or until golden brown. Cool slightly before slicing. Serve warm.

FAST FIX
Hot Dog Bean Soup

My husband fixed this soup for our three kids years ago. They always loved it and now prepare it for their own kids. It's a real favorite on camping trips.

—**MARY ANN KIME** STURGIS, MI

START TO FINISH: 10 MIN. • **MAKES:** 4 SERVINGS

- 3 hot dogs, halved lengthwise and sliced
- 1 teaspoon canola oil
- 1 can (16 ounces) kidney beans, rinsed and drained
- 1 can (11½ ounces) condensed bean and bacon soup, undiluted
- 1¼ cups water
- 1 teaspoon dried minced onion
- ¼ teaspoon pepper

1. In a large skillet, cook hot dogs in oil over medium heat for 3-4 minutes or until browned.
2. Meanwhile, in a 2-qt. microwave-safe bowl, combine the remaining ingredients. Cover and microwave on high for 2-3 minutes or until heated through, stirring once. Stir in hot dogs.

HOT DOG
BEAN SOUP

PESTO GRILLED CHEESE SANDWICHES

FAST FIX

Pesto Grilled Cheese Sandwiches

My daughter always says that with my cooking, I make the ordinary better. That's what this recipe is all about: an old favorite with a fresh new twist. Pair it with your favorite soup for a satisfying meal.

—**ARLENE REAGAN** LIMERICK, PA

START TO FINISH: 10 MIN.
MAKES: 4 SERVINGS

- 8 **slices walnut-raisin bread**
- 3 **to 4 tablespoons prepared pesto**
- 8 **slices provolone and mozzarella cheese blend**
- 8 **slices tomato**
- ¼ **cup butter, softened**

1. Spread four slices of bread with the pesto. Layer with cheese and tomato; top with remaining bread. Butter the outsides of sandwiches.
2. In a large skillet over medium heat, toast the sandwiches for 2-3 minutes on each side or until golden brown and the cheese is melted.

FAST FIX

Spicy Pumpkin & Corn Soup

A seriously quick dish, it can satisfy a hungry household in 20 minutes. My family loves this soup with a hot pan of corn bread.

—**HEATHER ROREX** WINNEMUCCA, NV

START TO FINISH: 20 MIN.
MAKES: 8 SERVINGS

- 1 **can (15 ounces) solid-pack pumpkin**
- 1 **can (15 ounces) black beans, rinsed and drained**
- 1½ **cups frozen corn**
- 1 **can (10 ounces) diced tomatoes and green chilies**
- 2 **cans (14½ ounces each) reduced-sodium chicken broth**
- ¼ **teaspoon pepper**

In a large saucepan, mix all ingredients. Bring to a boil. Reduce heat; simmer, uncovered, 10-15 minutes or until slightly thickened, stirring occasionally.
FREEZE OPTION *Freeze the cooled soup in freezer containers. To use, partially thaw in refrigerator overnight. Heat through in a saucepan, stirring occasionally and adding a little broth if necessary.*

SPICY PUMPKIN & CORN SOUP

Chipotle BLT Wraps

BLT sandwiches are so good, but they can make a lot of messy crumbs from the toasted bread. Since we also love wraps, I decided to make BLT's with tortillas instead. Warming the tortillas a little makes them pliable and easy to work with.

—**DARLENE BRENDEN** SALEM, OR

START TO FINISH: 15 MIN.
MAKES: 4 SERVINGS

- 3 **cups chopped romaine**
- 2 **plum tomatoes, finely chopped**
- 8 **bacon strips, cooked and crumbled**
- ⅓ **cup reduced-fat chipotle or regular mayonnaise**
- 4 **flour tortillas (8 inches), warmed**

1. In a large bowl, combine romaine, tomatoes and bacon. Add mayonnaise; toss to coat.
2. Spoon about 1 cup romaine mixture down center of each tortilla. Fold bottom of tortilla over filling; fold both sides to close. Serve immediately.

TOP TIP

Quick and easy! I couldn't find chipotle mayo, so I used tangy bacon French dressing instead, and it was perfect. Served with fries for a fast weeknight meal.
—**MINKS05** TASTEOFHOME.COM

CHIPOTLE BLT WRAPS

Sausage & Spinach Calzones

These are perfect for a quick lunch or a midnight snack. My co-workers always ask me to make them when it's my turn to bring in lunch.

—KOURTNEY WILLIAMS MECHANICSVILLE, VA

START TO FINISH: 30 MIN. • **MAKES:** 4 SERVINGS

- ½ **pound bulk Italian sausage**
- 1 **tube (13.8 ounces) refrigerated pizza crust**
- ¾ **cup shredded part-skim mozzarella cheese**
- 3 **cups fresh baby spinach**
- ½ **cup part-skim ricotta cheese**
- ¼ **teaspoon salt**
- ¼ **teaspoon pepper**

1. Preheat oven to 400°. In a large skillet, cook sausage over medium heat until no longer pink. Meanwhile, unroll the pizza crust; pat into a 15x11-in. rectangle. Cut into four rectangles. Sprinkle mozzarella cheese over half of each rectangle to within 1 in. of edges.

2. Drain sausage. Add spinach; cook and stir over medium heat until spinach is wilted. Remove from heat. Stir in ricotta cheese, salt and pepper; spread over mozzarella cheese. Fold dough over filling; press edges with a fork to seal.

3. Transfer to a greased baking sheet. Bake 10-15 minutes or until lightly browned.

SAUSAGE & SPINACH CALZONES

TURKEY SAUSAGE, BUTTERNUT & KALE SOUP

Turkey Sausage, Butternut & Kale Soup

Kale and butternut squash are two of my favorite fall veggies. This low-fat soup combines them. If you love sweet potatoes, sub them for the squash.

—LAURA KOCH LINCOLN, NE

PREP: 20 MIN. • **COOK:** 30 MIN.
MAKES: 10 SERVINGS (2½ QUARTS)

- 1 **package (19½ ounces) Italian turkey sausage links, casings removed**
- 1 **medium butternut squash (about 3 pounds), peeled and cubed**
- 2 **cartons (32 ounces each) reduced-sodium chicken broth**
- 1 **bunch kale, trimmed and coarsely chopped (about 16 cups)**
- ½ **cup shaved Parmesan cheese**

1. In a stockpot, cook sausage over medium heat 8-10 minutes or until no longer pink, breaking into crumbles.

2. Add squash and broth; bring to a boil. Gradually stir in kale, allowing it to wilt slightly between additions. Return to a boil. Reduce heat; simmer, uncovered, 15-20 minutes or until vegetables are tender. Top servings with cheese.

FAST FIX
Quick Clam Chowder

Not only is this soup a quick fix, but it's oh so tasty! Now you can enjoy the comfort of clam chowder with only a fraction of the work.

—**JUDY JUNGWIRTH** ATHOL, SD

START TO FINISH: 10 MIN. • **MAKES:** 5 SERVINGS

- 1 can (10¾ ounces) condensed cream of celery soup, undiluted
- 1 can (10¾ ounces) condensed cream of potato soup, undiluted
- 2 cups half-and-half cream
- 2 cans (6½ ounces each) minced/chopped clams, drained
- ¼ teaspoon ground nutmeg
  Pepper to taste

In a large saucepan, combine all ingredients. Cook and stir over medium heat until heated through.

FAST FIX
Grilled PBJ Sandwiches

I was going to make grilled cheese sandwiches one day and had already buttered several slices of bread when I found I was out of cheese. So I pulled out some peanut butter and jelly, and the result was this tasty version of a popular classic.

—**BARB TRAUTMANN** HAM LAKE, MN

START TO FINISH: 10 MIN. • **MAKES:** 2 SERVINGS

- 4 tablespoons peanut butter
- 2 tablespoons strawberry jam
- 4 slices English muffin or white toasting bread
- 2 tablespoons butter, softened
  Confectioners' sugar, optional

Spread peanut butter and jam on two slices of bread; top with remaining bread. Butter the outsides of sandwiches; cook in a large skillet over medium heat until golden brown on each side. Dust with confectioners' sugar if desired.

SIMPLY ELEGANT TOMATO SOUP

Simply Elegant Tomato Soup

If you've only had tomato soup from a can, you're going to be blown away when you try this. It's velvety, creamy and so delicious!

—HEIDI BLANKEN SEDRO-WOOLLEY, WA

PREP: 25 MIN. • **COOK:** 20 MIN. • **MAKES:** 4 SERVINGS

- 4 pounds tomatoes (about 10 medium)
- 1 tablespoon butter
- 3 tablespoons minced chives, divided
- 1 teaspoon salt
- ½ teaspoon pepper
- 2 cups half-and-half cream

1. In a large saucepan, bring 8 cups water to a boil. Using a slotted spoon, place tomatoes, one at a time, in boiling water for 30-60 seconds. Remove each tomato and immediately plunge in ice water. Peel and quarter tomatoes; remove seeds.

2. In another large saucepan, melt butter. Add tomatoes, 2 tablespoons chives, salt and pepper. Bring to a boil. Reduce heat; simmer, uncovered, for 6-7 minutes or until tender, stirring occasionally. Remove from the heat. Cool slightly.

3. In a blender, process soup until blended. Return to the pan. Stir in cream; heat through. Sprinkle each serving with remaining chives.

FAST FIX

Burger Americana

Here's a good basic burger your family will love. Grill the patties and load them sky high with everyone's favorite toppings. Cheese, lettuce and tomato are classics, but you could also go for bacon and blue cheese.

—SUSAN MAHANEY NEW HARTFORD, NY

START TO FINISH: 25 MIN. • **MAKES:** 4 SERVINGS

- ½ cup seasoned bread crumbs
- 1 egg, lightly beaten
- ½ teaspoon salt
- ½ teaspoon pepper
- 1 pound ground beef
- 1 tablespoon olive oil
- 4 sesame seed hamburger buns, split
  Toppings of your choice

1. In a large bowl, combine bread crumbs, egg, salt and pepper. Add beef; mix lightly but thoroughly. Shape into four ½-in.-thick patties. Press a shallow indentation in the center of each with your thumb. Brush both sides of patties with oil.

2. Grill burgers, covered, over medium heat or broil 4 in. from heat 4-5 minutes on each side or until a thermometer reads 160°. Serve on buns with the toppings of your choice.

FAST FIX

Egg Drop Soup

Planning an Asian-inspired meal? Start it off with this traditional Chinese soup that uses just five ingredients.

—MARY KELLEY MINNEAPOLIS, MN

START TO FINISH: 10 MIN. • **MAKES:** 4 SERVINGS

- 5 cups chicken broth
- ½ teaspoon sugar
- 1 egg, lightly beaten
- ⅓ cup sliced fresh spinach
- 2 green onions, sliced

In a large saucepan, bring broth and sugar to a boil over medium heat. Reduce heat to low. Drizzle beaten egg into hot broth, stirring constantly. Remove from the heat; stir in spinach and onions.

SLOW COOKER 🍲
Tex-Mex Shredded Beef Sandwiches

Slow cooker meals, like this shredded beef, are my favorite kind because after I combine a few ingredients and get them cooking, there is time for me to do my own thing. Plus, I have a hearty, satisfying and enticing meal when I come home!

—**KATHERINE WHITE** CLEMMONS, NC

PREP: 5 MIN. • **COOK:** 8 HOURS • **MAKES:** 8 SERVINGS

- 1 **boneless beef chuck roast (3 pounds)**
- 1 **envelope chili seasoning**
- ½ **cup barbecue sauce**
- 8 **onion rolls, split**
- 8 **slices cheddar cheese**

1. Cut roast in half; place in a 3-qt. slow cooker. Sprinkle with chili seasoning. Pour barbecue sauce over top. Cover and cook on low for 8-10 hours or until meat is tender.

2. Remove roast; cool slightly. Shred meat with two forks. Skim fat from cooking juices. Return meat to slow cooker; heat through. Using a slotted spoon, place ½ cup meat mixture on each roll bottom; top with cheese. Replace tops.

TEX-MEX SHREDDED BEEF SANDWICHES

VEGETABLE MEATBALL SOUP

FAST FIX ▶
Vegetable Meatball Soup

You can have this delicious soup on the table in less than 30 minutes. If you have leftover meatballs from a previous meal, it's a great way to use them up.

—**SUSAN WESTERFIELD** ALBUQUERQUE, NM

START TO FINISH: 25 MIN.
MAKES: 6 SERVINGS (2 QUARTS)

- 1 **package (12 ounces) frozen fully cooked Italian meatballs**
- 2 **cans (14½ ounces each) beef broth**
- 2 **cups frozen Italian vegetable blend**
- 1 **can (14½ ounces) Italian diced tomatoes, undrained**
- 1½ **cups water**
- ⅓ **cup small pasta shells**
   Shredded Parmesan cheese, optional

In a Dutch oven, combine the meatballs, broth, vegetable blend, tomatoes, water and pasta. Bring to a boil. Reduce heat; simmer, uncovered, for 10-12 minutes or until pasta is tender. Garnish servings with cheese if desired.

Pigs in a Blanket

Even my husband, Allan, admits to enjoying every bite of these baked hot dog sandwiches. We like to dip them in ketchup and mustard.
—**LINDA YOUNG** LONGMONT, CO

START TO FINISH: 25 MIN. • **MAKES:** 4 SERVINGS

- 1 **tube (8 ounces) refrigerated crescent rolls**
- 8 **hot dogs**
- 1 **egg, lightly beaten**
- 1 **tablespoon water**
   Caraway seeds

1. Preheat oven to 375°. Separate crescent dough into triangles. Place hot dogs at wide ends of triangles and roll up. Place on an ungreased baking sheet. Combine egg and water; brush over rolls. Sprinkle caraway over tops; press lightly into rolls.
2. Bake 12-15 minutes or until golden brown.

Wild Rice and Mushroom Soup

Frequently requested at family get-togethers, this rich and hearty soup is ready in a flash. Cooking for a vegetarian? Swap in vegetable stock for the beef broth.
—**DANIELLE NOBLE** FORT THOMAS, KY

PREP: 10 MIN. • **COOK:** 35 MIN.
MAKES: 8 SERVINGS (2 QUARTS)

- 1 **pound baby portobello mushrooms, chopped**
- 2 **tablespoons olive oil**
- 2 **packages (6 ounces each) long grain and wild rice mix**
- 1 **carton (32 ounces) reduced-sodium beef broth**
- ½ **cup water**
- 2 **cups heavy whipping cream**

In a Dutch oven, saute mushrooms in oil until tender. Add the rice, contents of seasoning packets, broth and water. Bring to a boil. Reduce heat; cover and simmer for 25 minutes. Add cream and heat through.

FAST FIX

Turkey-Cranberry Bagels

Take care of that leftover turkey in a way your family will love. It's good with all sorts of cranberry sauces and chutneys, so have fun playing around.

—TASTE OF HOME **TEST KITCHEN**

START TO FINISH: 10 MIN.
MAKES: 4 SERVINGS

- 4 **plain bagels, split and toasted**
- 8 **ounces thinly sliced cooked turkey**
- ½ **cup whole-berry cranberry sauce**
- 8 **slices provolone cheese**

Preheat broiler. Place bagel halves on a baking sheet; layer with turkey, cranberry sauce and cheese. Broil 4-6 in. from the heat 1-2 minutes or until heated through and cheese is melted.

TOP TIP

You can make countless variations of this recipe. For example, prepare the broiled sandwiches with ham, Swiss cheese, chutney and split biscuits or English muffins.

TURKEY-CRANBERRY BAGELS

Chipotle Pomegranate Pulled Pork

Once I was making pulled pork and wanted to kick it up a bit. Smoky chipotles and a sweet-tart jelly were the perfect addition.

—TATIANA HENDRICKS VISALIA, CA

PREP: 10 MIN. • **COOK:** 8½ HOURS
MAKES: 10 SERVINGS

- 1 boneless pork shoulder butt roast (3 pounds)
- 2 tablespoons steak seasoning
- ½ cup water
- 1 cup pomegranate or red currant jelly
- 3 tablespoons minced chipotle peppers in adobo sauce
- 10 kaiser rolls, split

1. Cut roast in half. Place in a 5-qt. slow cooker; sprinkle with steak seasoning. Add water. Cover and cook on low for 8-10 hours or until tender.
2. In a small saucepan, combine jelly and peppers. Cook over medium heat for 5 minutes or until heated through. Remove meat from slow cooker; discard cooking liquid. Shred pork with two forks. Return to the slow cooker; top with jelly mixture. Cover and cook on low for 30 minutes or until heated through. Spoon about ⅔ cup meat onto each roll.

NOTE *This recipe was tested with McCormick's Montreal Steak Seasoning. Look for it in the spice aisle.*

QUICK RAVIOLI
& SPINACH SOUP

Quick Ravioli & Spinach Soup

I love my Italian-American traditions, but I didn't have time to make a classic Italian wedding soup. So I created this shortcut version that uses ravioli.

—CYNTHIA BENT NEWARK, DE

START TO FINISH: 25 MIN.
MAKES: 6 SERVINGS

- 2 cartons (32 ounces each) chicken broth
- ¼ teaspoon onion powder
  Dash pepper
- 1 package (9 ounces) refrigerated small cheese ravioli
- 4 cups coarsely chopped fresh spinach (about 4 ounces)
- 3 cups shredded cooked chicken
  Grated Parmesan cheese, optional

1. In a large saucepan, combine the broth, onion powder and pepper; bring to a boil. Add the ravioli and cook, uncovered, for 7-10 minutes or until tender. Add spinach and chicken during the last 3 minutes of cooking.
2. If desired, serve with cheese.

CHIPOTLE POMEGRANATE
PULLED PORK

**MICHELE ORTHNER'S
TEX-MEX PASTA**
PAGE 82

Beef

**CAROL HILLE'S
SLOW COOKER BEEF
AU JUS** PAGE 75

**KAMI JONES' MOM'S
SLOPPY TACOS** PAGE 77

**JEAN FERGUSON'S QUICK
TATER TOT BAKE** PAGE 81

Cheeseburger Pockets

Ground beef is my favorite meat to cook with because it's so versatile and affordable. Refrigerated biscuits save the trouble of making dough from scratch.

—**PAT CHAMBLESS** CROWDER, OK

PREP: 30 MIN. • **BAKE:** 10 MIN. • **MAKES:** 5 SERVINGS

- ½ **pound ground beef**
- 1 **tablespoon chopped onion**
- ½ **teaspoon salt**
- ⅛ **teaspoon pepper**
- 1 **tube (12 ounces) refrigerated buttermilk biscuits**
- 5 **slices process American cheese**

1. Preheat oven to 400°. In a large skillet, cook beef, onion, salt and pepper over medium heat until meat is no longer pink; drain and cool.
2. Place two biscuits overlapping on a floured surface; roll out into a 5-in. oval. Place about ¼ cup of meat mixture on one side. Fold a cheese slice to fit over meat mixture. Fold dough over filling; press edges with a fork to seal. Repeat with remaining biscuits, meat mixture and cheese.
3. Place on a greased baking sheet. Prick tops with a fork. Bake 10 minutes or until golden brown.

NOTE *Pricking the tops of Cheeseburger Pockets helps steam escape during baking. If you don't do this, the pockets will puff up and may break open.*

Easy Skillet Supper

Between working and helping my husband on the farm, I don't have a lot of time to cook. That's why I love this quick dish. I used to rely on this recipe when all our kids were still at home.

—**LARUE FLAA** WAHPETON, ND

PREP: 15 MIN. • **COOK:** 45 MIN. • **MAKES:** 4-6 SERVINGS

- 1 **pound lean ground beef (90% lean)**
- 4 **medium potatoes, peeled and diced**
- 2 **cups fresh or frozen corn**
- 1 **small onion, chopped**
  Salt and pepper to taste
- 1 **can (10¾ ounces) condensed cream of mushroom soup, undiluted**

1. Crumble beef into a large skillet. Top with potatoes, corn and onion. Sprinkle with salt and pepper. Spread soup over the top.
2. Cover the pan and cook over medium heat for 10 minutes.
3. Reduce the heat; cover and simmer for 30-45 minutes or until meat is no longer pink and potatoes are tender.

MARINATED CHUCK ROAST

Mexican Stuffed Peppers

My homegrown peppers shine in this nutritious yet economical summer meal. I like to top the peppers with sour cream and serve tortilla chips and salsa alongside.
—KIM COLEMAN COLUMBIA, SC

PREP: 25 MIN. • **BAKE:** 30 MIN. • **MAKES:** 8 SERVINGS

- 8 **medium green peppers**
- 1 **pound lean ground beef (90% lean)**
- 1 **can (14½ ounces) diced tomatoes and green chilies, undrained**
- 1½ **cups water**
- 1 **envelope (5.4 ounces) Mexican-style rice and pasta mix**
- 2 **cups (8 ounces) shredded Mexican cheese blend**

1. Preheat oven to 375°. Cut tops off peppers and remove seeds. In a Dutch oven, cook peppers in boiling water 3-5 minutes. Drain and rinse in cold water; set aside.
2. In a large skillet, cook beef over medium heat until no longer pink; drain. Add diced tomatoes, water and pasta mix. Bring to a boil. Reduce heat; cover and simmer 6-8 minutes or until the liquid is absorbed.
3. Place ⅓ cup rice mixture in each pepper; sprinkle each with 2 tablespoons cheese. Top with remaining rice mixture. Place in a greased 13x9-in. baking dish. Cover and bake 25 minutes. Sprinkle with remaining cheese; bake 5-10 minutes longer or until the cheese is melted and peppers are tender.

Marinated Chuck Roast

The simple marinade of orange juice, soy sauce, brown sugar and Worcestershire sauce makes this beef roast so tasty and tender.
—MARY LEE BAKER ENON, OH

PREP: 10 MIN. + MARINATING • **BAKE:** 3 HOURS + STANDING
MAKES: 8-10 SERVINGS

- ½ **cup orange juice**
- 3 **tablespoons soy sauce**
- 3 **tablespoons brown sugar**
- 1 **teaspoon Worcestershire sauce**
- 1 **boneless beef chuck roast (3 to 4 pounds)**

1. In a large resealable plastic bag, combine he orange juice, soy sauce, brown sugar and Worcestershire sauce; add the roast. Seal bag and turn to coat; refrigerate for 8 hours or overnight.
2. Pour the marinade into a Dutch oven. Bring to a boil; boil for 2 minutes. Add roast to the pan. Cover and bake at 325° for 3 to 3½ hours or until the meat is tender. Let stand for 10 minutes before slicing. Thicken juices for gravy if desired.

MEXICAN STUFFED PEPPER

SOUTHWEST
BEEF PIE

FAST FIX

Southwest Beef Pie

This meaty delight will have the family coming back for seconds! Hearty and filling, it's sure to be an instant classic.

—*TASTE OF HOME* **TEST KITCHEN**

START TO FINISH: 30 MIN.
MAKES: 6 SERVINGS

- 2 cups coarsely crushed nacho-flavored tortilla chips
- 1½ pounds ground beef
- 1 can (8 ounces) tomato sauce
- ½ cup water
- 1 envelope taco seasoning
- ¼ teaspoon pepper
- 1 cup (4 ounces) shredded Monterey Jack cheese

1. Preheat oven to 375°. Place tortilla chips in an ungreased 9-in. pie plate; set aside. In a large skillet, cook beef over medium heat until no longer pink; drain. Add tomato sauce, water, taco seasoning and pepper. Bring to a boil; cook and stir 2 minutes or until thickened.
2. Spoon half of the meat mixture over chips; sprinkle with half of the cheese. Repeat layers.
3. Bake the pie uncovered, 10-15 minutes or until heated through and cheese is melted.

Lasagna Rolls

Folks can't believe these flavor-filled rolls use only five ingredients. Prepared spaghetti sauce saves a lot of cooking time. My family never complains when these are on the menu.

—**MARY LEE THOMAS** LOGANSPORT, IN

PREP: 25 MIN. • **BAKE:** 10 MIN.
MAKES: 6 SERVINGS

- 6 lasagna noodles
- 1 pound ground beef
- 1 jar (14 ounces) spaghetti sauce
- 1 teaspoon fennel seed, optional
- 2 cups (8 ounces) shredded part-skim mozzarella cheese, divided

1. Cook lasagna noodles according to package directions. Meanwhile, in a large skillet, cook beef over medium heat until no longer pink; drain. Stir in spaghetti sauce and, if desired, fennel seed; heat through.
2. Drain noodles. Spread ¼ cup meat sauce over each noodle; sprinkle with 2 tablespoons cheese. Carefully roll up noodles and place seam side down in an 8-in.-square baking dish. Top with remaining spaghetti sauce and cheese.
3. Bake, uncovered, at 400° for 10-15 minutes or until heated through and cheese is melted.

LASAGNA ROLLS

SLOW COOKER 🍲
Slow Cooker Beef au Jus

It's easy to fix this roast, which has lots of onion flavor. Sometimes I also add cubed potatoes and baby carrots to the slow cooker to make a terrific meal with plenty of leftovers.

—CAROL HILLE GRAND JUNCTION, CO

PREP: 20 MIN.
COOK: 6 HOURS + STANDING
MAKES: 10 SERVINGS

- 1 **beef rump roast or bottom round roast (3 pounds)**
- 1 **large onion, sliced**
- ¾ **cup reduced-sodium beef broth**
- 1 **envelope (1 ounce) au jus gravy mix**
- 2 **garlic cloves, halved**
- ¼ **teaspoon pepper**

1. Cut roast in half. In a large nonstick skillet coated with cooking spray, brown meat on all sides over medium-high heat.
2. Place onion in a 5-qt. slow cooker. Top with meat. Combine the broth, gravy mix, garlic and pepper; pour over meat. Cover and cook on low for 6-7 hours or until meat is tender.
3. Remove meat to a cutting board. Let stand for 10 minutes. Thinly slice meat and return to the slow cooker; serve with cooking juices and onion.

JAVA ROAST BEEF

SLOW COOKER 🍲
Java Roast Beef

Coffee adds richness to the gravy, which is perfect for sopping up with crusty bread or draping over mashed potatoes.

—**CHARLA SACKMANN** ORANGE CITY, IA

PREP: 10 MIN. • **COOK:** 8 HOURS • **MAKES:** 12 SERVINGS

- 5 garlic cloves, minced
- 1½ teaspoons salt
- ¾ teaspoon pepper
- 1 boneless beef chuck roast (3 to 3½ pounds)
- 1½ cups strong brewed coffee
- 2 tablespoons cornstarch
- ¼ cup cold water

1. In a small bowl, mix garlic, salt and pepper; rub over beef. Transfer to a 4-qt. slow cooker. Pour coffee around meat. Cook, covered, on low 8-10 hours or until tender.
2. Remove meat to a serving platter; keep warm. Skim fat from cooking juices; transfer to a small saucepan. Bring to a boil. In a small bowl, mix cornstarch and water until smooth; gradually stir into cooking juices. Bring to a boil; cook and stir for 1-2 minutes or until thickened. Serve with meat.

SLOW COOKER 🍲
Brisket with Cranberry Gravy

With just a few minutes of hands-on work, this tender beef brisket simmers into a delectable entree. The leftover meat and gravy are great for sandwiches the following day.

—**NOELLE LABRECQUE** ROUND ROCK, TX

PREP: 15 MIN. • **COOK:** 5½ HOURS • **MAKES:** 12 SERVINGS

- 1 medium onion, sliced
- 1 fresh beef brisket (3 pounds), halved
- 1 can (14 ounces) jellied cranberry sauce
- ½ cup thawed cranberry juice concentrate
- 2 tablespoons cornstarch
- ¼ cup cold water

1. Place onion in a 5-qt. slow cooker; top with brisket. Combine cranberry sauce and juice concentrate; pour over beef. Cover and cook on low for 5½ to 6 hours or until meat is tender.
2. Remove brisket and keep warm. Strain cooking juices, discarding onion; skim fat. Place in a small saucepan and bring to a boil. Combine cornstarch and cold water until smooth; gradually stir into the pan. Cook and stir for 2 minutes or until thickened. Thinly slice brisket across the grain and serve with the gravy.
NOTE *This is a fresh beef brisket, not corned beef.*

BRISKET WITH CRANBERRY GRAVY

FAST FIX
Mom's Sloppy Tacos

No matter how hectic the weeknight, there's always time to serve your family a healthy meal with a convenient recipe like this!

—KAMI JONES AVONDALE, AZ

START TO FINISH: 30 MIN. • **MAKES:** 6 SERVINGS

- 1½ pounds extra-lean ground beef (95% lean)
- 1 can (15 ounces) tomato sauce
- ¾ teaspoon garlic powder
- ½ teaspoon salt
- ¼ teaspoon pepper
- ¼ teaspoon cayenne pepper
- 12 taco shells, warmed
    Optional toppings: shredded lettuce and cheese, chopped tomatoes, avocado and olives

1. In a large skillet, cook beef over medium heat until no longer pink. Stir in the tomato sauce, garlic powder, salt, pepper and cayenne. Bring to a boil. Reduce heat; simmer, uncovered, for 10 minutes.
2. Fill each taco shell with ¼ cup beef mixture and toppings of your choice.

Pizza Crescent Bake

As a new bride, I didn't have a large collection of recipes. When my cousin heard, she wrote out nearly 50 of her favorites—including this pizza-like dish.

—LAURIE MALYUK RIVER FALLS, WI

PREP: 20 MIN. • **BAKE:** 30 MIN. • **MAKES:** 6-8 SERVINGS

- 2 tubes (8 ounces each) refrigerated crescent rolls
- 1½ pounds ground beef
- 1 can (15 ounces) pizza sauce
- 1 cup (4 ounces) shredded cheddar cheese
- 1 cup (4 ounces) shredded mozzarella cheese

1. Preheat oven to 350°. Unroll one tube of crescent dough; place in a lightly greased 13x9-in. baking dish. Press to seal perforations.
2. In a large skillet, cook beef over medium heat until no longer pink; drain. Sprinkle over dough. Top with pizza sauce and sprinkle with cheeses.
3. On a lightly floured surface, press or roll second tube of crescent dough into a 13x9-in. rectangle, sealing seams and perforations. Place over cheese. Bake, uncovered, 30 minutes or until golden brown.

EASY STUFFED SHELLS

Easy Stuffed Shells

I put this recipe together one day when we had unexpected guests. It was an immediate hit and is now a family favorite. Get the kids involved when putting together this simple, savory dish.

—**DOLORES BETCHNER** CUDAHY, WI

PREP: 20 MIN. • **BAKE:** 40 MIN. • **MAKES:** 12 SERVINGS

- 36 uncooked jumbo pasta shells
- 1 jar (24 ounces) spaghetti sauce
- 36 frozen fully cooked Italian meatballs (½ ounce each), thawed
- 2 cups (8 ounces) shredded part-skim mozzarella cheese

1. Preheat oven to 350°. Cook pasta shells according to package directions; drain and rinse in cold water.
2. Spread ½ cup sauce into a greased 13x9-in. baking dish. Fill each shell with a meatball; place over sauce. Top with remaining sauce and cheese.
3. Bake, covered, 35 minutes. Uncover and bake 3-5 minutes longer or until bubbly and the cheese is melted.

Slow-Cooked Swiss Steak

This is a favorite for me to make, because I can flour and season the steaks and refrigerate them overnight. The next morning, I just put all the ingredients in the slow cooker and I have a delicious dinner waiting when I arrive home from work.

—**SARAH BURKS** WATHENA, KS

PREP: 10 MIN. • **COOK:** 6 HOURS • **MAKES:** 6 SERVINGS

- 2 tablespoons all-purpose flour
- ½ teaspoon salt
- ¼ teaspoon pepper
- 1½ pounds beef round steak, cut into six pieces
- 1 medium onion, cut into ¼-inch slices
- 1 celery rib, cut into ½-inch slices
- 2 cans (8 ounces each) tomato sauce

1. In a large resealable plastic bag, combine the flour, salt and pepper. Add the steak; seal bag and shake to coat.
2. Place onion in a greased 3-qt. slow cooker. Top with the steak, celery and tomato sauce. Cover and cook on low for 6-8 hours or until meat is tender.

Simple Shepherd's Pie

Our son, Charlie, loves to help in the kitchen. When we have leftover mashed potatoes, he fixes this dish. It goes well with a green salad.

—**LERA JOE BAYER** WIRTZ, VA

PREP: 20 MIN. • **BAKE:** 30 MIN. • **MAKES:** 4 SERVINGS

- 1 pound ground beef
- 2 cans (10¾ ounces each) condensed cream of potato soup, undiluted
- 1½ cups frozen peas, thawed
- 1½ cups frozen sliced carrots, thawed
- 4 cups mashed potatoes (with added milk and butter)

1. Preheat oven to 350°. In a large skillet, cook beef over medium heat until no longer pink; drain. Add soup, peas and carrots. Pour into a greased 11x7-in. baking dish. Top with potatoes.
2. Bake, uncovered, 30-40 minutes or until heated through.

SLOW-COOKED
SWISS STEAK

Grilled Flank Steak

Friends shared this three-ingredient marinade years ago, and it's been a favorite since. Serve the steak with salad and grilled potatoes for a quick dinner.

—BEVERLY DIETZ SURPRISE, AZ

PREP: 5 MIN. + MARINATING • **GRILL:** 15 MIN. + STANDING
MAKES: 8 SERVINGS

- 1 **cup barbecue sauce**
- ½ **cup burgundy wine or beef broth**
- ¼ **cup lemon juice**
- 1 **beef flank steak (2 pounds)**

1. In a bowl, combine the barbecue sauce, wine and lemon juice. Pour 1 cup marinade into a large resealable plastic bag. Add beef; seal bag and turn to coat. Refrigerate 4 hours or overnight. Cover and refrigerate remaining marinade.

2. Drain beef, discarding marinade in bag. Grill steak, covered, over medium heat 6-8 minutes on each side or until meat reaches desired doneness (for medium-rare, a thermometer should read 145°; medium, 160°; well-done, 170°). Let stand for 10 minutes before slicing. To serve, thinly slice across the grain. Serve with reserved marinade.

HOW TO

GRILL STEAK WITH SUCCESS

❶ Trim steaks to avoid flare-ups, leaving a thin layer of fat if desired to help maintain juiciness. Pat dry with paper towels before grilling—a dry steak will brown better than a moist one.

❷ Avoid grilling at too high a temperature, which will char the outside of the steak before the inside reaches the desired doneness. Grill steaks to at least medium-rare, 145°, but do not overcook.

❸ To test for doneness, insert an instant-read thermometer horizontally from the side, making sure to get the reading in the center of the steak.

GRILLED FLANK STEAK

QUICK TATER
TOT BAKE

Quick Tater Tot Bake

I like to make this dish when time is short before supper.
It serves two to three people, but if we have unexpected
company I double the ingredients and use a 13x9-in. pan.
I call it my "Please Stay Casserole."

—**JEAN FERGUSON** ELVERTA, CA

PREP: 15 MIN. • **BAKE:** 30 MIN. • **MAKES:** 2-3 SERVINGS

- ¾ to 1 pound ground beef or turkey
- 1 small onion, chopped
   Salt and pepper to taste
- 1 package (16 ounces) frozen Tater Tot potatoes
- 1 can (10¾ ounces) condensed cream of
   mushroom soup, undiluted
- ⅔ cup water or milk
- 1 cup (4 ounces) shredded cheddar cheese

1. Preheat oven to 350°. In a large skillet, cook beef
and onion over medium heat until meat is no longer
pink; drain. Season with salt and pepper.
2. Transfer to a greased 2-qt. baking dish. Top
with potatoes. Combine soup and water; pour over
potatoes. Sprinkle with cheese. Bake, uncovered,
30-40 minutes or until heated through.

FAST FIX ▶
Potato Leek Skillet

Before sampling this recipe from a neighbor, I had never
eaten leeks. I've since fallen in love with their mellow,
slightly sweet flavor. This is a nice brunch dish.

—**SHARON BOYAJIAN** LINDEN, CA

START TO FINISH: 30 MIN. • **MAKES:** 4 SERVINGS

- ½ pound ground beef
- 2 medium potatoes, cubed and cooked
- 3 large leeks (white part only), cut into
   ½-inch slices
- ½ cup water
- 2 tablespoons olive oil
- 1 teaspoon salt
- ½ teaspoon pepper
- ½ teaspoon dill weed

In a skillet, cook beef over medium heat until no
longer pink; drain. Add the potatoes, leeks, water,
oil, salt, pepper and dill. Bring to a boil. Reduce heat;
simmer, uncovered, until leeks are tender, about
5 minutes.

FAST FIX ▶
Veggie Beef Patties

I created these speedy patties using ingredients I had on
hand. They make a nice entree for a dinner or potluck.
Or, you can serve them with barbecue sauce on a bun
for a casual lunch or cookout.

—**MELODY SMALLER** FOWLER, CO

START TO FINISH: 25 MIN. • **MAKES:** 4 SERVINGS

- ¼ cup grated carrot
- ¼ cup finely chopped onion
- ¼ cup finely chopped green pepper
- 1 pound ground beef
   Salt and pepper to taste

1. In a large bowl, combine the carrot, onion and
green pepper. Crumble beef over mixture and mix
well. Shape into four patties. Season with salt
and pepper.
2. In a large skillet, cook burgers over medium
heat for 4-6 minutes on each side or until meat is
no longer pink.

Tex-Mex Pasta

After a recent surgery, I wasn't able to stock up on groceries. One night, I looked in my pantry and created this. The results were fabulous!

—MICHELE ORTHNER LETHBRIDGE, AB

START TO FINISH: 30 MIN. • **MAKES:** 4 SERVINGS

- 2 cups uncooked spiral pasta
- 1 pound ground beef
- 1 jar (16 ounces) salsa
- 1 can (10¾ ounces) condensed cream of chicken soup, undiluted
- 1 cup (4 ounces) shredded Mexican cheese blend, divided

1. Preheat oven to 350°. Cook pasta according to package directions.
2. Meanwhile, cook beef in a Dutch oven over medium heat until no longer pink; drain. Stir in the salsa, soup and ½ cup cheese; heat through.
3. Drain pasta; stir into meat mixture. Transfer to a greased 11x7-in. baking dish. Sprinkle with the remaining cheese. Cover and bake 15-20 minutes or until cheese is melted.

BLUE CHEESE-STUFFED STEAKS FOR TWO

Blue Cheese-Stuffed Steaks for Two

For a fast, fancy dinner for two, try this tender beef with a mild blue cheese stuffing. Grape tomatoes sauteed in garlic make a flavorful accompaniment.

—TEDDY DEVICO WARREN, NJ

START TO FINISH: 30 MIN. • **MAKES:** 2 SERVINGS

- 5 garlic cloves, peeled
- 1 tablespoon canola oil
- 2 cups grape tomatoes
- 2 boneless beef top loin steaks (8 ounces each)
- ¼ cup crumbled blue cheese
- ¼ teaspoon salt
- ⅛ teaspoon pepper

1. In a large skillet, saute garlic in oil until tender. Cover and cook over low heat for 5-7 minutes or until golden and softened. Add tomatoes; cook and stir until tomatoes just begin to burst. Remove from the skillet; set aside and keep warm.
2. Cut a pocket in the thickest part of each steak; fill with blue cheese. Sprinkle with salt and pepper.
3. In the same skillet, cook steaks over medium heat for 4-5 minutes on each side or until meat reaches desired doneness (for medium-rare, a thermometer should read 145°; medium, 160°; well-done, 170°). Serve with tomato mixture.
NOTE *Top loin steak may be labeled as strip steak, Kansas City steak, New York strip steak, ambassador steak or boneless club steak in your region.*

TEX-MEX PASTA

SIRLOIN WITH
MUSHROOM SAUCE

FAST FIX ▶
Sirloin with Mushroom Sauce

A mouthwatering combination of rich mushroom sauce and peppery steak is a welcome way to finish off a busy day. Whenever visitors drop in around dinnertime, I pull out this recipe and it's ready before we know it.
—**JOE ELLIOTT** WEST BEND, WI

START TO FINISH: 30 MIN. • **MAKES:** 4 SERVINGS

- 1 boneless beef sirloin steak (1 pound and ¾ inch thick)
- 1 teaspoon coarsely ground pepper
- 2 teaspoons canola oil
- 1½ cups sliced fresh mushrooms
- ½ cup beef broth
- ½ cup dry red wine or additional beef broth

1. Preheat oven to 450°. Rub steak with pepper. In a heavy ovenproof skillet, heat oil over medium-high heat. Brown steak on both sides. Transfer to oven; roast 4 minutes or until meat reaches desired doneness (for medium-rare, a thermometer should read 145°; medium, 160°; well-done, 170°).
2. Remove steak from pan; tent with foil. Let stand 10 minutes before slicing.
3. Add mushrooms to same pan; cook and stir over medium-high heat until golden brown. Add broth and wine, stirring to loosen browned bits from pan. Bring to a boil; cook until liquid is reduced by half. Thinly slice steak; serve with mushroom sauce.

Pepper Jack Meat Loaf

This is a quick way to put a zesty twist on a traditional main dish. The meat loaf is stuffed with pepper jack cheese and has even more melted on top.
—**DEBRA HARTZE** ZEELAND, ND

PREP: 20 MIN. • **BAKE:** 55 MIN. + STANDING
MAKES: 6 SERVINGS

- 1 egg, lightly beaten
- 1 cup seasoned bread crumbs
- ¼ cup chopped onion
- ½ to 1 teaspoon salt
- ½ teaspoon pepper
- 1½ pounds lean ground beef (90% lean)
- 1 cup (4 ounces) pepper jack cheese, divided
- 1 cup salsa, optional

1. In a large bowl, combine the egg, bread crumbs, onion, salt and pepper. Crumble beef over mixture and mix well. Press half of the beef mixture onto the bottom and halfway up the sides of a greased 8x4-in. loaf pan. Sprinkle ¾ cup cheese over meat to within ½ in. of sides. Pat remaining beef mixture over cheese.
2. Bake, uncovered, at 350° for 50-55 minutes or until meat is no longer pink and a thermometer reads 160°. Sprinkle with remaining cheese. Bake 5 minutes longer or until cheese is melted. Let stand for 10 minutes before slicing. Serve meat loaf with salsa if desired.

Southwest Steak

For grilling, my husband and I make an easy marinade that bumps steak to a new level. Chili powder adds color and perks up the flavor.

—**CAROLINE SHIVELY** NEW YORK, NY

PREP: 15 MIN. + MARINATING
GRILL: 15 MIN. • **MAKES:** 8 SERVINGS

- ¼ **cup lime juice**
- 6 **garlic cloves, minced**
- 4 **teaspoons chili powder**
- 4 **teaspoons canola oil**
- 1 **teaspoon salt**
- 1 **teaspoon crushed red pepper flakes**
- 1 **teaspoon pepper**
- 2 **beef flank steaks (1 pound each)**

1. In a small bowl, mix the first seven ingredients; spread over both sides of steaks. Place in a large resealable plastic bag; refrigerate 6 hours or overnight, turning occasionally.

2. Moisten a paper towel with cooking oil; using long-handled tongs, rub on grill rack to coat lightly. Grill steaks, covered, over medium heat or broil 4 in. from heat 6-9 minutes on each side or until meat reaches desired doneness (for medium-rare, a thermometer should read 145°; medium, 160°; well-done, 170°).

3. Let steaks stand 5 minutes. Thinly slice across the grain.

SOUTHWEST STEAK

Black Bean and Beef Tostadas

Just a handful of ingredients add up to one of our family's favorites. It can be doubled for company!

—SUSAN BROWN KANSAS CITY, KS

START TO FINISH: 30 MIN.
MAKES: 4 SERVINGS

- ½ **pound lean ground beef (90% lean)**
- 1 **can (10 ounces) diced tomatoes and green chilies, undrained**
- 1 **can (15 ounces) black beans, rinsed and drained**
- 1 **can (16 ounces) refried beans, warmed**
- 8 **tostada shells**
  Optional toppings: shredded lettuce, shredded reduced-fat Mexican cheese blend, sour cream and/or salsa

1. In a large skillet, cook beef over medium heat until no longer pink; drain. Stir in tomatoes. Bring to a boil. Reduce heat; simmer, uncovered, for 6-8 minutes or until most of the liquid is evaporated. Stir in black beans; heat through.

2. Spread refried beans over tostada shells. Top with beef mixture. Serve with toppings of your choice.

BLACK BEAN AND BEEF TOSTADAS

Spinach Steak Pinwheels

I wow family and friends with this delicious and impressive yet deceptively simple dish. Even those who don't like spinach seem to enjoy it!

—MARY ANN MARINO WEST PITTSBURGH, PA

START TO FINISH: 30 MIN.
MAKES: 4 SERVINGS

- 1 **beef flank steak (1½ pounds)**
- 1 **package (10 ounces) frozen chopped spinach, thawed and squeezed dry**
- ¼ **cup grated Parmesan cheese**
- ¼ **cup sour cream**
  Dash each salt and pepper

1. Cut steak horizontally from a long side to within ½ in. of opposite side. Open meat so it lies flat; cover with plastic wrap. Flatten to ¼-in. thickness. Remove plastic.

2. In a small bowl, combine the spinach, cheese and sour cream; spread over steak to within ½ in. of edges. With the grain of the meat going from left to right, roll up jelly-roll style. Slice beef across the grain into eight slices.

3. Transfer to an ungreased baking sheet. Sprinkle with salt and pepper. Broil 4-6 in. from the heat for 5-7 minutes on each side or until meat reaches desired doneness (for medium-rare, a thermometer should read 145°; medium, 160°; well-done, 170°).

PEPPERED BEEF
TENDERLOIN

Peppered Beef Tenderloin

A pepper rub gives beef tenderloin a rich, bold flavor. It takes just minutes to prepare, and lining the pan with foil makes cleanup a breeze, too.

—DENISE BITNER REEDSVILLE, PA

PREP: 10 MIN. • **BAKE:** 45 MIN. + STANDING
MAKES: 10-12 SERVINGS

- 3 tablespoons coarsely ground pepper
- 2 tablespoons olive oil
- 1 tablespoon grated lemon peel
- 1 teaspoon salt
- 2 garlic cloves, minced
- 1 beef tenderloin roast (3 to 4 pounds)

1. Preheat oven to 400°. Combine pepper, oil, lemon peel, salt and garlic; rub over tenderloin. Place on a greased rack in a foil-lined roasting pan.
2. Bake, uncovered, 45-65 minutes or until beef reaches desired doneness (for medium-rare, a thermometer should read 145°; medium, 160°; well-done, 170°). Cover and let stand 10 minutes before slicing.

Spicy Meat Loaf

This is not your typical meat loaf! The green chili salsa really gives it some zip, and the pork sausage combined with the beef adds variety. Meat loaves of all kinds are a favorite at my house.

—MARIE HISKEY SPRINGFIELD, MO

PREP: 10 MIN. • **BAKE:** 1 HOUR • **MAKES:** 8-10 SERVINGS

- 2 eggs
- ½ cup green or red chili salsa
- 1 cup seasoned bread crumbs
- 2 pounds ground beef
- ½ pound bulk pork sausage
  Additional salsa, optional

1. Preheat oven to 350°. In a large bowl, combine eggs, salsa and bread crumbs. Crumble beef and sausage over mixture and mix well. Press into an ungreased 9x5-in. loaf pan.
2. Bake, uncovered, 1 hour or until no pink remains and a thermometer reads 160°; drain. Top with additional salsa if desired.

MASHED POTATO HOT DISH

Save a Penny Casserole

At the office where I worked years ago, we often shared our favorite recipes at lunchtime. This casserole came from a co-worker, and my family has enjoyed it for more than 30 years. It's ideal for weeknight preparation and very economical. They'll love it at church suppers and potlucks.

—JANICE MILLER WORTHINGTON, KY

PREP: 10 MIN. • **BAKE:** 30 MIN. • **MAKES:** 4-6 SERVINGS

- 1 **pound ground beef**
- 1 **can (10¾ ounces) condensed cream of mushroom soup, undiluted**
- 1 **can (14¾ ounces) spaghetti in tomato sauce with cheese**
- 1 **can (15 ounces) mixed vegetables, drained**
- 1 **cup (4 ounces) shredded cheddar cheese, optional**

1. Preheat oven to 350°. In a large skillet, cook beef until no longer pink; drain. Stir in soup, spaghetti and vegetables. Transfer to an ungreased 11x7-in. baking dish.
2. Bake, uncovered, 30 minutes or until heated through. Sprinkle with cheese if desired; bake for 5 minutes longer or until cheese is melted.

Fast Beef and Rice

I received a lot of recipe requests the first time I made this super simple dish. Just how easy it is can be your little secret!

—DEBORAH VAHLKAMP BELLEVILLE, IL

PREP: 5 MIN. • **COOK:** 35 MIN. • **MAKES:** 4 SERVINGS

- 1 **pound ground beef**
- 1 **package (6.8 ounces) beef-flavored rice and vermicelli mix**
- 2 **tablespoons butter or margarine**
- 2½ **cups water**

1. In a skillet, cook beef over medium heat until no longer pink; drain and set aside.
2. In the same skillet, brown rice mix in butter. Add water and contents of seasoning packet; mix well. Stir in beef. Cover and simmer for 15 minutes or until rice is tender.

Mashed Potato Hot Dish

My cousin gave me this simple but delicious recipe. Whenever I'm making homemade mashed potatoes, I throw in a few extra spuds so I can make this dish for supper the next night.

—TANYA ABERNATHY YACOLT, WA

PREP: 15 MIN. • **BAKE:** 20 MIN. • **MAKES:** 4 SERVINGS

- 1 **pound ground beef**
- 1 **can (10¾ ounces) condensed cream of chicken soup, undiluted**
- 2 **cups frozen French-style green beans**
- 2 **cups hot mashed potatoes (prepared with milk and butter)**
- ½ **cup shredded cheddar cheese**

1. In a large skillet, cook beef over medium heat until no longer pink; drain. Stir in soup and beans.
2. Transfer to a greased 2-qt. baking dish. Top with mashed potatoes; sprinkle with cheese. Bake, uncovered, at 350° for 20-25 minutes or until bubbly and cheese is melted.

JOANN BROWN'S CRANBERRY-APRICOT PORK TENDERLOINS
PAGE 100

Pork

KEITH MILLER'S BACON-SWISS PORK CHOPS *PAGE 96*

CONNIE FLECHLER'S HONEY-GLAZED SPIRAL HAM *PAGE 91*

ALPHA WILSON'S SLOW COOKER SPARERIBS *PAGE 94*

ORANGE-GLAZED
HAM STEAKS

FAST FIX ▶

Orange-Glazed Ham Steaks

These ham steaks combine orange marmalade and maple syrup for a terrific taste that goes beyond dinner. I like to serve the leftovers at brunch. You'll love it with fruit and scrambled eggs.

—**BONNIE HAWKINS** ELKHORN, WI

START TO FINISH: 20 MIN.
MAKES: 4 SERVINGS

- ½ cup orange marmalade
- 2 tablespoons maple syrup
- 4½ teaspoons orange juice
- 1½ teaspoons chili powder
- 4 boneless fully cooked ham steaks (5 ounces each)

1. In a small bowl, combine the marmalade, syrup, orange juice and chili powder.
2. Grill ham steaks, covered, over medium heat or broil 4 in. from the heat for 3-4 minutes on each side or until heated through, brushing occasionally with marmalade mixture.

Baked Pork Chops with Apple Slices

A friend who raises pork shared this recipe with me. The lightly breaded chops with simple glazed apples on the side make a mouthwatering meal.

—**BURLIN JONES** BELOIT, WI

PREP: 15 MIN. • **BAKE:** 1 HOUR
MAKES: 6 SERVINGS

- 3 tablespoons all-purpose flour
- 1½ teaspoons salt
- ½ teaspoon pepper
- 6 bone-in pork loin chops (1½ inches thick and 8 ounces each)
- ¼ cup water
- 1 jar (12 ounces) currant jelly
- 3 to 4 medium tart apples, thinly sliced

1. Preheat oven to 350°. In a shallow bowl, combine flour, salt and pepper. Coat pork chops. Place in a greased 15x10x1-in. baking pan. Add water to pan. Bake, uncovered, 1 hour or until a thermometer reads 145°. Let stand 5 minutes.
2. In a large skillet, melt the jelly. Add apples. Cook over low heat 5-7 minutes or until apples are tender, turning occasionally. Serve with pork chops.

BAKED PORK CHOPS
WITH APPLE SLICES

MARINATED PORK
MEDALLIONS

Marinated Pork Medallions

Serve this easy main dish with a green salad, corn and dinner rolls for a standout supper.

—**MELANIE MILLER** BASCOM, OH

PREP: 15 MIN. + MARINATING • **GRILL:** 10 MIN.
MAKES: 5 SERVINGS

- ½ **cup packed brown sugar**
- ½ **cup Italian salad dressing**
- ¼ **cup unsweetened pineapple juice**
- 3 **tablespoons soy sauce**
- 2 **pork tenderloins (1 pound each), cut into ¾-inch slices**

1. In a small bowl, combine brown sugar, salad dressing, pineapple juice and soy sauce until blended. Pour ½ cup of marinade into a large resealable plastic bag. Add pork; seal bag and turn to coat. Refrigerate overnight. Cover and refrigerate the remaining marinade.
2. Drain pork, discarding marinade in bag. Moisten a paper towel with cooking oil; using long-handled tongs, rub on grill rack to coat lightly.
3. Grill pork, covered, over medium heat or broil 4 in. from heat for 5-7 minutes on each side or until a thermometer reads 145°, basting occasionally with reserved marinade. Let stand 5 minutes before serving.

Honey-Glazed Spiral Ham

Celebrate a holiday with this big and savory ham. The spiraled pieces taste so good drenched in a sweet and tangy glaze. If you like extra glaze, simply double the recipe and drizzle away or serve some on the side.

—**CONNIE FLECHLER** LOUISVILLE, KY

PREP: 10 MIN. • **BAKE:** 1¼ HOURS
MAKES: 20-24 SERVINGS

- 1 **bone-in fully cooked spiral-sliced ham (7 to 8 pounds)**
- ½ **cup pear nectar**
- ½ **cup orange juice**
- ½ **cup packed brown sugar**
- ½ **cup honey**

1. Preheat oven to 325°. Line a roasting pan with heavy-duty foil. Place ham on a rack in pan. Combine pear nectar and orange juice; brush ⅓ cup over ham. Bake, uncovered, 30 minutes, brushing twice with remaining juice mixture.
2. Combine brown sugar and honey; spread over ham. Bake 45-55 minutes longer or until a thermometer reads 140°, basting occasionally with pan drippings.

CARNITAS TACOS

Carnitas Tacos

The aroma in the house is fantastic when I'm making this dish. The tacos deliver a lot of flavor, with just a little bit of work.

—**MARY WOOD** MAIZE, KS

PREP: 15 MIN. • **COOK:** 6 HOURS • **MAKES:** 12 SERVINGS

- 1 boneless pork shoulder butt roast (3 to 4 pounds)
- 1 envelope taco seasoning
- 1 can (10 ounces) diced tomatoes and green chilies, undrained
- 12 flour tortillas (8 inches), warmed
- 2 cups (8 ounces) shredded Colby-Monterey Jack cheese
  Sour cream, optional

1. Cut roast in half; place in a 4- or 5-qt. slow cooker. Sprinkle with taco seasoning. Pour tomatoes over top. Cover and cook on low for 6-8 hours or until meat is tender.

2. Remove meat from slow cooker; shred with two forks. Skim fat from cooking juices. Return meat to slow cooker; heat through. Using a slotted spoon, place ½ cup on each tortilla; top with cheese. Serve with sour cream if desired.

Ham with Ruby Red Glaze

I have used this recipe for over 40 years and it is still a favorite with my family. Children love the glaze with mashed potatoes.

—**BEVERLY PAYNE** EL SOBRANTE, CA

PREP: 5 MIN. • **BAKE:** 2 HOURS + STANDING
MAKES: 8-10 SERVINGS

- 1 boneless fully cooked ham (about 4 pounds)
- ¾ cup packed brown sugar
- ¾ cup creamy French salad dressing

1. Preheat oven to 325°. Place the ham on a rack in a shallow roasting pan. Bake, uncovered, 1½ hours.

2. Meanwhile, in a small microwave-safe bowl, combine brown sugar and salad dressing. Cover and microwave on high 30-60 seconds or until sugar is dissolved. Pour ¼ cup over the ham.

3. Bake, uncovered, 30-40 minutes longer or until a thermometer reads 140°. Let stand 10 minutes before slicing. Serve with remaining glaze.

Grilled Jerk Chops

Pork chops get a quick kiss of tropical flavor with this easy lime marinade. Grilled pineapple is naturally sweet, so it's the perfect complement.
—TASTE OF HOME TEST KITCHEN

PREP: 15 MIN. + MARINATING • **GRILL:** 10 MIN.
MAKES: 4 SERVINGS

- 4 **medium limes**
- 1 **tablespoon Caribbean jerk seasoning**
- 1 **tablespoon olive oil**
- 4 **bone-in pork loin chops (¾ inch thick)**
- 1 **small fresh pineapple**

1. Finely grate the peel from one lime; set aside. Squeeze juice from two limes. Cut remaining two limes in half; set aside.
2. In a small bowl, combine the jerk seasoning, oil, lime peel and half of the juice; rub over pork chops. Refrigerate for at least 30 minutes. Meanwhile, peel and quarter the pineapple; drizzle with remaining lime juice.
3. Moisten a paper towel with cooking oil; using a long-handled tongs, rub on grill rack to coat lightly. Grill pork chops and pineapple, covered, over medium heat for 4-5 minutes on each side or until a thermometer reads 160° and pineapple is tender. Grill the lime halves for 2-3 minutes or until heated through.
4. Chop the pineapple; serve with pork chops and lime halves.

GRILLED JERK CHOPS

BOW TIES WITH ASPARAGUS AND PROSCIUTTO

FAST FIX
Bow Ties with Asparagus and Prosciutto

For a main course, I like to serve a meal that lets the flavors of prosciutto and asparagus shine. With only five ingredients and a couple of tablespoons of water, this dish is as easy as it is elegant. Add a dash of nutmeg for a change of pace.
—JODI TRIGG TOLEDO, IL

START TO FINISH: 30 MIN. • **MAKES:** 6 SERVINGS

- 1 **package (16 ounces) bow tie pasta**
- 1½ **cups heavy whipping cream**
- 1 **pound fresh asparagus, trimmed and cut into 1-inch pieces**
- 3 **tablespoons water**
- ½ **cup shredded Parmesan cheese**
- 6 **ounces thinly sliced prosciutto or deli ham, cut into strips**

1. Cook pasta according to package directions. Meanwhile, in a small saucepan, bring cream to a boil. Reduce heat; simmer, uncovered, for 6-7 minutes or until slightly thickened.
2. Place asparagus and water in a microwave-safe dish. Cover; microwave on high for 3-4 minutes or until crisp-tender. Drain.
3. Drain pasta and place in a large serving bowl. Add the cream, asparagus, cheese and prosciutto; toss to coat.

SLOW COOKER SPARERIBS

Maple-Peach Glazed Ham

This is one of my husband's favorite recipes. He makes it regularly for his friends on the weekends because it's so simple and tasty.

—**BONNIE HAWKINS** ELKHORN, WI

PREP: 5 MIN. • **BAKE:** 2 HOURS
MAKES: 16 SERVINGS (ABOUT 2 CUPS SAUCE)

- 1 fully cooked bone-in ham (7 to 9 pounds)
- 2 cups peach preserves or orange marmalade
- ½ cup maple syrup
- ⅓ cup orange juice
- 2 tablespoons ground ancho chili pepper, optional

1. Preheat oven to 325°. Place ham on a rack in a shallow roasting pan. Cover and bake 1¾ to 2¼ hours or until a thermometer reads 130°.
2. Meanwhile, in a small saucepan, mix preserves, syrup, orange juice and, if desired, chili pepper until blended. Remove ¾ cup mixture for glaze.
3. Remove ham from oven; brush with some of the glaze. Bake, uncovered, 15-20 minutes longer or until a thermometer reads 140°, brushing occasionally with remaining glaze.
4. Bring preserves mixture in saucepan to a boil over medium heat, stirring occasionally. Cook and stir 1-2 minutes or until slightly thickened. Serve as a sauce with ham.

SLOW COOKER 🍲
Slow Cooker Spareribs

These minimal-prep ribs call for everyday ingredients. So I never complain when my family asks me to make them. Everyone enjoys their down-home goodness.

—**ALPHA WILSON** ROSWELL, NM

PREP: 25 MIN. + COOLING • **COOK:** 4 HOURS
MAKES: 4 SERVINGS

- 3 pounds pork spareribs
- ½ teaspoon salt
- ¼ teaspoon pepper
- 1¾ cups sliced onions
- 1 bottle (18 ounces) barbecue sauce

1. Place ribs, meat side up, on a broiling pan. Sprinkle with salt and pepper. Broil 6 in. from the heat for 15-20 minutes or until browned. Cool; cut into serving-size pieces.
2. Place onion in a 5-qt. slow cooker; top with ribs. Pour barbecue sauce over all. Cover and cook on high for 1 hour; reduce heat to low and cook 3-4 hours or until ribs are tender.

FAST FIX
Kielbasa Skillet

I created this meal by accident one day and have been making it ever since. It's also great if you're on a budget.

—**CHRISTINE GOMEZ** CORONA, CA

START TO FINISH: 25 MIN. • **MAKES:** 2 SERVINGS

- ½ pound smoked kielbasa or Polish sausage, sliced
- 1 cup frozen French-style green beans, thawed
- ½ cup sliced fresh mushrooms
- 1 tablespoon reduced-sodium soy sauce
- 1 cup hot cooked rice

In a large skillet coated with cooking spray, saute kielbasa until browned. Add the beans, mushrooms and soy sauce; saute 4-5 minutes longer or until vegetables are tender. Serve with rice.

**MAPLE-PEACH
GLAZED HAM**

Bacon-Swiss Pork Chops

I'm always looking for quick and easy recipes that are impressive enough to serve company. These pork chops smothered in bacon and Swiss cheese certainly deliver.
—**KEITH MILLER** FORT GRATIOT, MI

START TO FINISH: 25 MIN. • **MAKES:** 4 SERVINGS

- 2 **bacon strips, chopped**
- 1 **medium onion, chopped**
- 4 **boneless pork loin chops (4 ounces each)**
- ½ **teaspoon garlic powder**
- ¼ **teaspoon salt**
- 2 **slices reduced-fat Swiss cheese, halved**

1. In a nonstick skillet coated with cooking spray, cook bacon and onion over medium heat, stirring occasionally, until bacon is crisp. Drain on paper towels; discard drippings.

2. Sprinkle pork chops with garlic powder and salt. Add pork chops to same pan; cook over medium heat 3-4 minutes on each side or until a thermometer reads 145°. Top pork with bacon mixture and cheese. Cook, covered, on low heat for 1-2 minutes or until cheese is melted. Let stand 5 minutes before serving.

BACON-SWISS
PORK CHOPS

HAM & SPINACH
COUSCOUS

Ham & Spinach Couscous

A simple way to dress up couscous, this foolproof dish makes a tasty one-pot meal when time is tight.
—**LISA SHANNON** CULLMAN, AL

START TO FINISH: 20 MIN. • **MAKES:** 4 SERVINGS

- 2 **cups water**
- 1 **cup chopped fully cooked ham**
- 1 **cup chopped fresh spinach**
- ½ **teaspoon garlic salt**
- 1 **cup uncooked couscous**
- ¼ **cup shredded cheddar cheese**

In a large saucepan, combine the water, ham, spinach and garlic salt. Bring to a boil. Stir in couscous. Remove from the heat; cover and let stand for 5-10 minutes or until water is absorbed. Fluff with a fork. Sprinkle with cheese.

Tender Teriyaki Pork

My children really loved this dish growing up: it was the only meat they would gladly eat besides hot dogs! I got the recipe from my mother.

—DEBBIE DUNAWAY KETTERING, OH

PREP: 10 MIN. • **COOK:** 6¼ HOURS • **MAKES:** 6-8 SERVINGS

- 1 **boneless pork shoulder butt roast (3 to 4 pounds)**
- 1 **cup packed brown sugar**
- ⅓ **cup unsweetened apple juice**
- ⅓ **cup reduced-sodium soy sauce**
- ½ **teaspoon salt**
- ¼ **teaspoon pepper**
- 2 **tablespoons cornstarch**
- 3 **tablespoons cold water**

1. Cut roast in half; rub with brown sugar. Place in a 5-qt. slow cooker. Pour apple juice and soy sauce over roast. Sprinkle with salt and pepper. Cover and cook on low for 6-8 hours or until meat is tender.
2. Remove roast; cover and keep warm. Skim fat from cooking juices. Mix cornstarch and water until smooth; stir into juices. Cover and cook on high for 15 minutes or until thickened. Serve with pork.

TENDER
TERIYAKI PORK

MANDARIN PORK
AND WILD RICE

Mandarin Pork and Wild Rice

Mandarin oranges add a splash of color and citrus flavor to a tasty pork entree. With just a few minutes of prep, it's a complete meal in a flash.

—MELANIE GABLE ROSEVILLE, MI

START TO FINISH: 25 MIN. • **MAKES:** 4 SERVINGS

- 1¼ **pounds boneless pork loin chops, cut into strips**
- ¼ **teaspoon pepper**
- ⅛ **teaspoon salt**
- 1 **tablespoon canola oil**
- 1 **can (11 ounces) mandarin oranges**
- 1½ **cups water**
- 1 **package (6.2 ounces) fast-cooking long grain and wild rice mix**
- ¼ **cup thinly sliced green onions**

1. Sprinkle pork with pepper and salt. In a large skillet, brown pork in oil. Meanwhile, drain oranges, reserving juice; set oranges aside.
2. Add the water, rice mix with contents of seasoning packet, onions and reserved juice to the skillet. Bring to a boil. Reduce heat; cover and simmer for 10-12 minutes or until meat is no longer pink and liquid is absorbed. Stir in the oranges and heat through.

BBQ HOT DOG & POTATO PACKS

FAST FIX
Ham & Broccoli Pasta

You can create this meal in one pan, in just 30 minutes. And, your kids will actually thank you for making it! With all those benefits, this recipe page will be dog-eared in no time.

—**JANA CATHEY** ADA, MI

START TO FINISH: 30 MIN. • **MAKES:** 6 SERVINGS

- 4½ **cups uncooked bow tie pasta (12 ounces)**
- 1 **package (16 ounces) frozen broccoli florets**
- 3 **cups cubed fully cooked ham**
- 1 **carton (8 ounces) spreadable chive and onion cream cheese**
- ⅓ **cup milk**
- ¼ **teaspoon salt**
- ½ **teaspoon pepper**

1. In a Dutch oven, cook pasta according to package directions, adding the broccoli during the last 5 minutes of cooking; drain.
2. In same pan, combine remaining ingredients; cook and stir over medium heat until heated through and cream cheese is melted. Return pasta mixture to pan and toss to combine.

FAST FIX
BBQ Hot Dog & Potato Packs

The kids will have fun helping to assemble these nifty foil packs, then savoring the tasty results in short order. They're perfect for camping trips, or just camping in the backyard.

—**KELLY WESTPHAL** WIND LAKE, WI

START TO FINISH: 20 MIN. • **MAKES:** 4 SERVINGS

- 1 **package (20 ounces) refrigerated red potato wedges**
- 4 **hot dogs**
- 1 **small onion, cut into wedges**
- ¼ **cup shredded cheddar cheese**
- ½ **cup barbecue sauce**

1. Divide potato wedges among four pieces of heavy-duty foil (about 18 in. square). Top each with a hot dog, onion wedges and cheese. Drizzle with barbecue sauce. Fold foil around mixture, sealing tightly.
2. Grill, covered, over medium heat 10-15 minutes or until heated through. Open foil carefully to allow steam to escape.

HAM & BROCCOLI PASTA

Holiday Baked Ham

One of the best things about the yuletide season is the aroma of a baking ham—and the anticipation of the feast to come! The apricot glaze in this recipe is sure to please guests.

—STACY DUFFY CHICAGO, IL

PREP: 10 MIN. • **BAKE:** 1¾ HOURS • **MAKES:** 16 SERVINGS

- 1 **fully cooked smoked half ham (6 to 7 pounds)**
- 1 **tablespoon whole cloves**
- ¼ **cup apricot preserves**
- 1 **tablespoon butter**
- 2 **teaspoons Dijon mustard**

1. Preheat oven to 325°. Place ham on a rack in a shallow roasting pan. Using a sharp knife, score surface of ham with ¼-in.-deep cuts in a diamond pattern; insert a clove in each diamond. Bake, uncovered, 1¼ hours.
2. Meanwhile, in a small saucepan, combine preserves, butter and mustard; heat through. Remove ham from oven. Spoon preserves mixture over ham. Bake, uncovered, 30-40 minutes longer or until a thermometer reads 140°.

FAST FIX
Ravioli Carbonara

This ravioli has a gourmet-sounding name because it uses a classic Italian pairing of rich Alfredo sauce and crispy cooked bacon. The tempting recipe uses just a handful of ingredients!

—RONDA WEIRICH PLAINS, KS

START TO FINISH: 25 MIN. • **MAKES:** 3 SERVINGS

- 1 **package (16 ounces) frozen cheese ravioli**
- 8 **bacon strips, diced**
- 1 **cup prepared Alfredo sauce**
- ¼ **cup milk**
- 2 **to 3 teaspoons dried basil**
  Pepper to taste

1. Cook ravioli according to package directions. Meanwhile, in a large skillet, cook bacon over medium heat until crisp. Remove to paper towels; drain, reserving 2 teaspoons drippings.
2. Stir the Alfredo sauce, milk and basil into the drippings; heat through. Drain ravioli; add to sauce and toss to coat. Sprinkle with bacon and pepper.

Cranberry-Apricot Pork Tenderloins

A cranberry and apricot stuffing wonderfully complements pork tenderloin. This is an elegant entree that you can pull together in very little time.

—**JOANN BROWN** LOS ALAMOS, NM

PREP: 30 MIN. • **BAKE:** 30 MIN.
MAKES: 6-8 SERVINGS

- 1 **cup dried cranberries**
- 1 **cup chopped dried apricots**
- 3 **tablespoons water**
- 2 **teaspoons dried rosemary, crushed**
- ½ **teaspoon salt**
- ¼ **teaspoon pepper**
- 2 **pork tenderloins (1 pound each)**

1. In a small saucepan, combine the first six ingredients. Bring to a boil. Reduce heat; cover and simmer 10 minutes or until fruit is softened. Cool.

2. Preheat oven to 400°. Cut a lengthwise slit down the center of each tenderloin to within ½ in. of bottom. Open tenderloins so they lie flat; cover with plastic wrap. Flatten to ¾-in. thickness; remove plastic. Spread with fruit mixture to within ¾ in. of edges. Roll up jelly-roll style, starting with a long side; tie with kitchen string at 1½-in. intervals.

3. Line a shallow pan with heavy-duty foil. Place meat on a rack in prepared pan. Bake, uncovered, for 30-35 minutes or until a thermometer reads 145°. Let stand 5-10 minutes before slicing.

CRANBERRY-APRICOT PORK TENDERLOINS

Chipotle-Raspberry Pork Chops

My husband and I love this dinner because it comes together quickly after a long day of work. Also, we appreciate that it's tasty and healthy.

—**JENNIFER RAY** PONCHA SPRING, CO

START TO FINISH: 20 MIN.
MAKES: 4 SERVINGS (¼ CUP SAUCE)

- ½ cup seedless raspberry preserves
- 1 chipotle pepper in adobo sauce, finely chopped
- ½ teaspoon salt
- 4 bone-in pork loin chops (7 ounces each)

1. In a small saucepan, cook and stir preserves and chipotle pepper over medium heat until heated through. Reserve ¼ cup for serving. Sprinkle pork with salt; brush with remaining raspberry sauce.

2. Lightly grease a grill or broiler pan rack. Grill chops, covered, over medium heat or broil 4 in. from heat 4-5 minutes on each side or until a thermometer reads 145°. Let stand 5 minutes before serving. Serve with reserved sauce.

Southern Skillet Chops

Creole seasoning adds the right amount of heat to these pork chops. The black-eyed peas make the perfect accompaniment.

—**IRENE SULLIVAN** LAKE MILLS, WI

START TO FINISH: 25 MIN.
MAKES: 4 SERVINGS

- 4 bone-in pork loin chops (8 ounces each)
- 2 teaspoons plus ⅛ teaspoon Creole seasoning, divided
- 2 tablespoons canola oil

SOUTHERN SKILLET CHOPS

- 2 cans (14½ ounces each) diced tomatoes with mild green chilies, undrained
- 1 can (15½ ounces) black-eyed peas, rinsed and drained
  Shredded cheddar cheese, optional

1. Sprinkle pork chops with 2 teaspoons Creole seasoning. In a large skillet, brown pork chops in oil. Remove and keep warm.

2. Drain one can tomatoes; discard liquid. Add tomatoes to skillet with the remaining can of undrained tomatoes, black-eyed peas and remaining Creole seasoning, stirring to loosen browned bits from pan.

3. Bring to a boil and return chops to pan. Reduce heat; simmer, uncovered, for 2-4 minutes or until a thermometer reads 145°. Sprinkle with cheese if desired. Let stand for 5 minutes.

NOTE *The following spices may be substituted for 1 teaspoon Creole seasoning: ¼ teaspoon each salt, garlic powder and paprika; and a pinch each of dried thyme, ground cumin and cayenne pepper.*

CHIPOTLE-RASPBERRY PORK CHOPS

SLOW COOKER
Slow-Cooked Ribs

Nothing says comfort food like a plate of mouthwatering ribs smothered in barbecue sauce. These are delicious and tangy.

—**SHARON CRIDER** JUNCTION CITY, KS

PREP: 15 MIN. • **COOK:** 6 HOURS • **MAKES:** 8 SERVINGS

- 4 **pounds boneless country-style pork ribs**
- 1 **cup barbecue sauce**
- 1 **cup Catalina salad dressing**
- ½ **teaspoon minced garlic**
- 2 **tablespoons all-purpose flour**
- ¼ **cup cold water**

1. Cut ribs into serving-size pieces. Place in a 5-qt. slow cooker. Combine barbecue sauce and salad dressing; pour over ribs. Sprinkle with garlic. Cover and cook on low for 6-7 hours or until meat is tender.

2. Remove meat to a serving platter; keep warm. Skim fat from cooking juices; transfer to a small saucepan. Bring liquid to a boil.

3. Combine flour and water until smooth. Gradually stir into the pan. Bring to a boil; cook and stir for 2 minutes or until thickened. Serve with meat.

SLOW-COOKED RIBS

HAM & SWEET POTATO PACKETS

Ham & Sweet Potato Packets

I can my own peaches and use them in this recipe. Add a simple salad for a delicious meal.

—**JANET ERNSBARGER** SALINA, KS

PREP: 5 MIN. • **BAKE:** 30 MIN. • **MAKES:** 2 SERVINGS

- 2 **individual boneless fully cooked ham steaks (5 ounces each)**
- 1 **large sweet potato, peeled and thinly sliced**
- 2 **canned peach halves**
- 1 **tablespoon brown sugar**
- 1 **tablespoon butter**

1. Preheat oven to 350°. Place each ham steak on a double thickness of heavy-duty foil (about 12 in. square). Layer with sweet potato and peaches. Sprinkle with brown sugar; dot with butter. Fold foil around mixture and seal tightly. Place on a baking sheet.

2. Bake 30-35 minutes or until heated through and sweet potato is tender. Open foil carefully to allow steam to escape.

Rosemary Pork Tenderloin

I started growing rosemary in my garden after I discovered this pork recipe. My husband and I think it's restaurant-quality, and we look forward to making it after work.

—JUDY LEARNED BOYERTOWN, PA

PREP: 15 MIN. + STANDING • **GRILL:** 20 MIN.
MAKES: 4 SERVINGS

- 1 **garlic clove, minced**
- ¾ **teaspoon salt**
- 1 **tablespoon olive oil**
- 2 **teaspoons minced fresh rosemary**
- ¼ **teaspoon pepper**
- 1 **pork tenderloin (1 pound)**

1. Place garlic on a cutting board; sprinkle with salt. Using the flat side of a knife, mash garlic. Continue to mash until it reaches a paste consistency. Transfer to a small bowl.
2. Stir in the oil, rosemary and pepper; brush over pork. Let stand for 20 minutes.
3. Moisten a paper towel with cooking oil; using long-handled tongs, rub on grill rack to coat lightly. Grill pork, covered, over medium heat or broil 4 in. from the heat for 9-11 minutes on each side or until a thermometer reads 145°. Let stand for 5 minutes before slicing.

ROSEMARY
PORK TENDERLOIN

HAM & SUN-DRIED
TOMATO ALFREDO

FAST FIX
Ham & Sun-Dried Tomato Alfredo

This quick Alfredo dish seems decadent and special. No one will guess how little time you spent on it! Sun-dried tomatoes add the elegant touch.

—TASTE OF HOME TEST KITCHEN

START TO FINISH: 20 MIN. • **MAKES:** 4 SERVINGS

- 8 **ounces uncooked linguine**
- ¼ **cup chopped oil-packed sun-dried tomatoes**
- 1 **cup heavy whipping cream**
- ½ **cup grated Parmesan cheese**
- 1 **cup cubed fully cooked ham**

1. Cook linguine according to package directions.
2. Meanwhile, in a large skillet coated with cooking spray, saute tomatoes for 1 minute. Reduce heat; stir in cream and cheese. Bring to a gentle boil over medium heat. Simmer, uncovered, for 5-7 minutes or until thickened.
3. Drain linguine; stir into sauce mixture. Add ham; heat through.

HONEY LEMON
SCHNITZEL

PORK

Honey Lemon Schnitzel

These pork cutlets are coated in a sweet sauce with honey, lemon juice and butter. They're certainly good enough for company, but perfect for a weeknight meal, too. Very seldom are there any leftovers.

—CAROLE FRASER NORTH YORK, ON

START TO FINISH: 25 MIN. • **MAKES:** 4 SERVINGS

- 2 **tablespoons all-purpose flour**
- ½ **teaspoon salt**
- ½ **teaspoon pepper**
- 4 **pork sirloin cutlets (4 ounces each)**
- 2 **tablespoons butter**
- ¼ **cup lemon juice**
- ¼ **cup honey**

1. In a large resealable plastic bag, combine the flour, salt and pepper. Add pork, two pieces at a time, and shake to coat. In a large skillet, cook pork in butter over medium heat for 3-4 minutes on each side or until juices run clear. Remove and keep warm.
2. Add lemon juice and honey to the skillet; cook and stir for 3 minutes or until thickened. Return pork to pan; cook 2-3 minutes longer or until heated through.

Pineapple Ham Steaks

It's a snap to dress up ham steaks with a few kitchen staples. You won't believe how quickly this dish comes together before you pop it into the oven.

—RITA SHOLTZ TONAWANDA, NY

PREP: 10 MIN. • **BAKE:** 45 MIN. • **MAKES:** 6-8 SERVINGS

- 1 **can (8 ounces) unsweetened crushed pineapple**
- 1 **tablespoon whole cloves**
- 2 **bone-in fully cooked ham steaks (½ inch thick and 1 pound each)**
- ¼ **cup packed brown sugar**
- ½ **teaspoon ground mustard**

1. Preheat oven to 350°. Drain pineapple, reserving juice. Insert cloves into edges of ham steaks. Place one ham steak in a greased shallow baking pan. Spread pineapple over ham; top with the second ham steak. Pour reserved pineapple juice over ham. Combine brown sugar and mustard; sprinkle over the top.
2. Bake, uncovered, 40 minutes or until a thermometer reads 140°, basting occasionally with pan juices. Discard cloves.

TOP TIP

For easy cleanup, spritz the measuring cup with a little cooking spray before measuring sticky ingredients like honey and molasses.

PORK CHOPS WITH
APRICOT SAUCE

Ham & Noodles with Veggies

A hearty, healthy dinner has never been easier! I use frozen veggies in cheese sauce to make a quick sauce for ham and noodles.

—**JEANNIE KLUGH** LANCASTER, PA

START TO FINISH: 20 MIN. • **MAKES:** 6 SERVINGS

- 1 can (14½ ounces) chicken broth
- 1 cup water
- 3 cups uncooked egg noodles
- 2 packages (24 ounces each) frozen broccoli, carrots, cauliflower and cheese sauce
- 1 package (16 ounces) cubed fully cooked ham

1. Bring broth and water to a boil in a large saucepan. Add noodles; return to a boil. Cook for 8-10 minutes or until tender. Meanwhile, place vegetables and cheese sauce in a Dutch oven. Cover and cook over medium heat for 13-15 minutes or until heated through, stirring occasionally.
2. Pour noodles and cooking liquid into vegetable mixture. Stir in ham and heat through.

Pork Chops with Apricot Sauce

Apricot preserves gives a very special flavor to pork chops. I serve this entree with good, old-fashioned corn bread to make it a classic comfort-food meal.

—**PATRICIA SWART** GALLOWAY, NJ

START TO FINISH: 30 MIN. • **MAKES:** 6 SERVINGS

- 6 boneless pork loin chops (6 ounces each)
- ½ teaspoon garlic pepper blend
- 1 tablespoon olive oil
- 1 cup sugar-free apricot preserves
- 1 tablespoon minced chives
- ¼ teaspoon salt

1. Sprinkle pork with garlic pepper blend. In a large nonstick skillet coated with cooking spray, brown chops in oil on both sides.
2. Combine the preserves, chives and salt; spoon over chops. Reduce heat; cover and cook for 5-6 minutes or until a thermometer reads 145°. Let meat stand for 5 minutes before serving. Serve with sauce.

HAM & NOODLES
WITH VEGGIES

**TINA OLES' CHICKEN &
VEGETABLE KABOBS**
PAGE 113

Poultry

RITA REINKE'S HONEY-APPLE TURKEY BREAST
PAGE 109

LISA KEYS' CRISPY BUFFALO CHICKEN ROLL-UPS FOR TWO
PAGE 121

DIANE HIXON'S TENDER BARBECUED CHICKEN
PAGE 112

BALSAMIC CHICKEN WITH
ROASTED TOMATOES

FAST FIX

Balsamic Chicken with Roasted Tomatoes

The end of summer is the best time of year to make this entree. Flavorful vine-ripened tomatoes create a sweet, tangy accompaniment that's so delicious!

—**KAREN GEHRIG** CONCORD, NC

START TO FINISH: 25 MIN. • **MAKES:** 4 SERVINGS

- 2 **tablespoons honey**
- 2 **tablespoons olive oil, divided**
- 2 **cups grape tomatoes**
- 4 **boneless skinless chicken breast halves (6 ounces each)**
- ½ **teaspoon salt**
- ½ **teaspoon pepper**
- 2 **tablespoons balsamic glaze**

1. Preheat oven to 400°. In a small bowl, mix honey and 1 tablespoon oil. Add tomatoes and toss to coat. Transfer to a greased 15x10x1-in. baking pan. Bake 5-7 minutes or until softened.

2. Pound chicken breasts with a meat mallet to ½-in. thickness; sprinkle with salt and pepper. In a large skillet, heat remaining oil over medium heat. Add chicken; cook 5-6 minutes on each side or until no longer pink. Serve with roasted tomatoes; drizzle with glaze.

NOTE *To make about 2 tablespoons balsamic glaze, bring ½ cup balsamic vinegar to a boil in a small saucepan. Reduce heat to medium; simmer 10-12 minutes or until thickened to a glaze consistency.*

FAST FIX

Ranch Turkey Pasta Dinner

Here's a great way to showcase leftover turkey in a snap! At times, I use chicken if I have that on hand instead. Try sprinkling grated cheese over the top of each helping for extra flavor and color.

—**PEGGY KEY** GRANT, AL

START TO FINISH: 20 MIN. • **MAKES:** 4 SERVINGS

- 2½ **cups uncooked penne pasta**
- 6 **to 8 tablespoons butter, cubed**
- 1 **envelope ranch salad dressing mix**
- 1 **cup frozen peas and carrots, thawed**
- 3 **cups cubed cooked turkey**

Cook pasta according to package directions. Meanwhile, in a large skillet, melt butter. Stir in salad dressing mix until smooth. Add peas and carrots; cook and stir for 2-3 minutes. Drain pasta and add to skillet. Stir in turkey; cook for 3-4 minutes or until heated through.

CHICKEN TORTELLINI SKILLET

FAST FIX

Chicken Tortellini Skillet

I'm a graduate student, and I live alone, so the meals I make are inexpensive and yield just a few servings. This chicken and pasta dish is on the table in no time.

—**CHANDRA BENJAMIN** EDEN PRAIRIE, MN

START TO FINISH: 25 MIN. • **MAKES:** 2 SERVINGS

- 2 **cups frozen cheese tortellini**
- ½ **pound boneless skinless chicken breast, cubed**
- 1 **tablespoon canola oil**
- 1 **cup meatless spaghetti sauce**
- ½ **cup shredded part-skim mozzarella cheese**

1. Cook tortellini according to package directions. Meanwhile, in a large skillet, cook chicken in oil over medium heat until juices run clear.
2. Drain tortellini; add to skillet. Stir in spaghetti sauce. Sprinkle with cheese. Reduce heat to low. Cover and cook for 3-5 minutes or until cheese is melted.

Honey-Apple Turkey Breast

Apple juice and ground mustard give complex flavor to this turkey breast. The honey comes through nicely when leftovers are used in casseroles and soups.

—**RITA REINKE** WAUWATOSA, WI

PREP: 10 MIN. • **BAKE:** 2 HOURS + STANDING
MAKES: 12-14 SERVINGS

- ¾ **cup thawed apple juice concentrate**
- ⅓ **cup honey**
- 1 **tablespoon ground mustard**
- 1 **bone-in turkey breast (6 to 7 pounds)**

1. Preheat oven to 325°. In a small saucepan, combine apple juice concentrate, honey and mustard. Cook over low heat 2-3 minutes or just until blended, stirring occasionally.
2. Place turkey breast on a rack in a foil-lined shallow roasting pan; pour honey mixture over the top.
3. Bake, uncovered, 2 to 2½ hours or until a thermometer reads 170°, basting with pan juices every 30 minutes. (Cover loosely with foil if turkey browns too quickly.) Cover and let stand 15 minutes before carving.

Pretzel-Crusted Chicken

Crunchy pretzels, honey mustard and deli ham add scrumptious flavor to this change-of-pace entree. The combination's a hit with my fussy family.

—**MARIE MCCARTHY** COBLESKILL, NY

PREP: 10 MIN. • **BAKE:** 40 MIN. • **MAKES:** 4 SERVINGS

- 4 **boneless skinless chicken breast halves (6 ounces each)**
- ¼ **cup honey mustard**
- 8 **thin slices deli ham**
- 1 **tablespoon butter, melted**
- ½ **cup crushed pretzels**

1. Preheat oven to 350°. Cut a horizontal slit in one side of each chicken breast half to within ½ in. of the opposite side. Spread honey mustard inside each pocket; stuff with two ham slices.
2. Place in a greased 13x9-in. baking dish. Brush with butter; sprinkle with pretzels. Bake, uncovered, 40-45 minutes or until a thermometer inserted in chicken reads 165°.

NO-FUSS CHICKEN

No-Fuss Chicken

Here, chicken gets a wonderfully tangy taste from convenient ingredients such as bottled salad dressing and onion soup mix. No one will know your time-saving secrets...unless you share the recipe with them!

—**MARILYN DICK** CENTRALIA, MO

PREP: 5 MIN. • **BAKE:** 40 MIN.
MAKES: 16 SERVINGS

- 1 bottle (16 ounces) Russian or Catalina salad dressing
- ⅔ cup apricot preserves
- 2 envelopes onion soup mix
- 16 boneless skinless chicken breast halves
  Hot cooked rice

Preheat oven to 350°. In a bowl, combine dressing, preserves and soup mix. Place chicken in two ungreased 13x9-in. baking dishes; top with dressing mixture. Cover and bake 20 minutes; baste. Bake, uncovered, 20 minutes longer or until chicken juices run clear. Serve over rice.

African Chicken & Sweet Potatoes

I created this dish when I combined some of my favorite ingredients: sweet potatoes, chicken and peanut butter. Add tomatoes and mango chutney and you've got a fantastic weeknight recipe.

—**DEVON DELANEY** WESTPORT, CT

PREP: 10 MIN. • **BAKE:** 40 MIN.
MAKES: 6 SERVINGS

- 6 bone-in chicken thighs (about 2¼ pounds)
- ½ teaspoon salt
- ¼ teaspoon pepper
- 2 tablespoons canola oil
- 2 medium sweet potatoes, peeled and finely chopped (about 4 cups)
- ½ cup mango chutney
- ¼ cup creamy peanut butter
- 1 can (10 ounces) diced tomatoes and green chilies, undrained

1. Preheat oven to 375°. Place chicken in a greased 13x9-in. baking dish; sprinkle with salt and pepper. Bake, uncovered, for 30 minutes.
2. Meanwhile, in a large skillet, heat oil over medium-high heat. Add sweet potatoes; cook and stir 10-12 minutes or until tender. In a small bowl, mix chutney and peanut butter; stir into sweet potatoes. Add the tomatoes; heat through.
3. Spoon potato mixture over chicken. Bake 10-15 minutes longer or until a thermometer inserted in chicken reads 180°.

AFRICAN CHICKEN & SWEET POTATOES

Zesty Chicken Soft Tacos

We've made these tacos with corn and flour tortillas, but flatbread is our favorite wrap. Set out toppings and let everyone assemble his or her own taco.

—JESSIE GREARSON-SAPAT
FALMOUTH, ME

START TO FINISH: 25 MIN.
MAKES: 6 SERVINGS

- 1 cup (8 ounces) reduced-fat sour cream
- 2 tablespoons Sriracha Asian hot chili sauce
- 2 tablespoons lime juice
- 1½ teaspoons grated lime peel
- ½ teaspoon salt
- ⅛ teaspoon pepper
- 6 naan flatbreads, warmed
- 1 rotisserie chicken, skin removed, shredded
   Minced fresh cilantro, optional

In a small bowl, mix the first six ingredients. Spread over the flatbreads; top with chicken and, if desired, cilantro.

TOP TIP

These full-flavored tacos come together easily with a rotisserie chicken from the grocery store. Don't forget this dish, however, when you have leftover cooked chicken or turkey to use up! Top the tacos with shredded cheese, baby spinach leaves and salsa for extra flair.

ZESTY CHICKEN
SOFT TACOS

CRISPY BAKED CHICKEN

Crispy Baked Chicken

Mashed potato flakes and Parmesan cheese create an ultra-crunchy coating for oven-baked chicken. Best of all, the chicken turns out so tender and perfectly moist.

—**JUNE BROWN** VENETA, OR

PREP: 15 MIN. • **BAKE:** 50 MIN. • **MAKES:** 4 SERVINGS

- 2 **cups mashed potato flakes**
- 2 **tablespoons grated Parmesan cheese**
- 2 **to 3 teaspoons poultry seasoning**
- ½ **to 1 teaspoon pepper**
- ½ **cup butter, melted**
- 1 **broiler/fryer chicken (3½ to 4½ pounds), cut up**

1. Preheat oven to 375°. In a shallow dish, combine potato flakes, Parmesan cheese, poultry seasoning and pepper. Place the butter in another shallow dish. Dip chicken in butter, then coat with potato-flake mixture.

2. Place chicken on a lightly greased 15x10-in. baking pan. Bake, uncovered, 50-65 minutes or until juices run clear.

Tender Barbecued Chicken

When we can't barbecue on the grill, I bring out my pressure cooker for this fall-off-the-bone chicken. My jazzed-up BBQ sauce adds a lot of tangy flavor.

—**DIANE HIXON** NICEVILLE, FL

PREP: 20 MIN. • **COOK:** 10 MIN. + COOLING
MAKES: 4 SERVINGS

- 1 **broiler/fryer chicken (3 to 4 pounds), cut up**
- 2 **tablespoons canola oil**
- 2 **cups barbecue sauce**
- 1½ **cups coarsely chopped onions**
- 1 **large green pepper, chopped**

1. In a pressure cooker, brown chicken in oil in batches over medium heat. Remove chicken and keep warm. Combine the barbecue sauce, onions and green pepper in pressure cooker. Return the chicken to the pan; stir to coat.

2. Close cover securely; place pressure regulator on vent pipe. Bring cooker to full pressure over medium-high heat. Reduce heat to medium and cook for 10 minutes. (Pressure regulator should maintain a slow steady rocking motion; adjust heat if needed.) Remove from the heat; allow pressure to drop on its own.

NOTE *This recipe was tested at 13 pounds of pressure (psi).*

TENDER BARBECUED CHICKEN

CHICKEN &
VEGETABLE
KABOBS

FAST FIX
Chicken & Vegetable Kabobs

In the summer, my husband and I love to cook out, especially vegetables. These kabobs not only taste delicious but they look great, too!

—**TINA OLES** NASHWAUK, MN

START TO FINISH: 30 MIN. • **MAKES:** 4 SERVINGS

- **1 pound boneless skinless chicken breasts, cut into 1½ inch cubes**
- **1 medium sweet red pepper, cut into 1½ inch pieces**
- **1 medium zucchini, cut into 1½ inch pieces**
- **1 medium red onion, cut into thick wedges**
- **⅔ cup sun-dried tomato salad dressing, divided**

1. In a large bowl, combine chicken and vegetables. Drizzle with ⅓ cup of dressing and toss to coat. Alternately thread chicken and vegetables onto four metal or soaked wooden skewers.

2. Grill kabobs, covered, over medium heat or broil 4 in. from heat 8-10 minutes or until chicken is no longer pink, turning occasionally and basting with remaining dressing during the last 3 minutes.

FAST FIX
Raspberry Chicken

Basic skillet-cooked chicken gets a slightly sweet kick with this fresh, fun raspberry sauce. Serve it over cooked rice.

—**ANITA HENNESY** HAGERSTOWN, MD

START TO FINISH: 30 MIN. • **MAKES:** 4 SERVINGS

- **4 boneless skinless chicken breast halves (5 ounces each)**
- **¼ teaspoon salt**
- **¼ teaspoon pepper**
- **½ cup seedless raspberry jam**
- **2 tablespoons balsamic vinegar**
- **1 tablespoon reduced-sodium soy sauce**
- **⅛ teaspoon crushed red pepper flakes**

1. Sprinkle chicken with salt and pepper. In a large nonstick skillet coated with cooking spray, cook chicken over medium heat for 5-7 minutes on each side or until a thermometer reads 170°.

2. Meanwhile, in a small saucepan, combine the remaining ingredients. Bring to a boil; cook until liquid is reduced to ½ cup. Serve with chicken.

Chicken Caesar Florentine

I adapted this dish from my favorite chicken Caesar salad recipe. It has many of the same ingredients as the salad: croutons, grated Parmesan, chicken and creamy Caesar dressing. These chicken breasts are perfect for company, even on a busy weeknight.

—JOYCE CONWAY WESTERVILLE, OH

PREP: 15 MIN. • **BAKE:** 40 MIN. • **MAKES:** 4 SERVINGS

- 2 cups grated Parmesan cheese, divided
- 2 cups Caesar salad croutons, coarsely crushed, divided
- 1 cup fresh baby spinach
- 1 cup creamy Caesar salad dressing, divided
- 4 bone-in chicken breast halves, skin removed (8 ounces each)

1. Preheat oven to 375°. In a large bowl, combine 1 cup cheese, 1 cup crushed croutons, spinach and 1/2 cup salad dressing. Cut a pocket in the thickest part of each chicken breast; fill with cheese mixture.
2. Place remaining dressing and crushed croutons in separate shallow bowls. Dip chicken in dressing, then roll in croutons.
3. Transfer to a greased 13x9-in. baking dish. Bake, uncovered, 30 minutes. Sprinkle with remaining cheese; bake chicken 10-15 minutes longer or until a thermometer reads 170°.

OREGANO ROASTING CHICKEN

CHICKEN CAESAR FLORENTINE

Oregano Roasting Chicken

Roast chicken gets a Mediterranean makeover with oregano, lemon and Italian salad dressing mix.

—*TASTE OF HOME* TEST KITCHEN

PREP: 10 MIN. • **BAKE:** 2¼ HOURS • **MAKES:** 6 SERVINGS

- ¼ cup butter, melted
- 1 envelope Italian salad dressing mix
- 2 tablespoons lemon juice
- 1 roasting chicken (6 to 7 pounds)
- 2 teaspoons dried oregano

1. Preheat oven to 350°. In a small bowl, combine butter, salad dressing mix and lemon juice. Place chicken on a rack in an ungreased roasting pan. Spoon butter mixture over chicken.
2. Cover and bake for 45 minutes. Uncover; sprinkle with oregano. Bake chicken, uncovered, 1½ to 1¾ hours or until a thermometer inserted in thigh reads 170°-175°.

Chicken with Shallot Sauce

Even though it doesn't take long to put together, this flavorful chicken tastes as if it simmered all day. It's wonderful with mashed potatoes and a green vegetable.
—**KATHY ANDERSON** ROCKFORD, IL

PREP: 10 MIN. • **COOK:** 50 MIN. • **MAKES:** 4 SERVINGS

- 6 bacon strips, chopped
- 1 broiler/fryer chicken (3 to 4 pounds), cut up
- ½ teaspoon salt
- ½ teaspoon pepper
- 10 shallots, thinly sliced
- 1 cup water
- 1 whole garlic bulb, cloves separated and peeled
- ½ cup balsamic vinegar

1. In a large skillet, cook bacon over medium heat until crisp. Remove to paper towels with a slotted spoon; drain, reserving 2 tablespoons drippings.
2. Sprinkle chicken with salt and pepper; brown in drippings. Remove and keep warm. Add shallots; cook and stir until tender. Stir in water and garlic. Return chicken to pan. Bring to a boil. Reduce heat; cover and simmer for 30-35 minutes or until a thermometer inserted in thigh reads 170°-175°.
3. Remove chicken to a serving platter; keep warm. Skim the fat from cooking juices. Mash garlic; add vinegar. Bring liquid to a boil; cook until slightly thickened. Spoon over chicken; sprinkle with reserved bacon.

CHICKEN WITH SHALLOT SAUCE

HONEY HOISIN CHICKEN & POTATOES

Honey Hoisin Chicken & Potatoes

When I was little, Tutu (my grandma) cooked up this blend of Asian and American flavors. The potatoes are delicious drizzled with pan juices.
—**JANET YEE** PHOENIX, AZ

PREP: 10 MIN. • **BAKE:** 50 MIN. • **MAKES:** 4 SERVINGS

- 4 medium Yukon Gold potatoes (about 1¾ pounds), cut into 1-inch pieces
- 1 large onion, cut into 1-inch pieces
- ½ cup hoisin sauce
- 3 tablespoons honey
- ½ teaspoon salt, divided
- ½ teaspoon pepper, divided
- 4 bone-in chicken thighs (about 1½ pounds)

1. Preheat oven to 400°. Place potatoes and onion in a greased 13x9-in. baking pan. In a small bowl, mix hoisin, honey, ¼ teaspoon salt and ¼ teaspoon pepper; add to the potato mixture and toss to coat.
2. Place chicken over vegetables; sprinkle with remaining salt and pepper. Roast 50-60 minutes or until potatoes are tender and a thermometer inserted in chicken reads 170°-175°, basting occasionally with pan juices.

BBQ & RANCH CHICKEN PIZZA

FAST FIX
BBQ & Ranch Chicken Pizza
I wanted something different for dinner and came up with this pizza. The kids loved it, and so did my friends. Best of all, it uses leftover chicken and convenience items. What's not to love?
—**SUE SITLER** BLOOMSBURG, PA

START TO FINISH: 30 MIN. • **MAKES:** 8 SERVINGS

- 2 **tubes (8 ounces each) refrigerated crescent rolls**
- ½ **cup hickory smoke-flavored barbecue sauce, divided**
- ¼ **cup prepared ranch salad dressing**
- 3 **cups cubed cooked chicken breasts**
- 2 **cups (8 ounces) shredded pizza cheese blend**

1. Preheat oven to 375°. Unroll both tubes of crescent dough and press onto the bottom and up the sides of an ungreased 15x10x1-in. baking pan, pressing perforations to seal. Bake 8-10 minutes or until lightly browned.
2. In a small bowl, mix ¼ cup barbecue sauce and salad dressing; spread over crust. In another bowl, toss the chicken with remaining barbecue sauce; arrange over top. Sprinkle with cheese. Bake 15-20 minutes longer or until crust is golden brown and cheese is melted.

FAST FIX
Breaded Turkey Slices
Serve these turkey slices with a vegetable and bread for a complete meal in no time.
—**JULIE JAHNKE** GREEN LAKE, WI

START TO FINISH: 20 MIN. • **MAKES:** 6 SERVINGS

- 2 **eggs**
- 3 **tablespoons 2% milk**
- 2 **cups seasoned bread crumbs**
- ½ **teaspoon salt**
- 1½ **pounds turkey breast cutlets**
- ½ **cup butter, cubed**

1. In a shallow bowl, beat the eggs and milk. In another shallow bowl, combine bread crumbs and salt. Dip turkey slices in egg mixture, then coat with crumb mixture.
2. In a skillet, melt butter; brown turkey in batches for about 2 minutes on each side or until the juices run clear.

FAST FIX
Fried Chicken Tenders
This extra-special, extra-easy chicken nugget recipe relies on sesame crackers for a fun crust. Any night is the perfect night for this gravy and chicken specialty.
—**SHIRLEY LITTLE** ALVORD, TX

START TO FINISH: 25 MIN. • **MAKES:** 4 SERVINGS

- 2 **eggs**
- 1 **tablespoon water**
- 1 **pound boneless skinless chicken breasts, cut into 1-inch strips**
- 1 **package (8 ounces) sesame crackers, crushed (about 4 cups)**
- ¼ to ½ **cup canola oil**
- 1 **envelope instant chicken gravy mix, optional**

1. In a shallow bowl, combine eggs and water. Dip chicken in egg mixture, then coat with cracker crumbs. In an electric skillet, heat oil to 375°. Fry chicken strips, a few at a time, for 5-6 minutes or until golden brown. Drain on paper towels.
2. Meanwhile, prepare the gravy mix according to the package directions if desired. Serve with chicken strips.

Grilled Brown Sugar- Mustard Chicken

I came up with this recipe in college, and it's been a household staple ever since. I throw it together in a snap with items I usually have on hand.

—KENDRA DOSS COLORADO SPRINGS, CO

START TO FINISH: 20 MIN.
MAKES: 8 SERVINGS

- ½ cup yellow or Dijon mustard
- ⅓ cup packed brown sugar
- ½ teaspoon ground allspice
- ¼ teaspoon crushed red pepper flakes
- 8 boneless skinless chicken thighs (about 2 pounds)

1. In a large bowl, mix mustard, brown sugar, allspice and pepper flakes. Remove ¼ cup mixture for serving. Add chicken to the remaining mixture; toss to coat.
2. Grill chicken, covered, over medium heat or broil 4 in. from heat 6-8 minutes on each side or until a thermometer reads 170°. Serve with the reserved mustard mixture.

GRILLED BROWN SUGAR-MUSTARD CHICKEN

Greek Lemon Chicken

This is one of my family's summertime favorites. Feta, sun-dreid tomatoes, lemon and Greek vinaigrette create the Mediterranean flavor.

—DAWN ELLEN BISHOPVILLE, SC

PREP: 10 MIN. + MARINATING
GRILL: 10 MIN.
MAKES: 4 SERVINGS

- 1¼ cups Greek vinaigrette, divided
- 4 boneless skinless chicken breast halves (5 ounces each)
- 1 medium lemon, quartered
- 3 tablespoons sliced oil-packed sun-dried tomatoes
- ¼ cup crumbled feta cheese

1. Pour ¾ cup vinaigrette into a large resealable plastic bag. Add chicken; seal the bag and turn to coat. Refrigerate up to 4 hours. Cover and refrigerate remaining vinaigrette for basting.
2. Drain chicken, discarding marinade in bag. Grill chicken, covered, over medium heat or broil 4 in. from the heat for 4 minutes. Turn and baste with some of the reserved vinaigrette. Grill or broil 4-5 minutes longer or until a thermometer reads 165°, basting occasionally.
3. Squeeze lemon wedges over chicken. Sprinkle with tomatoes and cheese.

Mediterranean Stuffed Chicken Breasts

In my first apartment, I started cooking chicken with feta and sun-dried tomatoes. Ever since then, I serve the main course with rice pilaf and a salad.
—**AMANDA ROCHETTE** WATERTOWN, MA

PREP: 20 MIN. • **BAKE:** 30 MIN. • **MAKES:** 4 SERVINGS

- 1 **cup (4 ounces) crumbled feta cheese**
- ⅓ **cup chopped oil-packed sun-dried tomatoes**
- 4 **boneless skinless chicken breast halves (6 ounces each)**
- 2 **tablespoons olive oil from sun-dried tomatoes, divided**
- 1 **teaspoon Greek seasoning**

1. Preheat oven to 375°. In a small bowl, mix cheese and tomatoes. Pound chicken breasts with a meat mallet to ¼-in. thickness. Brush with 1 tablespoon oil; sprinkle with Greek seasoning. Top with cheese mixture. Roll up chicken from a short side; secure with a toothpick.
2. Place in a greased 11x7-in. baking dish, seam side down; brush with remaining oil. Bake, uncovered, 30-35 minutes or until a thermometer reads 165°. Discard toothpicks before serving.

GLAZED CORNISH HENS

Glazed Cornish Hens

If you're looking to add a touch of elegance to your dinner table, try these Cornish game hens. Topped with a sweet apricot glaze, the no-fuss entree is sure to impress for weeknights and holidays alike.
—*TASTE OF HOME* TEST KITCHEN

PREP: 5 MIN. • **BAKE:** 1 HOUR • **MAKES:** 4 SERVINGS

- 2 **Cornish game hens (20 to 24 ounces each), split lengthwise**
- ¼ **teaspoon salt**
- ⅛ **teaspoon white pepper**
- ⅓ **cup apricot spreadable fruit**
- 1 **tablespoon orange juice**

1. Preheat oven to 350°. Place hens, breast side up, on a rack in a shallow roasting pan. Sprinkle with salt and pepper. Bake, uncovered, 30 minutes.
2. In a small bowl, combine spreadable fruit and orange juice. Spoon some of the apricot mixture over the hens. Bake 30-35 minutes longer or until golden brown and juices run clear, basting several times with remaining apricot mixture. Let stand 5 minutes before serving.

MEDITERRANEAN STUFFED
CHICKEN BREASTS

CRANBERRY
TURKEY BREAST
WITH GRAVY

Cranberry Turkey Breast with Gravy

Here's a way to make large holiday meals a little easier on yourself. The turkey turns out so tender and moist, and because it's made in a slow cooker, you can use the oven for your side dishes.

—**SHIRLEY WELCH** TULSA, OK

PREP: 15 MIN. • **COOK:** 5 HOURS
MAKES: 12 SERVINGS (3 CUPS GRAVY)

- 1 **bone-in turkey breast (5 to 6 pounds)**
- 1 **can (14 ounces) whole-berry cranberry sauce**
- ¼ **cup orange juice**
- 1 **envelope onion soup mix**
- ¼ **teaspoon salt**
- ¼ **teaspoon pepper**
- 3 **to 4 teaspoons cornstarch**
- 1 **tablespoon water**

1. Place turkey in a 5-qt. slow cooker. In a small bowl, combine the cranberry sauce, orange juice, onion soup mix, salt and pepper; pour over turkey. Cover and cook on low for 5-6 hours or until tender.
2. Remove turkey to a serving platter; keep warm. Skim fat from cooking juices; transfer to a small saucepan. Bring to a boil. Combine cornstarch and water until smooth. Gradually stir into the pan. Bring to a boil; cook and stir for 2 minutes or until thickened. Serve with turkey.

Chicken Enchilada Bake

Give store-bought rotisserie chicken a fun, new twist with this casserole. It almost resembles a lasagna, only you're using tortillas instead of noodles. Add a green salad or serve it alongside chips and salsa if you'd like.

—**MELANIE BURNS** PUEBLO WEST, CO

PREP: 20 MIN. • **BAKE:** 50 MIN. + STANDING
MAKES: 10 SERVINGS

- 4½ **cups cubed rotisserie chicken**
- 1 **can (28 ounces) green enchilada sauce**
- 1¼ **cups (10 ounces) sour cream**
- 9 **corn tortillas (6 inches), cut into 1½-inch pieces**
- 4 **cups (16 ounces) shredded Monterey Jack cheese**

1. Preheat oven to 375°. In a greased 13x9-in. baking dish, layer half of the chicken, enchilada sauce, sour cream, tortilla pieces and cheese. Repeat layers.
2. Cover and bake 40 minutes. Uncover; bake 10 minutes longer or until bubbly. Let stand 15 minutes before serving.

Roasted Turkey with Maple Cranberry Glaze

A sweet maple flavor comes through even in the breast meat in this no-fuss turkey entree. You may start to notice its caramelized color after about two hours. That's when I cover it loosely with foil while it finishes cooking. The meat always stays tender and juicy.

—**SUZANNE ANCTIL** WEST VANCOUVER, BC

PREP: 10 MIN.
BAKE: 3 HOURS + STANDING
MAKES: 12 SERVINGS

- 1 **turkey (12 to 14 pounds)**
- 1 **cup maple syrup**
- ¾ **cup whole-berry cranberry sauce**
- ¼ **cup finely chopped walnuts**

1. Place turkey on a rack in a shallow roasting pan, breast side up. Tuck wings under turkey; tie drumsticks together. In a small bowl, combine the maple syrup, cranberry sauce and walnuts. Pour over turkey.

2. Bake, uncovered, at 325° for 3 to 3¾ hours or until a thermometer inserted in thigh reads 180°, basting occasionally with pan drippings. Cover loosely with foil if turkey browns too quickly. Cover and let stand for 20 minutes before carving.

ROASTED TURKEY WITH MAPLE CRANBERRY GLAZE

Cheesy Bow Tie Chicken

Here's a super-simple dish that tastes as if it's straight from an Italian restaurant. Spinach-artichoke dip is usually available at the supermarket deli, but it comes frozen, too. Just make sure to thaw it according to the package directions before dinnertime rolls around.

—**SALLY SIBTHORPE** SHELBY TOWNSHIP, MI

START TO FINISH: 30 MIN.
MAKES: 4 SERVINGS

- 2 **packages (8 ounces each) frozen spinach and artichoke cheese dip**
- 3 **cups uncooked bow tie pasta**
- 3 **cups cubed rotisserie chicken**
- 1 **cup chopped roasted sweet red peppers**
- ⅓ **cup pitted Greek olives, halved**
- ½ **teaspoon salt**
- ¼ **teaspoon pepper**

1. Heat cheese dip according to package directions. Meanwhile, in a Dutch oven, cook the pasta according to package directions; drain, reserving ½ cup pasta water. Return to pan.

2. Stir in chicken, cheese dip, peppers, olives, salt and pepper, adding enough reserved pasta water to achieve a creamy consistency; heat through.

Crispy Buffalo Chicken Roll-Ups for Two

These winning chicken rolls are both impressive and easy to make. My family and friends absolutely love the crispy crust!
—**LISA KEYS** KENNET SQUARE, PA

PREP: 15 MIN. • **BAKE:** 30 MIN.
MAKES: 2 SERVINGS

- 2 **boneless skinless chicken breast halves (6 ounces each)**
- ¼ **teaspoon salt**
- ¼ **teaspoon pepper**
- 2 **tablespoons crumbled blue cheese**
- 2 **tablespoons hot pepper sauce**
- 1 **tablespoon mayonnaise**
- ½ **cup crushed cornflakes**

1. Preheat oven to 400°. Flatten the chicken breasts to ¼-in. thickness. Season with salt and pepper; sprinkle with blue cheese. Roll up each from a short side and secure with toothpicks.

2. In a shallow bowl, combine pepper sauce and mayonnaise. Place cornflakes in a separate shallow bowl. Dip chicken in pepper sauce mixture, then coat with cornflakes. Place seam side down in a greased 11x7-in. baking dish.

3. Bake chicken, uncovered, 30-35 minutes or until chicken is no longer pink. Discard toothpicks.

CHEESY BOW TIE CHICKEN

Homemade Italian Turkey Sausage

When the stores in my area stopped carrying our favorite turkey sausage, I was desperate. I went to the library for some cookbooks on sausage, and I was surprised how easy it is to make! We use this from-scratch sweet-spicy sausage for pizza, spaghetti sauce, casseroles and even breakfast patties.

—JOYCE HAWORTH DES PLAINES, IL

PREP: 10 MIN. + CHILLING
COOK: 10 MIN.
MAKES: 8 SERVINGS

- 1 **pound lean ground turkey**
- 2 **teaspoons garlic powder**
- 1½ **teaspoons fennel seed, crushed**
- 1½ **teaspoons sugar**
- 1 **teaspoon salt**
- 1 **teaspoon dried oregano**
- ½ **teaspoon pepper**

1. In a bowl, combine the turkey, garlic powder, fennel seed, sugar, salt, oregano and pepper. Cover turkey and refrigerate for at least 8 hours or overnight. Shape into eight patties.

2. Cook in a nonstick skillet coated with cooking spray for about 3 minutes on each side or until a thermometer reads 165°.

3. Or crumble turkey into a nonstick skillet coated with cooking spray. Cook and stir for about 4 minutes or until meat is no longer pink.

SLOW COOKER

Southwest Chicken

Add some Southwestern flair to plain chicken breasts with corn, beans, cheese and salsa. A variety of fresh garnishes really complete the meal.

—MADDYMOO TASTEOFHOME.COM

PREP: 15 MIN. • **COOK:** 4 HOURS
MAKES: 6 SERVINGS

- 1 **can (15¼ ounces) whole kernel corn, drained**
- 1 **can (15 ounces) black beans, rinsed and drained**
- 1 **jar (16 ounces) mild salsa**
- 4 **boneless skinless chicken breast halves (5 ounces each)**
    Sweet red and yellow pepper strips, sour cream, shredded cheddar cheese and sliced green onions, optional

1. In a 3-qt. slow cooker, layer three-fourths each of the corn and beans and half of the salsa. Arrange chicken over salsa; top with remaining corn, beans and salsa. Cover and cook on low for 4-5 hours or until chicken is tender.

2. Shred chicken with two forks and return to the slow cooker; heat through. Top with peppers, sour cream, cheese and onions if desired.

SOUTHWEST CHICKEN

MANGO CHUTNEY
CHICKEN CURRY

FAST FIX ▶

Mango Chutney Chicken Curry

My father dreamed up this curry and chutney combination. Now my family cooks it on road trips: in rain and sun, in the mountains, even on the beach. Adjust the curry for your taste and spice tolerance.
—**DINA MORENO** SEATTLE, WA

START TO FINISH: 25 MIN. • **MAKES:** 4 SERVINGS

- 1 tablespoon canola oil
- 1 pound boneless skinless chicken breasts, cubed
- 1 tablespoon curry powder
- 2 garlic cloves, minced
- ¼ teaspoon salt
- ¼ teaspoon pepper
- ½ cup mango chutney
- ½ cup half-and-half cream

1. In a large skillet, heat oil over medium-high heat; brown chicken. Stir in curry powder, garlic, salt and pepper; cook 1-2 minutes longer or until aromatic.
2. Stir in chutney and cream. Bring to a boil. Reduce the heat; simmer, uncovered, 4-6 minutes or until chicken is no longer pink, stirring occasionally.

FAST FIX ▶

Pesto-Olive Chicken

Pesto, mushrooms and olives dress up chicken for a weeknight dinner that feels weekend-special. You can keep the ingredients handy right in your pantry.
—**CRISTY KING** SCOTT DEPOT, WV

START TO FINISH: 30 MIN. • **MAKES:** 4 SERVINGS

- 4 boneless skinless chicken breast halves (6 ounces each)
- ½ cup prepared pesto
- 2 jars (4½ ounces each) sliced mushrooms, drained
- 1 can (4½ ounces) chopped ripe olives
- 1 cup (4 ounces) shredded provolone cheese

1. Preheat oven to 400°. Flatten chicken slightly. Place in an ungreased 13x9-in. baking dish. Spoon pesto over chicken; top with mushrooms and olives.
2. Bake, uncovered, 15-18 minutes or until a thermometer reads 165°. Sprinkle with cheese; bake 1-2 minutes longer or until cheese is melted.

**CATHY HUDAK'S
PISTACHIO BAKED
SALMON** *PAGE 139*

Fish & Seafood

**PAM CORDERS'
LIME-MARINATED FISH**
PAGE 134

**JANA RIPPEE'S THAI SHRIMP
PASTA** *PAGE 129*

**PATTI BAILEY'S BAKED
PARMESAN FLOUNDER**
PAGE 127

TERIYAKI MAHI MAHI

Scallops in Sage Cream

I didn't want to hide the ocean freshness of the scallops I bought on the dock from a local fisherman, so I used simple ingredients to showcase them.

—JOAN CHURCHILL DOVER, NH

START TO FINISH: 20 MIN. • **MAKES:** 4 SERVINGS

- 1½ **pounds sea scallops**
- ¼ **teaspoon salt**
- ⅛ **teaspoon pepper**
- 3 **tablespoons olive oil, divided**
- ½ **cup chopped shallots**
- ¾ **cup heavy whipping cream**
- 6 **fresh sage leaves, thinly sliced**
  Hot cooked pasta, optional

1. Sprinkle scallops with salt and pepper. In a large skillet, cook scallops in 2 tablespoons oil for 1½ to 2 minutes on each side or until firm and opaque. Remove and keep warm.

2. In the same skillet, saute shallots in remaining oil until tender. Add cream; bring to a boil. Cook and stir for 30 seconds or until slightly thickened.

3. Return scallops to the pan; heat through. Stir in sage. Serve with pasta if desired.

SCALLOPS IN SAGE CREAM

FAST FIX ▸
Teriyaki Mahi Mahi

This recipe is good with rice, vegetables or salad, and it works well with cod or halibut fillets, too. Blot the fish thoroughly with paper towels before cooking to allow a nice brown crust to form.

—MICHELLE IBARRIENTOS TORRANCE, CA

START TO FINISH: 20 MIN. • **MAKES:** 4 SERVINGS

- 4 **mahi mahi fillets (6 ounces each)**
- ¼ **teaspoon garlic powder**
- ¼ **teaspoon pepper**
- 1 **tablespoon canola oil**
- 1 **teaspoon minced fresh gingerroot**
- ¼ **cup reduced-sodium teriyaki sauce**

1. Sprinkle mahi mahi with garlic powder and pepper. In a large skillet, cook mahi mahi in oil over medium-high heat for 4-5 minutes on each side or until fish flakes easily with a fork. Remove fillets and keep warm.

2. In the same skillet, saute ginger for 30 seconds. Stir in the teriyaki sauce; heat through. Serve over mahi mahi.

LEMON-GARLIC SALMON STEAKS

Lemon-Garlic Salmon Steaks

I always enjoy making this easy recipe for my husband, Jim, and myself. He absolutely loves salmon and garlic, and they go together well in this recipe.
—**MARY LYNN BARONETT** WAYNESBURG, PA

PREP: 10 MIN. • **BAKE:** 25 MIN. • **MAKES:** 6 SERVINGS

- 6 **to 8 garlic cloves, minced**
- 4 **tablespoons olive oil, divided**
- 6 **salmon steaks (6 ounces each)**
- ⅔ **cup lemon juice**
- ¼ **cup minced fresh parsley**
  Salt and pepper to taste

1. Preheat oven to 350°. In a small skillet, saute garlic in 1 tablespoon oil for 1 minute.
2. Arrange salmon steaks in a greased 13x9-in. baking dish. Combine lemon juice, parsley, salt, pepper and remaining oil; pour over salmon. Top with garlic mixture.
3. Bake, uncovered, 25-30 minutes or until fish flakes easily with a fork.

FAST FIX
Baked Parmesan Flounder

My family and friends adore this light and crispy fish. It's table-ready in minutes, yet special enough to serve to company.
—**PATTI BAILEY** CHANUTE, KS

START TO FINISH: 25 MIN. • **MAKES:** 6 SERVINGS

- ¾ **cup crushed cornflakes**
- ½ **cup grated Parmesan cheese**
- ½ **teaspoon salt**
- 2 **eggs, lightly beaten**
- 2 **tablespoons 2% milk**
- 2 **pounds flounder fillets**

1. Preheat oven to 450°. In a large resealable plastic bag, combine cornflakes, cheese and salt. In a shallow bowl, combine eggs and milk. Dip fish fillets in egg mixture, then shake in cornflake mixture.
2. Transfer to a greased 15x10x1-in. baking pan. Bake 15-20 minutes or until the fish flakes easily with a fork.

Grilled Lobster Tails

I had never made lobster at home until I tried this convenient and deliciously different grilled recipe. It turned out amazing, and has left me with little reason to ever order lobster at a restaurant again.

—KATIE RUSH KANSAS CITY, MO

PREP: 15 MIN. + MARINATING
GRILL: 10 MIN.
MAKES: 6 SERVINGS

- 6 **frozen lobster tails (8 to 10 ounces each), thawed**
- ¾ **cup olive oil**
- 3 **tablespoons minced fresh chives**
- 3 **garlic cloves, minced**
- ½ **teaspoon salt**
- ½ **teaspoon pepper**

1. Using scissors, cut top of lobster shell lengthwise down the center, leaving tail fin intact. Loosen meat from shell, keeping the fin end attached; lift meat and lay over shell. With a knife, cut a slit, ½ in. deep, down center of meat.

2. In a small bowl, combine the remaining ingredients; spoon over lobster meat. Cover and refrigerate for 20 minutes.

3. Place lobster tails, meat side up, on grill rack. Grill, covered, over medium heat for 10-12 minutes or until meat is opaque.

GRILLED LOBSTER TAILS

Thai Shrimp Pasta

I came up with this dish when my son was home from the Navy. He loves Thai food, and I wanted to make something special but simple. There wasn't a noodle left in the bowl.

—JANA RIPPEE CASA GRANDE, AZ

START TO FINISH: 30 MIN.
MAKES: 4 SERVINGS

- 8 **ounces thin flat rice noodles**
- 1 **tablespoon curry powder**
- 1 **pound uncooked shrimp (31-40 per pound), peeled and deveined**
- 1 **can (13.66 ounces) light coconut milk**
- ¼ **teaspoon salt**
- ¼ **teaspoon pepper**
- ½ **cup minced fresh cilantro Lime wedges, optional**

1. Soak noodles according to package directions. Meanwhile, in a large dry skillet over medium heat, toast curry powder until aromatic, about 1-2 minutes. Stir in shrimp, coconut milk, salt and pepper. Bring to a boil. Reduce heat; simmer, uncovered, for 5-6 minutes or until the shrimp turn pink.

2. Drain noodles. Add noodles and cilantro to the pan; heat through. If desired, serve with lime wedges.

SALMON WITH
LEMON-DILL BUTTER

Salmon with Lemon-Dill Butter

Fast and healthy, this recipe has it all. I recommend rounding out the meal with steamed sugar snap peas.

—JENNIE RICHARDS RIVERTON, UT

START TO FINISH: 15 MIN.
MAKES: 2 SERVINGS

- 2 **salmon fillets (4 ounces each)**
- 5 **teaspoons reduced-fat butter, melted**
- ¾ **teaspoon lemon juice**
- ½ **teaspoon grated lemon peel**
- ½ **teaspoon snipped fresh dill**

Place salmon, skin side down, on a broiler pan. Combine the butter, lemon juice, lemon peel and dill. Brush one-third of mixture over salmon. Broil 3-4 in. from the heat 7-9 minutes or until fish flakes easily with a fork, basting occasionally with remaining butter mixture.
NOTE *This recipe was tested with Land O'Lakes light stick butter.*

THAI SHRIMP PASTA

CRUMB-COATED
RED SNAPPER

Crumb-Coated Red Snapper

It's true: You can eat well *and* take care of yourself.
Here's a delicious way to get heart-healthy omega-3 oils.
—CHARLOTTE ELLIOTT NEENAH, WI

START TO FINISH: 30 MIN. • **MAKES:** 4 SERVINGS

- ½ cup dry bread crumbs
- 2 tablespoons grated Parmesan cheese
- 1 teaspoon lemon-pepper seasoning
- ¼ teaspoon salt
- 4 red snapper fillets (6 ounces each)
- 2 tablespoons olive oil

1. In a shallow bowl, combine the bread crumbs, cheese, lemon pepper and salt; add fillets, one at a time, and turn to coat.
2. In a heavy skillet over medium heat, cook fillets in oil in batches for 4-5 minutes on each side or until fish flakes easily with a fork.

Greek Grilled Catfish

Temperatures here on the Gulf Coast are moderate year-round, so we grill out a lot. My husband, Larry, came up with this recipe by experimenting. Our whole family likes the unique taste of this dish.
—RITA FUTRAL STARKVILLE, MS

START TO FINISH: 30 MIN. • **MAKES:** 6 SERVINGS

- 6 catfish fillets (8 ounces each)
  Greek seasoning to taste
- 4 ounces feta cheese, crumbled
- 1 tablespoon dried mint
- 2 tablespoons olive oil

1. Sprinkle both sides of fillets with Greek seasoning. Sprinkle each fillet with 1 rounded tablespoon feta cheese and ½ teaspoon mint. Drizzle 1 teaspoon oil over each. Roll up fillets and secure with toothpicks.
2. Grill over medium heat 20-25 minutes or until fish flakes easily with a fork. Or, place fillets in a greased baking dish and bake at 350° 30-35 minutes or until fish flakes easily with fork.

THAI BARBECUED SALMON

FAST FIX ▶
Thai Barbecued Salmon

The blend of both Thai chili and barbecue sauces gives my salmon a sweet, spicy kick that's festive to serve dinner guests. And with only four ingredients, this entree comes together in a flash.

—**PAMELA BRICK** CHICAGO, IL

START TO FINISH: 15 MIN. • **MAKES:** 4 SERVINGS

- ⅔ cup barbecue sauce
- ⅓ cup Thai chili sauce
- ¼ cup minced fresh cilantro
- 4 salmon fillets (1 inch thick and 4 ounces each)

1. In a small bowl, combine the barbecue sauce, chili sauce and cilantro. Set aside ¼ cup for serving.
2. Cook salmon on an indoor grill coated with cooking spray for 4-5 minutes or until fish flakes easily with a fork, basting frequently with sauce mixture. Serve salmon with reserved sauce.

FAST FIX ▶
Creole Baked Tilapia

Since I'm originally from Louisiana, I love Creole cooking. Just a bit of seasoning gives this fish regional flavor. Serve it with your favorite rice dish.

—**CAROLYN COLLINS** FREEPORT, TX

START TO FINISH: 25 MIN. • **MAKES:** 4 SERVINGS

- 4 tilapia fillets (6 ounces each)
- 1 can (8 ounces) tomato sauce
- 1 small green pepper, thinly sliced
- ½ cup chopped red onion
- 1 teaspoon Creole seasoning

1. Preheat oven to 350°. Place tilapia in an ungreased 13x9-in. baking dish. In a small bowl, combine tomato sauce, green pepper, onion and Creole seasoning; pour over the fillets.
2. Bake, uncovered, 20-25 minutes or until fish flakes easily with a fork.
NOTE *The following spices may be substituted for 1 teaspoon Creole seasoning: ¼ teaspoon each salt, garlic powder and paprika; and a pinch each of dried thyme, ground cumin and cayenne pepper.*

CREOLE BAKED TILAPIA

BUTTERY GRILLED SHRIMP

Buttery Grilled Shrimp

Have a little decadence for dinner. These shrimp pair well with steak. For a special occasion, brush the sauce over lobster tails and grill.

—**SHERYL SHENBERGER** ALBUQUERQUE, NM

START TO FINISH: 25 MIN. • **MAKES:** 8 SERVINGS

- ½ **cup butter, melted**
- 3 **tablespoons lemon juice**
- 2 **teaspoons chili powder**
- 1 **teaspoon ground ginger**
- ¼ **teaspoon salt**
- 2 **pounds uncooked jumbo shrimp, peeled and deveined**

1. In a small bowl, combine the first five ingredients; set aside ¼ cup. Thread shrimp onto eight metal or soaked wooden skewers.
2. Grill the shrimp, covered, over medium heat for 3-5 minutes on each side or until shrimp turn pink, basting occasionally with butter mixture. Remove from the grill; brush with reserved butter mixture.

Spaghetti with Creamy White Clam Sauce

A handful of ingredients is all you need for this must-try main dish. I often make it when time is short.

—**LINDA EVANCOE-COBLE** LEOLA, PA

START TO FINISH: 20 MIN. • **MAKES:** 4 SERVINGS

- 1 **can (15 ounces) ready-to-serve reduced-fat New England clam chowder**
- 1 **can (6½ ounces) chopped clams, undrained**
- 1 **tablespoon minced fresh parsley**
- ¼ **teaspoon garlic powder**
- ⅛ **teaspoon salt**
  Dash white pepper
- 8 **ounces uncooked spaghetti**

1. In a large saucepan, combine the first six ingredients; bring to a boil. Reduce heat; cook and stir for 5 minutes until slightly thickened.
2. Meanwhile, cook spaghetti according to package directions; drain. Pour sauce over spaghetti.

Tarragon Flounder

I enjoy using tarragon in a number of dishes, but especially in this flounder recipe that makes just enough for two.

—**DONNA SMITH** FAIRPORT, NY

START TO FINISH: 30 MIN. • **MAKES:** 2 SERVINGS

- 2 **flounder fillets (4 ounces each)**
- ½ **cup chicken broth**
- 2 **tablespoons butter, melted**
- 1 **tablespoon minced fresh tarragon or 1 teaspoon dried tarragon**
- 1 **teaspoon ground mustard**

1. Preheat oven to 350°. Place fillets in a greased 11x7-in. baking dish. Combine the remaining ingredients; pour over fish.
2. Bake, uncovered, 20-25 minutes or until fish flakes easily with a fork. Remove to a serving plate with a slotted spatula. Serve immediately.

Tasty Maple-Glazed Salmon

This tasty salmon wonderfully balances sweet and savory in just four delicious ingredients.

—**JEANNIE KLUGH** LANCASTER, PA

START TO FINISH: 20 MIN. • **MAKES:** 4 SERVINGS

- 2 **tablespoons hoisin sauce**
- 2 **tablespoons maple syrup**
- 2 **teaspoons prepared mustard**
- 4 **salmon fillets (6 ounces each)**

1. In a small bowl, combine the hoisin sauce, syrup and mustard; set aside. Place salmon, skin side down, on a greased broiler pan.

2. Broil 4-6 in. from the heat for 5 minutes. Brush half of the sauce over salmon. Broil 7-10 minutes longer or until the fish flakes easily with a fork, brushing occasionally with remaining sauce.

Tuna Alfredo

When it's just my husband and I for dinner, I often prepare this easy favorite. It tastes like old-fashioned tuna noodle casserole, but a packaged mix makes it quick to whip up.

—**VICKI DIDIER** MACHESNEY PARK, IL

START TO FINISH: 20 MIN. • **MAKES:** 2-3 SERVINGS

- 1 **package (4.4 ounces) quick-cooking Alfredo noodles and sauce mix**
- 1 **can (5 ounces) tuna, drained and flaked**
- 1 **tablespoon chopped green onion**

Prepare noodles and sauce mix according to package directions. Stir in the tuna and onion; heat through.

TASTY
MAPLE-GLAZED
SALMON

TOMATO SALMON BAKE

Tomato Salmon Bake

I was looking for a healthy alternative to beef and chicken when I found this recipe and decided to personalize it. My husband doesn't usually like fish unless it's fried, but he loves the Italian flavor in this dish. Serve it with a green salad for a great meal any time of year.

—**LACEY PARKER** CARY, NC

START TO FINISH: 30 MIN. • **MAKES:** 4 SERVINGS

    4 **salmon fillets (6 ounces each)**
    1 **can (14½ ounces) diced tomatoes, drained**
    ½ **cup sun-dried tomato salad dressing**
    2 **tablespoons shredded Parmesan cheese**
       Hot cooked rice

1. Preheat oven to 375°. Place salmon in a greased 13x9-in. baking dish. Combine tomatoes and salad dressing; pour over salmon. Sprinkle with cheese.
2. Bake, uncovered, 20-25 minutes or until fish flakes easily with a fork. Serve with rice.

Lime-Marinated Fish

This dish is simple, flavorful and light. And since it's so quick, you can have company over and spend all your time visiting.

—**PAM CORDER** MONROE, LA

PREP: 10 MIN. + MARINATING • **BROIL:** 10 MIN.
MAKES: 4 SERVINGS

    4 **tilapia fillets (6 ounces each)**
    ⅓ **cup water**
    ⅓ **cup lime juice**
    2 **tablespoons honey**
    1 **tablespoon canola oil**
    ½ **teaspoon dill weed**

1. Place fillets in a 13x9-in. baking dish. For marinade, in a small bowl, whisk remaining ingredients until blended. Set aside 3 tablespoons marinade. Pour remaining marinade over fillets; turn to coat. Cover and refrigerate for 1 hour.
2. Drain and discard marinade. Transfer fillets to a broiler pan coated with cooking spray. Broil 4-6 in. from heat 4-6 minutes on each side or until fish flakes easily with a fork, basting frequently with reserved marinade.

LIME-MARINATED FISH

GRILLED TUNA STEAKS

Grilled Tuna Steaks

After enjoying yellowfin tuna at a restaurant in southwest Florida, I came up with this recipe so I could enjoy the flavor of my favorite fish at home.
—JAN HUNTINGTON PAINESVILLE, OH

PREP: 10 MIN. + MARINATING • **GRILL:** 10 MIN.
MAKES: 4 SERVINGS

- 2 **tablespoons lemon juice**
- 1 **tablespoon olive oil**
- 2 **garlic cloves, minced**
- 2 **teaspoons minced fresh thyme or**
     ½ teaspoon dried thyme
- 4 **tuna steaks (6 ounces each)**
- ¼ **teaspoon salt**
- ¼ **teaspoon pepper**

1. In a large resealable plastic bag, combine the lemon juice, oil, garlic and thyme. Add tuna; seal bag and turn to coat. Chill for up to 30 minutes, turning occasionally.
2. Remove tuna from bag; sprinkle with salt and pepper. Drain and discard marinade. Moisten a paper towel with cooking oil; using long-handled tongs, lightly coat the grill rack.
3. Grill tuna, covered, over medium-hot heat or broil 4 in. from the heat for 3-4 minutes on each side for medium-rare or until slightly pink in the center.

Flounder Florentine

A mixture of garden vegetable cream cheese and healthy chopped spinach lends rich flavor to these tender fish fillets. You'll have an elegant meal on the table in just over 30 minutes.
—BOBBY TAYLOR LAPORTE, IN

PREP: 10 MIN. • **BAKE:** 25 MIN. • **MAKES:** 4 SERVINGS

- 1 **package (10 ounces) frozen chopped spinach,**
     thawed and squeezed dry
- 1 **carton (8 ounces) spreadable garden vegetable**
     cream cheese, divided
- 4 **flounder or sole fillets (3 ounces each)**
- 2 **tablespoons 2% milk**
- ½ **teaspoon lemon juice**
- ⅛ **teaspoon salt**
- ⅛ **teaspoon pepper**

1. Preheat oven to 375°. In a small bowl, combine spinach and ¾ cup cream cheese. Spoon onto each fillet; roll up. Place seam side down in a greased 8-in.-square baking dish.
2. Bake, uncovered, 25-30 minutes or until fish flakes easily with a fork.
3. In a small microwave-safe bowl, combine milk, lemon juice, salt, pepper and remaining cream cheese. Microwave on high 30-60 seconds; stir until smooth. Spoon over fish.

PESTO HALIBUT

FAST FIX

Pesto Halibut

The mildness of halibut contrasts perfectly with the robust flavor of pesto in this recipe. It takes only minutes to get the fish ready for the oven, so you can start quickly on your side dishes. Nearly anything goes well with this entree.

—APRIL SHOWALTER INDIANAPOLIS, IN

START TO FINISH: 20 MIN.
MAKES: 6 SERVINGS

2 tablespoons olive oil
1 envelope pesto sauce mix
1 tablespoon lemon juice
6 halibut fillets
(4 ounces each)

1. Preheat oven to 450°. In a small bowl, combine oil, sauce mix and lemon juice; brush over both sides of fillets. Place in a greased 13x9-in. baking dish.
2. Bake fillets, uncovered, for 12-15 minutes or until fish flakes easily with a fork.

Orange-Pecan Salmon

I first made this baked salmon for a friend's luncheon, and everyone loved it. It was especially nice that I could pop it into the oven just before the guests arrived and still serve lunch within minutes.

—PAT NEAVES LEES SUMMIT, MO

PREP: 10 MIN. + MARINATING
BAKE: 20 MIN.
MAKES: 4 SERVINGS

1 cup orange marmalade
½ cup reduced-sodium soy sauce
¼ teaspoon salt
¼ teaspoon pepper
4 salmon fillets
(6 ounces each)
1 cup chopped pecans, toasted

1. In a small bowl, combine marmalade, soy sauce, salt and pepper. Pour ⅔ cup marinade into a large resealable plastic bag. Add the salmon; seal bag and turn to coat. Refrigerate for up to 30 minutes. Set aside the remaining marinade.
2. Preheat oven to 350°. Drain and discard marinade from salmon. Place salmon in a greased 11x7-in. baking dish. Bake, uncovered, 20-25 minutes or until the fish flakes easily with a fork.
3. In a small saucepan, bring reserved marinade to a boil; cook and stir until slightly thickened. Stir in pecans; serve with salmon.

ORANGE-PECAN SALMON

Shrimp Pasta Alfredo

My son loves any recipe with Alfredo sauce. When he was a bachelor, shrimp pasta was one of the first dishes he put together. Now his children ask him to make it.

—GAIL LUCAS OLIVE BRANCH, MS

START TO FINISH: 25 MIN.
MAKES: 4 SERVINGS

- 3 **cups uncooked bow tie pasta**
- 2 **cups frozen peas**
- 1 **pound peeled and deveined cooked medium shrimp, tails removed**
- 1 **jar (15 ounces) Alfredo sauce**
- ¼ **cup shredded Parmesan cheese**

1. In a Dutch oven, cook pasta according to package directions, adding peas during the last 3 minutes of cooking; drain and return to pan.

2. Stir in shrimp and sauce; heat through over medium heat, stirring occasionally. Sprinkle with cheese.

TOP TIP

To keep pasta from sticking together when cooking, use a large pot with plenty of water. Add a little cooking oil if desired (this also helps prevent the pot from boiling over).

SHRIMP PASTA
ALFREDO

BAKED ITALIAN
TILAPIA

Baked Italian Tilapia

This colorful dish is so simple, it will soon be on your list of go-to recipes.

—KIMBERLY MCGEE MOSHEIM, TN

PREP: 10 MIN. • **BAKE:** 40 MIN. • **MAKES:** 4 SERVINGS

- 4 tilapia fillets (6 ounces each)
- ¼ teaspoon pepper
- 1 can (14½ ounces) diced tomatoes with basil, oregano and garlic, drained
- 1 large onion, halved and thinly sliced
- 1 medium green pepper, julienned
- ¼ cup shredded Parmesan cheese

1. Preheat oven to 350°. Place tilapia in a 13x9-in. baking dish coated with cooking spray; sprinkle with pepper. Spoon tomatoes over tilapia; top with onion and green pepper.

2. Cover and bake 30 minutes. Uncover; sprinkle with cheese. Bake 10-15 minutes longer or until fish flakes easily with a fork.

Bacon Honey Walleye

The texture and flavor of the walleye are only enhanced by this recipe's savory-sweet topping. It takes only a few minutes to grill.

—LINDA NEUMANN ALGONAC, MI

PREP: 20 MIN. • **GRILL:** 15 MIN. • **MAKES:** 8 SERVINGS

- 16 bacon strips, partially cooked
- 4 walleye fillets (2½ pounds)
- 1 cup thinly sliced onion
- ¼ cup butter, melted
- 2 tablespoons honey
- ½ teaspoon salt
- ¼ teaspoon pepper

1. Fold four 18x15-in. pieces of heavy-duty aluminum foil in half; fold up edges to make pans about 12x7 in. Place four strips of bacon in each foil pan; top each with a fillet and ¼ cup onion. Drizzle with butter and honey. Sprinkle with salt and pepper.

2. Grill, covered, over medium heat 12-15 minutes or until fish flakes easily with a fork. Open foil carefully to allow steam to escape. Cut fillets in half; serve each with two bacon strips.

PISTACHIO
BAKED SALMON

Scalloped Shrimp and Potatoes

Shrimp and spinach take the flavors up a notch in our cheesy potato main dish. It couldn't be much easier to fix. Fresh spinach really packs in the nutrients.

—*TASTE OF HOME* TEST KITCHEN

START TO FINISH: 20 MIN. • **MAKES:** 4 SERVINGS

- 1 package (4.9 ounces) scalloped potatoes
- 2¼ cups water
- ⅓ cup 2% milk
- 1 pound peeled and deveined cooked medium shrimp
- 3 cups fresh baby spinach, coarsely chopped
- 1 cup (4 ounces) shredded Colby-Monterey Jack cheese

1. In a large skillet, combine the potatoes, contents of sauce mix packet, water and milk. Bring to a boil. Reduce heat; cover and simmer for 8-10 minutes or until potatoes are tender, stirring occasionally.
2. Add shrimp and spinach. Cook and stir until spinach is wilted. Stir in cheese until melted.

Pistachio Baked Salmon

Next time you have last-minute guests, try this fancy, flavorful salmon. With pistachios, brown sugar and dill, it's a guaranteed hit.

—**CATHY HUDAK** WADSWORTH, OH

START TO FINISH: 25 MIN. • **MAKES:** 6 SERVINGS

- 6 salmon fillets (6 ounces each)
- 1 cup pistachios, chopped
- ½ cup packed brown sugar
- 3 tablespoons lemon juice
- 1 teaspoon dill weed
- 1 teaspoon pepper

1. Preheat oven to 425°. Place salmon in a greased 13x9-in. baking dish. Combine remaining ingredients; spoon over salmon.
2. Bake, uncovered, 12-15 minutes or until fish flakes easily with a fork.

SCALLOPED SHRIMP
AND POTATOES

JERRY GULLEY'S PERSONAL MARGHERITA PIZZAS *PAGE 144*

Meatless

RUTH WUNDER'S CHEESY CHILI FRIES *PAGE 143*

CHASE MILLER'S THREE-VEGETABLE PASTA SAUCE *PAGE 147*

BRITTANY HUBBARD'S SWEET POTATO & BEAN QUESADILLAS *PAGE 146*

ARTICHOKE BLUE
CHEESE FETTUCCINE

MEATLESS

FAST FIX
Artichoke
Blue Cheese Fettuccine

This flavorful entree comes together in a snap. I use dried fettuccine, but you can make the recipe even faster with the fresh variety.

—**JOLANTHE ERB** HARRISONBURG, VA

START TO FINISH: 20 MIN. • **MAKES:** 4 SERVINGS

- 1 **package (12 ounces) fettuccine**
- 1 **can (14 ounces) water-packed artichoke hearts, rinsed, drained and chopped**
- 1 **cup sliced fresh mushrooms**
- 1½ **cups Alfredo sauce**
- ¼ **cup crumbled blue cheese**

1. Cook fettuccine according to package directions. Meanwhile, in a large nonstick skillet coated with cooking spray, saute artichokes and mushrooms until tender. Stir in Alfredo sauce. Bring to a boil. Reduce heat; simmer, uncovered, for 4-5 minutes or until heated through, stirring occasionally.
2. Drain fettuccine; add to artichoke mixture and toss to coat. Sprinkle with blue cheese.

FAST FIX
Polenta Lasagna

Using polenta instead of pasta puts a fresh spin on lasagna. We love the easy assembly.

—**YEVGENIYA FARRER** FREMONT, CA

START TO FINISH: 25 MIN. • **MAKES:** 4 SERVINGS

- 1½ **cups marinara sauce**
- 1 **teaspoon garlic powder**
- 1 **teaspoon herbes de Provence**
- 1 **tube (18 ounces) polenta, cut into 10 slices**
- 1½ **cups (6 ounces) shredded part-skim mozzarella cheese**

1. In a small bowl, mix marinara sauce, garlic powder and herbes de Provence. Arrange half of the polenta slices in a greased 8-in. skillet. Top with half of the sauce; sprinkle with ¾ cup cheese. Repeat layers.
2. Cook, uncovered, over medium heat for 12-14 minutes or until bubbly. Cover; cook 2-3 minutes longer or until cheese is melted.
NOTE *Look for herbes de Provence in the spice aisle.*

CHEESY CHILI FRIES

Cheesy Chili Fries

My family is all about chili fries, but the ones you find at restaurants aren't always the healthiest. Here's a better-for-you way to satisfy the craving.

—**RUTH WUNDER** FORTUNA, CA

START TO FINISH: 30 MIN. • **MAKES:** 4 SERVINGS

- 5 cups frozen seasoned curly fries
- 1 tablespoon olive oil
- 1 can (15 ounces) vegetarian chili with beans
- 1 cup (4 ounces) shredded cheddar cheese
  Optional toppings: sour cream, thinly sliced green onions and cubed avocado

1. Preheat oven to 450°. Place fries in an ungreased 15x10x1-in. baking pan; drizzle with oil and toss to coat. Bake according to package directions.
2. Divide fries among four 2-cup baking dishes; top each with chili and cheese. Bake 5-7 minutes or until the cheese is melted. Serve with toppings as desired.
NOTE *You may use an 8-in.-square baking dish instead of four 2-cup baking dishes. Bake as directed.*

Peppered Portobello Penne

Meaty mushrooms and a kickin' hot cheese sauce take this simple pasta toss from drab to fab! My family loves that it tastes like a restaurant dish, but it's made at home.

—**VERONICA CALLAGHAN** GLASTONBURY, CT

START TO FINISH: 30 MIN. • **MAKES:** 4 SERVINGS

- 2 cups uncooked penne pasta
- 4 large portobello mushrooms, stems removed, halved and thinly sliced
- 2 tablespoons olive oil
- ½ cup heavy whipping cream
- ¾ teaspoon salt
- ¼ teaspoon pepper
- 1 cup (4 ounces) shredded pepper jack cheese

1. Cook pasta according to package directions.
2. Meanwhile, in a large skillet, saute mushrooms in oil until tender. Stir in the cream, salt and pepper; heat through. Stir in cheese until melted. Drain pasta. Add to skillet and toss to coat.

Tomato Spinach Spirals

Convenience and economy blend with tomatoes and spinach to make this a tasty meatless main course.

—**JANET MONTANO** TEMECULA, CA

START TO FINISH: 25 MIN. • **MAKES:** 4 SERVINGS

- 1 package (8 ounces) spiral pasta
- 1 package (10 ounces) frozen creamed spinach
- 1 can (14½ ounces) diced tomatoes, undrained
- 3 tablespoons grated Romano cheese, divided
- 3 tablespoons grated Parmesan cheese, divided
- ½ teaspoon salt

Cook pasta according to package directions. Meanwhile, prepare spinach according to package directions. Drain pasta; place in a large bowl. Add the spinach, tomatoes, 2 tablespoons of Romano cheese, 2 tablespoons of Parmesan cheese and salt; toss to coat. Sprinkle with the remaining cheeses.

Polenta Chili Casserole

Combine spicy chili, mixed veggies and homemade polenta for a hearty dinner bake. It's a warm and comfy casserole sure to please everyone.

—DAN KELMENSON
WEST BLOOMFIELD, MI

PREP: 20 MIN.
BAKE: 35 MIN. + STANDING
MAKES: 8 SERVINGS

- 4 **cups water**
- ½ **teaspoon salt**
- 1¼ **cups yellow cornmeal**
- 2 **cups (8 ounces) shredded cheddar cheese, divided**
- 3 **cans (15 ounces each) vegetarian chili with beans**
- 1 **package (16 ounces) frozen mixed vegetables, thawed and well drained**

1. Preheat oven to 350°. In a large heavy saucepan, bring water and salt to a boil. Reduce heat to a gentle boil; slowly whisk in cornmeal. Cook and stir with a wooden spoon 15-20 minutes or until polenta is thickened and pulls away cleanly from sides of the pan.

2. Remove from the heat. Stir in ¼ cup cheese until melted.

3. Spread into a 13x9-in. baking dish coated with cooking spray. Bake, uncovered, 20 minutes. Meanwhile, heat chili according to package directions.

4. Spread vegetables over polenta; top with chili. Sprinkle with remaining cheese. Bake 12-15 minutes longer or until cheese is melted. Let stand for 10 minutes before serving.

FAST FIX

Personal Margherita Pizzas

This family-friendly supper is simplicity at its finest. Delectable fresh mozzarella and a sprinkling of basil give these little pies Italian flair.

—JERRY GULLEY SAN FRANCISCO, CA

START TO FINISH: 25 MIN.
MAKES: 3 SERVINGS

- 1 **package (6½ ounces) pizza crust mix**
- ½ **teaspoon dried oregano**
- ¾ **cup pizza sauce**
- 6 **ounces fresh mozzarella cheese, thinly sliced**
- ¼ **cup thinly sliced fresh basil leaves**

1. Preheat oven to 425°. Prepare pizza dough according to package directions, adding oregano before mixing. Divide dough into three portions.

2. Pat each portion of dough into an 8-in. circle on greased baking sheets. Bake 8-10 minutes or until edges are lightly browned.

3. Spread each crust with ¼ cup pizza sauce to within ½ in. of edge. Top with cheese. Bake for 5-10 minutes longer or until crust is golden and cheese is melted. Sprinkle with basil.

TOP TIP

To make a delicious herbed pizza crust, I add 1 teaspoon each of basil and oregano to a boxed pizza crust mix. It's an excellent way to give a little added zip to homemade pizza.

—**MICHELLE DURFEE** GREGORY, MI

PERSONAL MARGHERITA PIZZAS

SPINACH-ARTICHOKE RIGATONI

FAST FIX

Spinach-Artichoke Rigatoni

I love pasta, and so does my family. However, they are not so keen on their veggies. This one-pot meal gets us all eating our spinach.

—**YVONNE STARLIN** HERMITAGE, TN

START TO FINISH: 30 MIN. • **MAKES:** 4 SERVINGS

- 3 cups uncooked rigatoni or large tube pasta
- 1 package (10 ounces) frozen creamed spinach
- 1 can (14 ounces) water-packed artichoke hearts, rinsed, drained and quartered
- 2 cups (8 ounces) shredded part-skim mozzarella cheese, divided
- ¼ cup grated Parmesan cheese
- ½ teaspoon salt
- ¼ teaspoon pepper

1. Preheat broiler. Prepare rigatoni and spinach according to package directions.

2. Drain pasta, reserving ½ cup pasta water; return to pan. Add artichoke hearts, ½ cup mozzarella cheese, Parmesan cheese, salt, pepper and creamed spinach; toss to combine, adding some of the reserved pasta water to thin, if desired.

3. Transfer to a greased 2-qt. broiler-safe baking dish; sprinkle with remaining mozzarella cheese. Broil 4-6 in. from heat 2-3 minutes or until cheese is melted.

FAST FIX

Nutty Cheese Tortellini

I like to plant Italian flat-leaf parsley in a long terra-cotta planter so I have it on hand. The homegrown herb really lends itself to this pasta dish.

—**BARBARA PENATZER** VESTAL, NY

START TO FINISH: 20 MIN.
MAKES: 3 SERVINGS

- 1 package (9 ounces) refrigerated cheese tortellini
- ½ cup butter, cubed
- ½ cup minced fresh parsley
- ⅓ cup chopped walnuts, toasted
- ¼ cup shredded Parmesan cheese
  Coarsely ground pepper to taste

Cook tortellini according to package directions; drain and keep warm. In the same pan, melt butter. Stir in the tortellini, parsley and walnuts; toss to coat. Sprinkle with cheese and pepper.

FAST FIX

Jazzy Mac 'n' Cheese

Adding Parmesan and mozzarella to already cheesy macaroni will have your clan clamoring for this tried-and-true classic. Diced tomatoes and chilies lend a little zip.

—*TASTE OF HOME* TEST KITCHEN

START TO FINISH: 20 MIN. • **MAKES:** 4 SERVINGS

- 1 package (7¼ ounces) macaroni and cheese dinner mix
- 1 can (10 ounces) diced tomatoes and green chilies, undrained
- ¼ cup butter, cubed
- ½ cup grated Parmesan cheese
- ½ cup shredded part-skim mozzarella cheese

1. In a medium saucepan, bring 6 cups water to a boil. Add macaroni; set aside cheese packet. Cook, uncovered, for 6-8 minutes or until tender. Drain and return to saucepan.

2. Add tomatoes and butter; mix until butter is melted. Add the reserved cheese packet; mix well. Remove from heat; stir in the Parmesan and mozzarella cheeses.

Asparagus Souffle

I'm not sure where I found this recipe, but being an asparagus lover, I knew I'd like it. I've tried it out on several guests, and all have enjoyed it.

—**PATRICIA PATTON** JAL, NM

START TO FINISH: 30 MIN. • **MAKES:** 2 SERVINGS

- 1 package (8 ounces) frozen cut asparagus, thawed and well drained
- ⅓ cup finely shredded cheddar cheese
- ⅓ cup mayonnaise
- ¼ cup chopped onion
- 1 egg white

1. Preheat oven to 350°. In a large bowl, combine asparagus, cheese, mayonnaise and onion. In a small bowl, beat egg white on medium speed until soft peaks form. Fold into asparagus mixture.
2. Transfer to a greased 2½-cup baking dish. Bake, uncovered, 20-25 minutes or until lightly browned.

Ravioli Casserole

The whole family loves this yummy dish that tastes like lasagna without all the fuss. Time-saving ingredients such as spaghetti sauce and frozen ravioli speed up assembly. So simple, the kids can help, too!

—**MARY ANN ROTHERT** AUSTIN, TX

PREP: 10 MIN. • **BAKE:** 30 MIN. • **MAKES:** 6-8 SERVINGS

- 3½ cups spaghetti sauce
- 1 package (25 ounces) frozen cheese ravioli, cooked and drained
- 2 cups (16 ounces) 4% cottage cheese
- 4 cups (16 ounces) shredded mozzarella cheese
- ¼ cup grated Parmesan cheese

1. Spread 1 cup of spaghetti sauce in an ungreased 13x9-in. baking dish. Layer with half of the ravioli, 1¼ cups of sauce, 1 cup cottage cheese and 2 cups mozzarella cheese. Repeat layers. Sprinkle with Parmesan cheese.
2. Bake, uncovered, at 350° for 30-40 minutes or until bubbly. Let casserole stand for 5-10 minutes before serving.

SWEET POTATO &
BEAN QUESADILLAS

Sweet Potato & Bean Quesadillas

Stuff your quesadillas with added nutrients and sustenance via black beans and sweet potatoes.

—**BRITTANY HUBBARD** ST. PAUL, MN

START TO FINISH: 30 MIN. • **MAKES:** 4 SERVINGS

- 2 medium sweet potatoes
- 4 whole wheat tortillas (8 inches)
- ¾ cup canned black beans, rinsed and drained
- ½ cup shredded pepper jack cheese
- ¾ cup salsa

1. Scrub sweet potatoes; pierce several times with a fork. Place on a microwave-safe plate. Microwave, uncovered, on high 7-9 minutes or until very tender, turning once.
2. When cool enough to handle, cut each potato lengthwise in half. Scoop out pulp. Spread onto one half of each tortilla; top with beans and cheese. Fold other half of tortilla over filling.
3. Heat a griddle or skillet over medium heat. Cook quesadillas 2-3 minutes on each side or until golden brown and cheese is melted. Serve with salsa.

Three-Vegetable Pasta Sauce

In an effort to sneak vegetables into my family's food, I created this zesty sauce of cauliflowerets, baby spinach and tomatoes.

—CHASE MILLER GATESVILLE, TX

PREP: 20 MIN. • **COOK:** 2 HOURS • **MAKES:** 3 CUPS

- 2 **cups fresh cauliflowerets**
- 2 **cans (14½ ounces each) diced tomatoes, undrained**
- 4 **cups fresh baby spinach (about 4 ounces)**
- ½ **teaspoon salt**
- ½ **teaspoon garlic powder**
  Hot cooked pasta

1. In a saucepan, place a steamer basket over 1 in. of water. Place cauliflowerets in basket. Bring water to a boil. Reduce heat to a simmer; steam, covered, 10-12 minutes or until tender. Cool slightly.
2. Place cauliflower in a food processor; process until pureed. Transfer to a large saucepan; stir in tomatoes, spinach, salt and garlic powder. Bring to a boil. Reduce heat; simmer, uncovered, about 2 hours or until flavors are blended, stirring occasionally. Serve with pasta.

FAST FIX

Spinach Pizza

Looking for a fun twist on a traditional favorite? Veggies and Alfredo sauce add complexity to simple pizza.

—DAWN BARTHOLOMEW RALEIGH, NC

START TO FINISH: 25 MIN. • **MAKES:** 4-6 SERVINGS

- 1 **package (6½ ounces) pizza crust mix**
- ½ **cup Alfredo sauce**
- 2 **medium tomatoes**
- 4 **cups chopped fresh spinach**
- 2 **cups (8 ounces) shredded Italian cheese blend**

1. Prepare pizza dough according to package directions. With floured hands, press dough onto a greased 12-in. pizza pan.
2. Spread Alfredo sauce over dough to within 1 in. of edges. Thinly slice or chop tomatoes; top pizza with spinach, tomatoes and cheese.
3. Bake at 450° for 10-15 minutes or until cheese is melted and crust is golden brown.

FAST FIX

Zucchini-Parmesan Bake

When my garden is overflowing with zucchini, I turn to this recipe as a tasty way to use up the bounty.

—SHANNON DAVIS MASON, MI

START TO FINISH: 30 MIN.
MAKES: 6 SERVINGS

- 3 eggs
- ½ cup canola oil
- 3 cups shredded zucchini (about 1 pound)
- 1 cup reduced-fat biscuit/baking mix
- ½ cup shredded Parmesan cheese

1. Preheat the oven to 375°. In a large bowl, whisk eggs and oil until blended. Stir in the remaining ingredients.
2. Transfer to a greased 10-in. ovenproof skillet. Bake for 25-30 minutes or until golden brown.

TOP TIP

Thought this was delicious. Easy to make and few ingredients. Next time I may add some onion, as the flavor is pretty delicate. I did add some shredded cheddar too and would add a little more next time. I used a pie plate and it cooked up fine. Would be interesting to try with other types of veg.

—FEEN TASTEOFHOME.COM

ZUCCHINI-PARMESAN BAKE

Sage & Browned Butter Ravioli

After enjoying a similar dish in Italy, we came home and planted sage in our garden to be sure we could re-create it. This winning weeknight supper uses the fruits of our labor and always brings back fond memories of our trip.

—RHONDA HAMILTON PORTSMOUTH, OH

START TO FINISH: 30 MIN.
MAKES: 4 SERVINGS

- 1 package (20 ounces) refrigerated cheese ravioli or 2 packages (9 ounces each) mushroom agnolotti
- ½ cup butter, cubed
- ½ cup coarsely chopped fresh sage
- ½ teaspoon salt
- 2 tablespoons lemon juice
- ¼ cup shredded Parmesan cheese

1. Cook ravioli according to package directions. In a large heavy saucepan, melt butter over medium heat. Heat 5-7 minutes or until golden brown, stirring constantly. Immediately stir in sage and salt; remove from heat.
2. Drain ravioli, reserving 2 tablespoons pasta water. Add ravioli, pasta water and lemon juice to butter mixture; gently toss to coat. Serve with cheese.

PESTO PORTOBELLO PIZZAS

Pesto Portobello Pizzas

These little pizzas substitute mushrooms for crust. You can also quarter them and serve as an appetizer with toothpicks.

—LAURIE BARMORE WATERFORD, WI

START TO FINISH: 30 MIN.
MAKES: 4 SERVINGS

- 4 large portobello mushrooms (4 to 4½ inches)
- ½ cup prepared pesto
- 1 roma tomato, thinly sliced
- 1 cup (4 ounces) shredded part-skim mozzarella cheese
- 4 fresh basil leaves, thinly sliced

1. Preheat oven to 400°. Remove and discard stems and gills from mushrooms. Place mushrooms, stem side up, on a greased baking sheet.
2. Spoon pesto over the mushrooms. Top with tomato slices; sprinkle with cheese. Bake 15-20 minutes or until the mushrooms are tender. Sprinkle with basil.

SAGE & BROWNED BUTTER RAVIOLI

SARAH EIDEN'S LOW-FAT TANGY TOMATO DRESSING *PAGE 160*

Salads & Salad Dressings

MARYROSE DEGROOT'S EASY CAESAR COLESLAW
PAGE 153

LINDA STRUBHAR'S RHUBARB PEAR GELATIN *PAGE 156*

SUSAN DAVIS' SIMPLE LETTUCE SALAD *PAGE 157*

KALE SALAD

FAST FIX ▶
Kale Salad

I love to make meals that wow. The flavor and nutrition in this kale dish set it apart from other creations.
—**GINA MYERS** SPOKANE, WA

START TO FINISH: 15 MIN. • **MAKES:** 8 SERVINGS

- 10 cups sliced kale (about 1 bunch)
- 1 medium apple, thinly sliced
- 3 tablespoons olive oil
- 2 tablespoons lemon juice
- 1 teaspoon salt
- ½ teaspoon pepper
- ¼ cup crumbled feta cheese
- ¼ cup salted pumpkin seeds or pepitas

1. Place kale in a large bowl. With clean hands, massage kale until leaves become soft and darkened, about 2-3 minutes; stir in apple.
2. In a small bowl, whisk oil, lemon juice, salt and pepper until blended. Drizzle over salad; toss to coat. Sprinkle with cheese and pumpkin seeds.

Southwestern Corn Salad

This flavor-packed salad mellows as it chills and stays fresh in the fridge for several days. It's a nice make-ahead dish, ideal for potlucks and picnics.
—*TASTE OF HOME* TEST KITCHEN

PREP: 10 MIN. + CHILLING • **MAKES:** 9 SERVINGS

- 6 cans (7 ounces each) white or shoepeg corn, drained
- 8 green onions, chopped
- 3 jalapeno peppers, seeded and chopped
- ¼ cup minced fresh cilantro
- ½ cup mayonnaise
- ½ teaspoon salt
- ¼ teaspoon pepper

In a large bowl, combine the corn, onions, jalapenos and cilantro. Combine mayonnaise, salt and pepper; gently stir into corn mixture. Cover and refrigerate for 4 hours.
NOTE *Wear disposable gloves when cutting hot peppers; the oils can burn skin. Avoid touching your face.*

BERRY VINAIGRETTE

Applesauce-Raspberry Gelatin Mold

The children in our families especially enjoy this tangy, refreshing salad. Its pretty, bright red color makes it a festive addition to any special occasion.

—**KATHY SPANG** MANHEIM, PA

PREP: 15 MIN. + CHILLING • **MAKES:** 10 SERVINGS

    3 cups unsweetened applesauce
    ¼ cup orange juice
    2 packages (3 ounces each) raspberry gelatin
    1½ cups lemon-lime soda

1. In a large saucepan, bring applesauce and orange juice to a boil. Remove from the heat; stir in gelatin until dissolved. Slowly add soda.
2. Pour into a 6-cup mold coated with cooking spray. Refrigerate until firm. Unmold onto a serving platter.

FAST FIX ▶
Easy Caesar Coleslaw

Cool, crisp coleslaw is a fine compliment to any meal. I adapted it from a more time-consuming recipe. It's easy to double or triple for potlucks, too.

—**MARYROSE DEGROOT** STATE COLLEGE, PA

START TO FINISH: 10 MIN. • **MAKES:** 6 SERVINGS

    1 package (14 ounces) coleslaw mix
    1 cup grape tomatoes
    ¼ cup shredded Parmesan cheese
    ¾ cup creamy Caesar salad dressing
    1 green onion, sliced

In a salad bowl, combine the coleslaw mix, tomatoes and cheese. Add salad dressing; toss to coat. Chill until serving. Sprinkle with green onion.

FAST FIX ▶
Berry Vinaigrette

This dressing is wonderful on tossed fresh salad greens and your other favorite salad ingredients. Because the raspberry flavor comes from jam, this versatile vinaigrette is convenient to make year-round.

—**BARBARA MCCALLEY** ALLISON PARK, PA

START TO FINISH: 5 MIN. • **MAKES:** 1 CUP

    3 tablespoons seedless raspberry jam
    ⅔ cup canola oil
    ⅓ cup red wine vinegar
    ¼ teaspoon salt
    ¼ teaspoon pepper

Place jam in a small microwave-safe bowl. Microwave, uncovered, on high for 10-15 seconds or until melted. Whisk in the oil, vinegar, salt and pepper. Store in the refrigerator.

BUTTERMILK SALAD DRESSING

FAST FIX ▸
Buttermilk Salad Dressing

Buttermilk gives a tangy twist to this mild and creamy salad dressing. You'll love drizzling it on your favorite fresh greens and vegetables.

—*TASTE OF HOME* TEST KITCHEN

START TO FINISH: 5 MIN.
MAKES: 2 CUPS

- 1 cup mayonnaise
- 1 cup buttermilk
- ½ teaspoon onion salt
- ¼ teaspoon paprika
- ⅛ teaspoon pepper

In a bowl, whisk mayonnaise, buttermilk, onion salt, paprika and pepper.

Poppy Seed Slaw

This tasty side can be made in minutes. It's an easy addition to any backyard barbecue.

—**MARY MCRAE** COLDWATER, MI

PREP: 10 MIN. + CHILLING
MAKES: 5 SERVINGS

- 1 package (10 ounces) angel hair coleslaw
- ¾ cup dried cranberries
- ¾ cup honey-roasted sliced almonds
- ¾ cup poppy seed salad dressing
- ½ teaspoon salt
- ½ teaspoon pepper

In a large bowl, combine the coleslaw, cranberries and almonds. Combine the salad dressing, salt and pepper; drizzle over salad and toss to coat. Refrigerate slaw for 1 hour before serving.

FAST FIX ▸
Lemon Dijon Dressing

With lemon juice and Dijon mustard, this super-fast dressing has a nice tartness that's balanced by a hint of sweetness. Try it on a spinach salad or mixed greens with cucumber and tomatoes.

—**BRYAN BRAACK** ELDRIDGE, IA

START TO FINISH: 10 MIN.
MAKES: ABOUT 1 CUP

- ½ cup lemon juice
- ⅓ cup light corn syrup
- ¼ cup canola oil
- 1 tablespoon finely chopped red onion
- 2 teaspoons Dijon mustard
- ½ teaspoon salt

Place all ingredients in a jar with a tight-fitting lid; shake well. Just before serving, shake dressing and drizzle over salad and toss to coat.

POPPY SEED SLAW

FAST FIX ▸

Minty Watermelon-Cucumber Salad

Capturing the fantastic flavors of summer, this beautiful salad will be the talk of any picnic or potluck.

—**ROBLYNN HUNNISETT** GUELPH, ON

START TO FINISH: 20 MIN.
MAKES: 16 SERVINGS (¾ CUP EACH)

- 8 **cups cubed seedless watermelon**
- 2 **medium English cucumbers, halved lengthwise and sliced**
- 6 **green onions, chopped**
- ¼ **cup minced fresh mint**
- ¼ **cup balsamic vinegar**
- ¼ **cup olive oil**
- ½ **teaspoon salt**
- ½ **teaspoon pepper**

In a bowl, combine watermelon, cucumbers, onions and mint. In a small bowl, whisk remaining ingredients. Pour over salad and toss to coat. Serve immediately or refrigerate, covered, for up to 2 hours before serving.

TOP TIP

Balsamic vinegar gets much of its flavor from barrel aging. The longer it ages, the more thick and sweet it becomes. Highly aged vinegars are expensive and best enjoyed drizzled over cheese or used for dipping with oil and bread. Moderately priced vinegar works fine for most recipes. If needed, add a little sugar to taste.

MINTY WATERMELON-CUCUMBER SALAD

Rhubarb Pear Gelatin

When rhubarb season rolls around, this is one of my family's favorite ways to eat it. I love the combination of fruits with the marshmallows, and my family of 12 can't get enough.
—LINDA STRUBHAR CATALDO, ID

PREP: 25 MIN. + CHILLING • **MAKES:** 12 SERVINGS

- 2 packages (6 ounces each) strawberry gelatin
- 2 cups miniature marshmallows, divided
- 4 cups sliced fresh or frozen rhubarb
- 2 cups water
- ⅔ cup sugar
- 2 cups cold water
- 1 can (15¼ ounces) sliced pears, drained and chopped

1. Place gelatin and 1 cup marshmallows in a large bowl; set aside.
2. In a large saucepan, combine the rhubarb, water and sugar. Bring to a boil. Reduce heat; cover and simmer for 3-4 minutes or until rhubarb is tender. Remove from the heat; pour over marshmallow mixture, stirring to dissolve gelatin. Stir in the cold water, pears and remaining marshmallows.
3. Transfer to a 13x9-in. dish. Refrigerate for at least 6 hours or until firm.

RHUBARB
PEAR GELATIN

BLT Salad with Pasta

This simple pasta salad is a hit at gatherings and a favorite of everyone I know. I like to keep the ingredients in separate containers in the fridge and just toss them together for one or more servings whenever needed.
—MARY SIGFUSSON MANKATO, MN

PREP: 25 MIN. + CHILLING • **MAKES:** 6 SERVINGS

- 2 cups uncooked spiral pasta
- 1 package (1 pound) sliced bacon, chopped
- 1 large tomato, seeded and chopped
- ½ cup ranch salad dressing
- 3 cups torn romaine

1. Cook pasta according to package directions. Meanwhile, in a large skillet, cook bacon over medium heat until crisp. Remove to paper towels with a slotted spoon to drain.
2. Drain pasta and rinse in cold water; place in a large bowl. Add the bacon, tomato and dressing. Toss to coat. Refrigerate until serving.
3. Just before serving, add romaine and toss to coat.

FAST FIX ▶
Chunky Blue Cheese Dressing

This full-bodied, flavorful dressing is better than any bottled dressing I've ever tasted, and it's easy to prepare, too! I found the recipe in a church cookbook.
—LEONA LUECKING WEST BURLINGTON, IA

START TO FINISH: 10 MIN. • **MAKES:** ABOUT 4 CUPS

- ¼ cup milk
- 3 cups mayonnaise
- 1 cup (8 ounces) sour cream
- 4 ounces crumbled blue cheese
- 2 teaspoons garlic salt

Place the milk, mayonnaise, sour cream, blue cheese and garlic salt in a blender. Cover and process until smooth. Refrigerate until serving.

SIMPLE LETTUCE
SALAD

FAST FIX ▶
Simple Lettuce Salad

My mother often fixed this salad when I was a child. I grew up on a farm and most of our food came right from the garden. We especially liked this in the spring, when early leaf lettuce appeared. After a long winter of cooked vegetables, it was a real treat.

—**SUSAN DAVIS** VALE, NC

START TO FINISH: 10 MIN. • **MAKES:** 2 SERVINGS

- 2 cups torn leaf lettuce
- 1 hard-cooked egg, chopped
- 1 green onion, sliced
- 2 tablespoons mayonnaise
- 1 teaspoon cider vinegar
- ⅛ teaspoon pepper

In a salad bowl, combine the lettuce, egg and onion. In a small bowl, whisk the mayonnaise, vinegar and pepper. Pour over salad and toss to coat.

FAST FIX ▶
Dilled Potatoes with Feta

Here's a unique potato salad you can eat warm or cold. It's perfect for picnics, potlucks or dinner on the patio.

—**SHERRY JOHNSTON** GREEN COVE SPRINGS, FL

START TO FINISH: 25 MIN. • **MAKES:** 4 SERVINGS

- 1 pound small red potatoes, halved
- 1 cup (4 ounces) crumbled feta cheese
- ¼ cup snipped fresh dill
- 2 tablespoons olive oil
- 1 tablespoon lemon juice
- ¼ teaspoon salt
- ¼ teaspoon pepper

1. Place potatoes in a large saucepan and cover with water. Bring to a boil. Reduce heat; cover and cook for 10-15 minutes or until tender. Drain.
2. In a serving bowl, combine the cheese, dill, oil, lemon juice, salt and pepper. Add potatoes and toss gently to coat.

BALSAMIC ASIAGO SALAD

FAST FIX
Balsamic Asiago Salad

You can toss this tasty salad together in 10 minutes flat. Simply drizzle bottled dressing over the colorful blend of greens, tomato and pepper, add a quick sprinkle of garlic-seasoned cheese...and serve.
—*TASTE OF HOME* TEST KITCHEN

START TO FINISH: 10 MIN. • **MAKES:** 2 SERVINGS

- 2 cups torn mixed salad greens
- 1 plum tomato, cut into wedges
- ½ cup chopped sweet yellow pepper
- 2 tablespoons balsamic vinaigrette
- 2 tablespoons shredded mozzarella and Asiago cheese with roasted garlic

In a small serving bowl, combine the salad greens, tomato and yellow pepper. Drizzle with vinaigrette and toss to coat. Sprinkle with cheese.

TOP TIP

When setting up a reunion, block party or potluck, mark the table with sticky notes labeled for main dishes, sides, salads, drinks and desserts. Attendees will know where to place items and not have to ask.

Mediterranean Orange Salad

A friend gave me this old Sicilian recipe, featuring a refreshing mix of oranges, onion and oil dressing. It's the kind of salad I can imagine enjoying by the sea.
—**AMELIA MEAUX** CROWLEY, LA

PREP: 10 MIN. + CHILLING • **MAKES:** 2 SERVINGS

- 2 medium navel oranges, peeled and sliced
- 2 slices red onion, separated into rings
- 2 tablespoons olive oil
- ¼ teaspoon salt
- ⅛ teaspoon pepper
- 2 lettuce leaves

1. In a large bowl, combine the oranges, onion, oil, salt and pepper; gently toss to coat. Cover and refrigerate for 2 hours.
2. Using a slotted spoon, remove orange mixture to lettuce-lined plates.

FAST FIX
Fresh Mozzarella Tomato Salad

It takes only a few minutes to prepare this attractive salad and have it ready when a hungry bunch is coming to eat. Basil is the finishing touch.
—**REGINA WOOD** MACKENZIE, BC

START TO FINISH: 15 MIN. • **MAKES:** 6 SERVINGS

- 3 medium tomatoes, sliced
- 8 ounces fresh mozzarella cheese, thinly sliced
- ¼ cup olive oil
- 2 tablespoons minced fresh basil
- ¼ teaspoon salt
- ¼ teaspoon coarsely ground pepper

Alternate tomato and cheese slices on a platter. Drizzle with oil; sprinkle with the basil, salt and pepper. Serve immediately.

GREEN FLOP
JELL-O

Banana Split Fruit Salad

Whether you're celebrating or just relaxing after a long day, you'll definitely enjoy these whimsical parfaits. Watermelon, bananas and raspberries combine for a deliciously healthy treat.
—**TASTE OF HOME** TEST KITCHEN

START TO FINISH: 20 MIN.
MAKES: 4 SERVINGS

- 2 medium bananas
- ¼ medium seedless watermelon
- 1 carton (6 ounces) vanilla custard-style yogurt
- 1 cup fresh raspberries
- ¼ cup chopped walnuts

1. Cut bananas in half widthwise. Cut each half lengthwise into quarters. Using an ice cream scoop, scoop four balls from watermelon (save the remaining watermelon for another use).
2. Arrange four banana pieces in each shallow dessert bowl; top with watermelon. Spoon yogurt over melon. Sprinkle with raspberries and walnuts. Serve immediately.

Green Flop Jell-O

Get ready for fluffy lemon-lime goodness. Try it with any flavor Jell-O!
—**MICHELLE GAUER** SPICER, MN

PREP: 15 MIN. + CHILLING
MAKES: 16 SERVINGS (¾ CUP EACH)

- 2 cups lemon-lime soda
- 2 packages (3 ounces each) lime gelatin
- 6 ounces cream cheese, softened
- 2 cups lemon-lime soda, chilled
- 1 carton (12 ounces) frozen whipped topping, thawed

1. Microwave 2 cups soda on high for 1-2 minutes or until hot. Place hot soda and gelatin in a blender; cover and process until gelatin is dissolved. Add cream cheese; process until blended.
2. Transfer to a large bowl; stir in chilled soda. Whisk in whipped topping. Refrigerate, covered, 4 hours or until firm.

Pesto Tortellini Salad

I came up with this recipe when I tried re-creating a pasta salad I had at a wedding rehearsal. It's easy to make and I'm always asked to bring it to potlucks and parties.
—**DANIELLE WEETS** GRANDVIEW, WA

START TO FINISH: 20 MIN.
MAKES: 5 SERVINGS

- 1 package (19 ounces) frozen cheese tortellini
- ¾ cup shredded Parmesan cheese
- 1 can (2¼ ounces) sliced ripe olives, drained
- 5 bacon strips, cooked and crumbled
- ¼ cup prepared pesto

Cook tortellini according to package directions; drain and rinse in cold water. Place in a small bowl. Add remaining ingredients; toss to coat.

BANANA SPLIT
FRUIT SALAD

Low-Fat Tangy Tomato Dressing

Here's a dressing that's lovely over greens, pasta salad or summer vegetables. It's a healthier alternative to oil-heavy store-bought dressings. I think you'll agree it's a slam dunk!
—**SARAH EIDEN** ENID, OK

START TO FINISH: 5 MIN.
MAKES: 2 CUPS

- 1 can (14½ ounces) no-salt-added diced tomatoes, undrained
- 1 envelope Italian salad dressing mix
- 1 tablespoon cider vinegar
- 1 tablespoon olive oil

Place all ingredients in a blender; cover and process until blended.

Balsamic Arugula Salad

With just four ingredients, this arugula salad comes together in a flash and makes a sophisticated side.
—**LISA SPEER** PALM BEACH, FL

START TO FINISH: 5 MIN.
MAKES: 4 SERVINGS

- 6 cups fresh arugula or baby spinach
- ½ cup cherry tomatoes, halved
- ¼ cup grated Parmesan cheese
- ¼ cup balsamic vinaigrette

In a large bowl, combine the arugula, tomatoes and cheese. Drizzle with vinaigrette; toss to coat. Serve immediately.

LOW-FAT TANGY TOMATO DRESSING

FAST FIX
No-Fuss Avocado Onion Salad

My mother, Nena, grew up in Cuba and learned many styles of cooking. She had a knack for making something incredibly simple taste incredibly amazing. This salad is proof. By itself, the dressing is really tart, but add the avocados and onions and it's the perfect complement.

—MARINA CASTLE CANYON COUNTRY, CA

START TO FINISH: 15 MIN.
MAKES: 12 SERVINGS

- 3 medium ripe avocados, peeled and thinly sliced
- 1 large sweet onion, halved and thinly sliced
- ⅓ cup olive oil
- ¼ cup stone-ground mustard
- 2 tablespoons lemon juice
- 1 tablespoon honey

Arrange avocado and onion slices on a large platter. In a small bowl, whisk remaining ingredients; drizzle over salad. Serve immediately.

FAST FIX
Super Spinach Salad

You can make this elegant salad in a snap. Good-for-you spinach is the perfect backdrop for salty bacon bits and tangy balsamic vinaigrette.

—MARY "PEGGY" HARRIS SHIVELY, KY

START TO FINISH: 15 MIN.
MAKES: 8 SERVINGS

- 1 package (9 ounces) fresh baby spinach
- ½ pound sliced fresh mushrooms
- 2 hard-cooked eggs, chopped
- 2 tablespoons bacon bits
- ½ cup balsamic vinaigrette

In a large salad bowl, combine spinach, mushrooms, eggs and bacon. Drizzle with vinaigrette; toss to coat.

FAST FIX
Fiesta Corn Chip Salad

Whenever I bring this tasty corn salad to a gathering, someone requests the recipe. The fun texture of the salad pairs well with any main course.

—MANDY MCKINNON NORTH CANTON, OH

START TO FINISH: 10 MIN.
MAKES: 10 SERVINGS

- 2 cans (15¼ ounces each) whole kernel corn, drained
- 2 cups (8 ounces) shredded Mexican cheese blend
- 1 medium sweet red pepper, chopped
- 1 cup mayonnaise
- ⅛ teaspoon salt
- ⅛ teaspoon pepper
- 1 package (9¼ ounces) chili cheese-flavored corn chips, crushed

In a large bowl, combine the corn, cheese, red pepper, mayonnaise, salt and pepper. Chill until serving. Just before serving, stir in corn chips.

NO-FUSS AVOCADO ONION SALAD

CHRISTINE BERGMAN'S ZESTY GARLIC GREEN BEANS *PAGE 178*

Sides & Condiments

KELLY WALMSLEY'S BACON-PARMESAN BRUSSELS SPROUTS *PAGE 180*

MARGIE WAMPLER'S GARLIC LEMON BUTTER *PAGE 187*

MAE CRAFT'S RANCH POTATO CUBES *PAGE 169*

ROASTED CAULIFLOWER
& BRUSSELS SPROUTS

Roasted Cauliflower
& Brussels Sprouts

Here's my surefire way to get my husband to eat Brussels sprouts. The roasted flavor of the veggies and the crisp, smoky bacon will convert even the pickiest eaters and have them asking for seconds.

—**LISA SPEER** PALM BEACH, FL

PREP: 30 MIN. • **BAKE:** 20 MIN. • **MAKES:** 10 SERVINGS

- 2 **pounds fresh Brussels sprouts, thinly sliced**
- 1 **pound fresh cauliflowerets (about 7 cups), thinly sliced**
- ¼ **cup olive oil**
- 1 **teaspoon freshly ground pepper**
- ½ **teaspoon salt**
- 1 **pound bacon strips, cooked and crumbled**
- ⅓ **to ½ cup balsamic vinaigrette**

1. Preheat oven to 375°. In a very large bowl, toss the Brussels sprouts and cauliflower with oil, pepper and salt. Transfer to two greased 15x10x1-in. baking pans.
2. Roast 20-25 minutes or until vegetables are tender. Transfer to a serving bowl. Just before serving, add bacon and drizzle with vinaigrette; toss to coat.

FAST FIX ▸
Dilled Peas with Walnuts

This delicious side dish is a family favorite. Dill, onion and walnut dress up green peas without overpowering them.

—**KRISTEN JOHNSON** ALOHA, OR

START TO FINISH: 20 MIN. • **MAKES:** 2 SERVINGS

- 1 **cup frozen peas**
- 2 **tablespoons chopped onion**
- 1½ **teaspoons butter**
- ¾ **teaspoon snipped fresh dill or**
   ¼ teaspoon dill weed
- ⅛ **teaspoon salt**
- ⅛ **teaspoon pepper**
- 1 **tablespoon chopped walnuts**

1. In a small saucepan, combine peas and onion. Cover with water. Bring to a boil. Reduce heat; cover and simmer for 4-5 minutes or until peas are tender. Drain.
2. Stir in the butter, dill, salt and pepper; heat through. Sprinkle with walnuts.

Herbed Potato Packs

Fingerlings are small, waxy and tender, and are often sold in bags of assorted colors (red, purple and gold). These little potatoes look festive in convenient single-serve foil packs.

—TASTE OF HOME TEST KITCHEN

START TO FINISH: 25 MIN. • **MAKES:** 4 SERVINGS

- 2 pounds fingerling potatoes
- 2 tablespoons olive oil
- 2 garlic cloves, minced
- 1 teaspoon salt
- 2 teaspoons minced fresh thyme
- ½ teaspoon coarsely ground pepper

1. Pierce potatoes with a fork. Place in a large microwave-safe dish; cover and microwave for 4-7 minutes or until crisp-tender, stirring halfway. Add the remaining ingredients; toss to coat.
2. Place one-fourth of the potatoes on a double thickness of heavy-duty foil (about 14x12 in.). Fold foil around potatoes and seal tightly. Repeat with remaining potatoes.
3. Grill, covered, over medium-high heat for 6-9 minutes on each side or until potatoes are tender. Open foil carefully to allow steam to escape.

BROCCOLI SAUTE

Broccoli Saute

When I needed a new recipe for cooking broccoli, I came up with my own. It goes well with most entrees.
—JIM MACNEAL WATERLOO, NY

START TO FINISH: 20 MIN. • **MAKES:** 10 SERVINGS

- 1 cup chopped onion
- 1 cup julienned sweet red pepper
- ¼ cup olive oil
- 12 cups fresh broccoli florets
- 1⅓ cups water
- 3 teaspoons minced garlic
- ½ teaspoon salt
- ½ teaspoon pepper

In a Dutch oven, saute onion and red pepper in oil for 2-3 minutes or until crisp-tender. Stir in the broccoli, water, garlic, salt and pepper. Cover and cook over medium heat for 5-6 minutes or until broccoli is crisp-tender.

HERBED POTATO PACKS

HAWAIIAN BARBECUE BEANS

SLOW COOKER

Hawaiian Barbecue Beans

Guests rave and wonder about the unique flavor in this recipe—fresh ginger is the hidden surprise. It's a hit at every barbecue.

—HELEN REYNOLDS QUINCY, CA

PREP: 10 MIN. • **COOK:** 5 HOURS
MAKES: 9 SERVINGS

- 4 cans (15 ounces each) black beans, rinsed and drained
- 1 can (20 ounces) crushed pineapple, drained
- 1 bottle (18 ounces) barbecue sauce
- 1½ teaspoons minced fresh gingerroot
- ½ pound bacon strips, cooked and crumbled

In a 4-qt. slow cooker, combine the beans, pineapple, barbecue sauce and ginger. Cover and cook on low for 5-6 hours. Stir in bacon before serving.

FAST FIX

Chive Buttered Carrots

It's nice to have a reliable side dish like this to round out any meal. A friend shared the recipe with me several years ago, and now I use it all the time.

—OPAL SNELL JAMESTOWN, OH

START TO FINISH: 25 MIN.
MAKES: 8 SERVINGS

- 2½ pounds carrots, diagonally sliced ½ inch thick
- 6 tablespoons butter, cubed
- ¼ to ½ teaspoon seasoned salt
- ¼ teaspoon pepper
- 1 to 2 tablespoons minced fresh chives

1. Place 1 in. of water and carrots in a large saucepan; bring to a boil. Cook, covered, 3-4 minutes or until crisp-tender. Drain well.
2. In a large skillet, heat the butter over medium-high heat. Add carrots, seasoned salt and pepper; cook and stir for 1-2 minutes or until carrots are tender. Sprinkle with chives.

CHIVE BUTTERED CARROTS

Quick & Easy Honey Mustard

Add tang and sweetness to mustard with rice vinegar and honey. I prefer it to any other honey mustard I've tried.

—**SHARON REHM** NEW BLAINE, AR

START TO FINISH: 5 MIN.
MAKES: 1 CUP

- ½ cup stone-ground mustard
- ¼ cup honey
- ¼ cup rice vinegar

In a small bowl, whisk all ingredients. Refrigerate until serving.

Chinese-Style Zucchini

A quick side, this fresh-tasting dish pairs nicely with salmon. The toasted sesame seeds add Asian flair.

—**MARIE RIZZIO** INTERLOCHEN, MI

START TO FINISH: 20 MIN.
MAKES: 4 SERVINGS

- 1 pound medium zucchini, thinly sliced
- 4 teaspoons olive oil
- 2 garlic cloves, minced
- 2 tablespoons reduced-sodium soy sauce
- ½ teaspoon sesame seeds, toasted

In a large nonstick skillet, saute zucchini in oil until tender. Add garlic; cook 1 minute longer. Stir in soy sauce; sprinkle with sesame seeds.

QUICK & EASY HONEY MUSTARD

GARLIC-CHIVE BAKED FRIES

Garlic-Chive Baked Fries

No one can resist golden brown fries seasoned with garlic and fresh chives. They're especially great with a juicy steak.

—**STEVE WESTPHAL** WIND LAKE, WI

PREP: 15 MIN. • **BAKE:** 20 MIN. • **MAKES:** 4 SERVINGS

- 4 **medium russet potatoes**
- 1 **tablespoon olive oil**
- 4 **teaspoons dried minced chives**
- ½ **teaspoon salt**
- ½ **teaspoon garlic powder**
- ¼ **teaspoon pepper**

1. Preheat oven to 450°. Cut potatoes into ¼-in. julienne strips. Rinse well and pat dry.
2. Transfer potatoes to a large bowl. Drizzle with oil; sprinkle with the remaining ingredients. Toss to coat. Arrange in a single layer in two 15x10x1-in. baking pans coated with cooking spray.
3. Bake 20-25 minutes or until lightly browned, turning once.

FAST FIX
Spaetzle Dumplings

These tender homemade noodles take only minutes to make and are a natural accompaniment to chicken. You can enjoy them with chicken gravy or simply buttered and sprinkled with parsley.

—**PAMELA EATON** MONCLOVA, OH

START TO FINISH: 15 MIN. • **MAKES:** 6 SERVINGS

- 2 **cups all-purpose flour**
- 4 **eggs, lightly beaten**
- ⅓ **cup 2% milk**
- 2 **teaspoons salt**
- 8 **cups water**
- 1 **tablespoon butter**

1. In a large bowl, stir the flour, eggs, milk and salt until smooth (dough will be sticky). In a large saucepan, bring water to a boil. Pour dough into a colander or spaetzle maker coated with cooking spray; place over boiling water.
2. With a wooden spoon, press dough until small pieces drop into boiling water. Cook for 2 minutes or until dumplings are tender and float. Remove with a slotted spoon; toss with butter.

SPAETZLE DUMPLINGS

RANCH
POTATO CUBES

Broccoli Casserole

People who don't even like broccoli ask me to make this. It's similar to a green bean casserole, but the melted cheese just puts it over the top.

—**ELAINE HUBBARD** POCONO LAKE, PA

PREP: 20 MIN. • **BAKE:** 35 MIN. • **MAKES:** 6-8 SERVINGS

- 2 packages (16 ounces each) frozen broccoli florets
- 1 can (10¾ ounces) condensed cream of mushroom soup, undiluted
- 1 cup (8 ounces) sour cream
- 1½ cups (6 ounces) shredded sharp cheddar cheese, divided
- 1 can (6 ounces) French-fried onions, divided

1. Preheat oven to 325°. Cook broccoli according to package directions; drain well. In a large saucepan, combine soup, sour cream, 1 cup of cheese and 1¼ cups onions. Cook over medium heat 4-5 minutes or until heated through. Stir in the broccoli.

2. Pour into a greased 2-qt. baking dish. Bake, uncovered, 25-30 minutes or until bubbly. Sprinkle with the remaining cheese and onions. Bake 10-15 minutes longer or until cheese is melted.

FAST FIX
Maple-Honey Cranberry Sauce

This recipe is simple, quick and a family favorite. I'll often make a double batch for us to use on meats, spread on toast or even garnish desserts.

—**REBECCA ISRAEL** MANSFIELD, PA

START TO FINISH: 25 MIN. • **MAKES:** 2 CUPS

- 2 cups fresh or frozen cranberries
- ½ cup maple syrup
- ½ cup honey
- 1 tablespoon grated orange peel

In a large saucepan, combine the cranberries, syrup, honey and orange peel. Cook over medium heat until the berries pop, about 15 minutes. Cover and store in the refrigerator.

Ranch Potato Cubes

I love to cook for my children, grandchildren and the folks at church. I've never taken this dish anywhere where it wasn't cleaned out. It's so simple, but so good and different, that it's always a hit.

—**MAE CRAFT** CLARKSVILLE, AR

PREP: 10 MIN. • **BAKE:** 65 MIN. • **MAKES:** 8 SERVINGS

- 7 medium potatoes, cut into ½-inch cubes
- ¼ cup butter, cubed
- 1 cup (8 ounces) sour cream
- 1 envelope ranch salad dressing mix
- 1 cup (4 ounces) shredded cheddar cheese

1. Preheat oven to 325°. Place potatoes in a greased 11x7-in. baking dish; dot with butter. Cover and bake 60-65 minutes or until tender.

2. Combine sour cream and salad dressing mix; spoon over potatoes. Sprinkle with cheese. Bake, uncovered, 5-10 minutes or until cheese is melted.

Simple Spanish Rice

I prefer this version of the dish to traditional recipes because it's vegetarian and lower in fat. While you're preparing the rest of your meal, it simmers on the stove, allowing the flavors to blend beautifully.

—**EMILY HOCKETT** FEDERAL WAY, WA

PREP: 5 MIN. • **COOK:** 45 MIN. • **MAKES:** 6 SERVINGS

- 1 **cup uncooked brown rice**
- 1 **large onion, chopped**
- 1 **medium green pepper, chopped**
- 2 **tablespoons butter**
- 1 **can (14½ ounces) diced tomatoes with mild green chilies, undrained**
- ¼ **teaspoon salt**

1. Cook brown rice according to package directions. Meanwhile, in a large nonstick skillet, saute onion and pepper in butter until tender. Stir in tomatoes and salt. Bring to a boil.

2. Reduce the heat; simmer, uncovered, for 5-10 minutes or until slightly thickened. Stir in cooked rice; heat through.

SIMPLE
SPANISH RICE

**BROILED TOMATOES
WITH ARTICHOKES**

FAST FIX ▶
Broiled Tomatoes with Artichokes

These fresh-tasting stuffed tomatoes make a lovely side dish or hearty appetizer. You'll appreciate the simplicity and quickness of this recipe.

—**TASTE OF HOME** TEST KITCHEN

START TO FINISH: 15 MIN. • **MAKES:** 6 SERVINGS

- 3 **small tomatoes, halved**
- 1 **jar (7½ ounces) marinated artichoke hearts, drained and chopped**
- ½ **cup crumbled feta cheese**
- ⅓ **cup dry bread crumbs**
- 2 **tablespoons butter, melted**

1. With a sharp knife, remove the seeds and pulp from the center of each tomato half. Place cut side up on a foil-lined baking sheet.

2. Combine artichoke hearts and cheese; place 2 tablespoons in center of each tomato. Broil 3-4 in. from the heat for 2-3 minutes or until bubbly.

3. Toss the bread crumbs and butter; sprinkle over tomatoes. Broil 3-4 in. from the heat for 1-2 minutes or until browned.

FREEZER
RASPBERRY
SAUCE

Freezer Raspberry Sauce

This is a fun topping for ice cream, and—since it's thicker than sweetened berries—it's nice over sponge cake or shortcake, too. My family enjoys spreading it over waffles with plain yogurt or sour cream. In fact, no one asks for maple syrup anymore!

—KATIE KOZIOLEK HARTLAND, MN

PREP: 20 MIN. + STANDING • **MAKES:** 4 PINTS

- 10 **cups fresh raspberries, divided**
- 3 **cups sugar**
- 1 **cup light corn syrup**
- 1 **package (3 ounces) liquid fruit pectin**
- 2 **tablespoons lemon juice**

1. Rinse four 1-pint plastic containers and lids with boiling water. Dry thoroughly. Thoroughly crush 6 cups raspberries, 1 cup at a time, to measure exactly 3 cups; transfer to a large bowl. Stir in sugar and corn syrup; let stand 10 minutes, stirring occasionally.

2. In a small bowl, mix liquid pectin and lemon juice. Add to raspberry mixture; stir constantly for 3 minutes to evenly distribute pectin. Stir in remaining whole raspberries.

3. Immediately fill all containers to within ½ in. of tops. Wipe off top edges of containers; immediately cover with lids. Let stand at room temperature 24 hours or until partially set. Refrigerate up to 3 weeks or freeze up to 12 months.

4. Thaw frozen sauce in refrigerator before using.

FAST FIX ▶

Creamy Herb Spread

This fresh-flavored spread is ideal for chicken, turkey, veggie wraps and salads.

—TASTE OF HOME TEST KITCHEN

START TO FINISH: 5 MIN. • **MAKES:** ½ CUP

- 1 **package (3 ounces) cream cheese, softened**
- ¼ **cup loosely packed basil leaves**
- ¼ **cup mayonnaise**
- 1 **tablespoon minced fresh parsley**
- ½ **teaspoon cider vinegar**
- ⅛ **teaspoon pepper**
  Dash salt

Place all ingredients in a small food processor; cover and process until blended. Store in the refrigerator.

FAST FIX

Browned Butter Red Potatoes

I've been making my version of Dad's potatoes for years, and it goes great with any meal. Browning the butter gives the potatoes a rich and hearty taste.

—**ANNE PAVELAK** ENDICOTT, WA

START TO FINISH: 30 MIN.
MAKES: 12 SERVINGS (¾ CUP EACH)

- 16 **medium red potatoes (about 4 pounds), quartered**
- 1 **cup butter, cubed**
- 8 **garlic cloves, minced**
- 2 **teaspoons salt**
- 1 **teaspoon pepper**

1. Place potatoes in a Dutch oven; add water to cover. Bring to a boil. Reduce heat; cook, uncovered, 15-20 minutes or until tender.

2. Meanwhile, in a small heavy saucepan, melt the butter over medium heat. Heat 5-7 minutes or until light golden brown, stirring constantly. Stir in garlic; cook 30 seconds longer or until butter is golden brown. Remove from heat.

3. Drain potatoes; transfer to a bowl. Sprinkle with salt and pepper. Drizzle with browned butter and toss to coat.

BROWNED BUTTER RED POTATOES

Cheddar Creamed Corn

SLOW COOKER

I brought this super-easy recipe to a school potluck once and it was gone in no time. I've been asked to bring it to every function since.

—**JESSICA MAXWELL** ENGLEWOOD, NJ

PREP: 10 MIN. • **COOK:** 3 HOURS
MAKES: 9 SERVINGS

- 2 packages (one 16 ounces, one 12 ounces) frozen corn, thawed
- 1 package (8 ounces) cream cheese, cubed
- ¾ cup shredded cheddar cheese
- ¼ cup butter, melted
- ¼ cup heavy whipping cream
- ½ teaspoon salt
- ¼ teaspoon pepper

In a 3- or 4-qt. slow cooker, combine all ingredients. Cook, covered, on low 3 to 3½ hours or until cheese is melted and corn is tender. Stir just before serving.

Crisp Sweet Pickles

My mom's delicious pickles, a Christmas tradition, are a cinch to make since they start with a jar of store-bought pickles which are then dressed up. They make a nice homemade gift in a pretty glass jar with ribbon tied around the top.

—**DENISE BITNER** REEDSVILLE, PA

PREP: 10 MIN. + CHILLING
MAKES: 1 QUART

- 1 jar (32 ounces) whole kosher dill pickles, drained
- 1¼ cups sugar
- 3 tablespoons cider vinegar
- 1 tablespoon dried minced onion
- 1 tablespoon celery seed

Cut pickles into ½-in. slices; return to the jar. Add the remaining ingredients. Cover and shake until coated. Refrigerate for at least 1 week, shaking occasionally. Serve with a slotted spoon.

Honey-Spice Acorn Squash

I've made this simple side dish for more than 35 years. Cinnamon and ginger give a warm spiced flavor to the tender squash.

—**ALPHA WILSON** ROSWELL, NM

PREP: 15 MIN. • **BAKE:** 70 MIN.
MAKES: 8 SERVINGS

- ⅓ cup honey
- ¼ cup butter, melted
- ½ teaspoon salt
- ¼ teaspoon ground cinnamon
- ¼ teaspoon ground ginger
- 4 medium acorn squash

1. Preheat oven to 375°. In a large bowl, combine honey, butter, salt, cinnamon and ginger. Cut squash in half; discard the seeds. Fill squash halves with butter mixture.
2. Place in a greased 15x10x1-in. baking pan. Cover and bake 1 hour or until squash is tender. Uncover; bake 10 minutes longer or until filling is bubbly.

FREEZE OPTION *If there are leftover squash halves, scrape the pulp along with the honey mixture into a bowl and mash. Place cooled squash mixture in freezer bags and freeze up to 3 months. Reheat in the microwave.*

CHEDDAR CREAMED CORN

Mushroom & Peas Rice Pilaf

Anything goes in a rice pilaf, so add peas and baby portobello mushrooms for a springlike burst of color and a variety of textures.
—**STACY MULLENS** GRESHAM, OR

START TO FINISH: 25 MIN. • **MAKES:** 6 SERVINGS

- 1 **package (6.6 ounces) rice pilaf mix with toasted almonds**
- 1 **tablespoon butter**
- 1½ **cups fresh or frozen peas**
- 1 **cup sliced baby portobello mushrooms**

1. Prepare pilaf according to package directions.
2. In a large skillet, heat butter over medium heat. Add the peas and mushrooms; cook and stir 6-8 minutes or until tender. Stir in rice.

Sauteed Corn with Tomatoes & Basil

We harvest the veggies and basil from our backyard garden just minutes before fixing this recipe. It's so fresh and easy—and always delicious with grilled fish or meat.
—**PATRICIA NIEH** PORTOLA VALLEY, CA

START TO FINISH: 15 MIN. • **MAKES:** 4 SERVINGS

- 1 **cup fresh or frozen corn**
- 1 **tablespoon olive oil**
- 2 **cups cherry tomatoes, halved**
- ¼ **teaspoon salt**
- ¼ **teaspoon pepper**
- 3 **fresh basil leaves, thinly sliced**

In a large skillet, saute corn in oil until crisp-tender. Stir in the tomatoes, salt and pepper; cook 1 minute longer. Remove from the heat; sprinkle with basil.

**MUSHROOM &
PEAS RICE PILAF**

PICKLED SWEET ONIONS

3. Carefully ladle hot mixture into four hot half-pint jars, leaving 1/2-in. headspace. Remove air bubbles and adjust headspace, if necessary, by adding hot mixture. Wipe rims. Center lids on jars; screw on bands until fingertip tight.

4. Place jars into canner with simmering water, ensuring that they are completely covered with water. Bring to a boil; process for 10 minutes. Remove jars and cool.

NOTE *The processing time listed is for altitudes of 1,000 feet or less. For altitudes up to 3,000 feet, add 5 minutes; 6,000 feet, add 10 minutes; 8,000 feet, add 15 minutes; 10,000 feet, add 20 minutes.*

Pickled Sweet Onions

These slightly crunchy pickled onions are not only a great gift for Christmas, but also a terrific contribution to a backyard barbecue as a relish for burgers and hot dogs. They're a great hostess gift, too.
—**LAURA WINEMILLER** DELTA, PA

PREP: 30 MIN. + STANDING • **PROCESS:** 10 MIN.
MAKES: 4 HALF-PINTS

- 8 cups thinly sliced sweet onions
- 2 tablespoons canning salt
- 1¾ cups white vinegar
- 1 cup sugar
- 1 teaspoon dried thyme

1. Place onions in a colander over a plate; sprinkle with canning salt and toss. Let stand for 1 hour. Rinse and drain onions, squeezing to remove the excess liquid.

2. In a Dutch oven, combine vinegar, sugar and thyme; bring to a boil. Add onions and return to a boil. Reduce heat; simmer, uncovered, 10 minutes. Remove from heat.

Potato Gnocchi

My Italian mother remembers her mother making these dumplings for special occasions. She still has the bowl Grandma mixed the dough in, which will be passed down to me some day.
—**TINA REPAK MIRILOVICH** JOHNSTOWN, PA

PREP: 30 MIN. • **COOK:** 10 MIN./BATCH
MAKES: 6-8 SERVINGS

- 4 medium potatoes, peeled and quartered
- 1 egg, lightly beaten
- 1½ teaspoons salt, divided
- 1¾ to 2 cups all-purpose flour
- 3 quarts water
  Spaghetti sauce, warmed

1. Place potatoes in a saucepan and cover with water. Bring to a boil. Reduce heat; cover and cook for 15-20 minutes or until tender. Drain and mash.

2. Place 2 cups mashed potatoes in a large bowl (save any remaining mashed potatoes for another use). Stir in egg and 1 teaspoon salt. Gradually beat in flour until blended (dough will be firm and elastic).

3. Turn onto a lightly floured surface and knead 15 times. Roll into 1/2-in.-wide ropes. Cut ropes into 1-in. pieces. Press down with a lightly floured fork.

4. In a Dutch oven, bring water and remaining salt to a boil. Add gnocchi in small batches; cook for 8-10 minutes or until gnocchi float to the top and are cooked through. Remove with a slotted spoon. Serve immediately with spaghetti sauce.

SPICY OLIVE RELISH

FAST FIX
Spicy Olive Relish

I was looking for a zippy relish to jazz up plain hot dogs. Not wanting to make a run to the store, I rummaged through my refrigerator, found these items and thought they would be good together—and I was right! This relish is also good on toasted bagel bites.

—JAMES MACGILLIVRAY SAN MARCOS, CA

START TO FINISH: 10 MIN. • **MAKES:** 2 CUPS

- 1 jar (16 ounces) pickled hot cherry peppers, drained
- 1 jar (7 ounces) pimiento-stuffed olives, drained
- 1 small onion, quartered
- 1 tablespoon yellow mustard

Place peppers, olives and onion in a food processor; cover and process until finely chopped. Transfer to a bowl; stir in mustard.

HOW TO

CLEAN MUSHROOMS

Gently remove dirt by rubbing with a mushroom brush or wipe mushrooms with a damp paper towel. Or quickly rinse under cold water, drain and pat dry with paper towels. Trim stems if they are dry or woody.

SLOW COOKER
Easy Beans & Potatoes with Bacon

I love the combination of green beans with bacon, so I created this recipe. When you have company, you can start it in the slow cooker and continue preparing the rest of your dinner.

—BARBARA BRITTAIN SANTEE, CA

PREP: 15 MIN. • **COOK:** 6 HOURS • **MAKES:** 10 SERVINGS

- 8 bacon strips, chopped
- 1½ pounds fresh green beans, trimmed and cut into 2-inch pieces (about 4 cups)
- 4 medium potatoes, peeled and cut into ½-inch cubes
- 1 small onion, halved and sliced
- ¼ cup reduced-sodium chicken broth
- ½ teaspoon salt
- ¼ teaspoon pepper

1. In a large skillet, cook bacon over medium heat until crisp, stirring occasionally. Remove to paper towels with a slotted spoon; drain, reserving 1 tablespoon drippings. Cover and refrigerate bacon until serving.
2. In a 5-qt. slow cooker, combine the remaining ingredients; stir in reserved drippings. Cover and cook on low for 6-8 hours or until potatoes are tender. Stir in bacon; heat through.

FAST FIX
Sauteed Garlic Mushrooms

These tasty mushrooms are a wonderful accompaniment to meat, but you could also serve them as an appetizer.

—JOAN SCHROEDER MESQUITE, NV

START TO FINISH: 15 MIN. • **MAKES:** 6 SERVINGS

- ¾ pound sliced fresh mushrooms
- 2 to 3 teaspoons minced garlic
- 1 tablespoon seasoned bread crumbs
- ⅓ cup butter, cubed

In a large skillet, saute the mushrooms, garlic and bread crumbs in butter until mushrooms are tender.

SPICY GRILLED EGGPLANT

FAST FIX

Spicy Grilled Eggplant

This versatile recipe goes well with pasta or grilled meats. Thanks to the Cajun seasoning, it gets more attention than ordinary veggies.

—**GREG FONTENOT** THE WOODLANDS, TX

START TO FINISH: 20 MIN.
MAKES: 10 SERVINGS

- 2 **small eggplants, cut into ½-inch slices**
- ¼ **cup olive oil**
- 2 **tablespoons lime juice**
- 1 **tablespoon Cajun seasoning**

1. Brush eggplant slices with oil on both sides. Drizzle with lime juice; sprinkle with Cajun seasoning. Let stand for 5 minutes.
2. Grill eggplant, covered, over medium heat or broil 4 in. from the heat for 4-5 minutes on each side or until tender.

FAST FIX

Zesty Garlic Green Beans

If you're looking for a change from the traditional green bean casserole, try this fresh take.

—**CHRISTINE BERGMAN** SUWANEE, GA

START TO FINISH: 25 MIN.
MAKES: 10 SERVINGS

- ½ **cup oil-packed sun-dried tomatoes**
- 1 **cup sliced sweet onion**
- 3 **garlic cloves, minced**
- 1½ **teaspoons lemon-pepper seasoning**
- 2 **packages (16 ounces each) frozen French-style green beans**

1. Drain the tomatoes, reserving 2 tablespoons of oil. In a Dutch oven, saute onion in reserved oil for 8-10 minutes or until tender.
2. Add the tomatoes, garlic and lemon pepper; cook and stir for 2 minutes. Add frozen green beans and stir to coat. Cover and cook 8 minutes or just until hot, stirring occasionally.
3. Uncover: cook 2-3 minutes longer or until the liquid is almost evaporated.

ZESTY GARLIC GREEN BEANS

All-Day Apple Butter

I make several batches of this simple and delicious apple butter to freeze in jars. Depending on the sweetness of the apples, you can adjust the sugar to taste.

—BETTY RUENHOLL SYRACUSE, NE

PREP: 20 MIN. • **COOK:** 11 HOURS
MAKES: 4 PINTS

- 5½ **pounds apples, peeled and finely chopped**
- 4 **cups sugar**
- 2 **to 3 teaspoons ground cinnamon**
- ¼ **teaspoon ground cloves**
- ¼ **teaspoon salt**

1. Place apples in a 3-qt. slow cooker. Combine sugar, cinnamon, cloves and salt; pour over apples and mix well. Cover and cook on high for 1 hour.

2. Reduce heat to low; cover and cook for 9-11 hours or until thickened and dark brown, stirring occasionally (stir more frequently as it thickens to prevent sticking).

3. Uncover and cook on low 1 hour longer. If desired, stir with a wire whisk until smooth. Spoon into freezer containers, leaving ½-in. headspace. Cover and refrigerate or freeze.

ALL-DAY APPLE BUTTER

FAST FIX ▶
Bacon-Parmesan Brussels Sprouts

I never thought I liked Brussels sprouts until someone gave me this recipe. It's delicious and just may change your mind about them, too! I've substituted broccoli and cauliflower for the sprouts, and they're also tasty cooked this way. The only change I make is that I generally use a microwave steamer to cook the broccoli and cauliflower.

—**KELLY WALMSLEY** LEWISTOWN, IL

START TO FINISH: 25 MIN. • **MAKES:** 4 SERVINGS

- 5 bacon strips, chopped
- 1 package (16 ounces) frozen Brussels sprouts, thawed
- ⅓ cup sliced onion
- 2 tablespoons water
- ¼ teaspoon pepper
- 1 tablespoon grated Parmesan cheese

1. Cook bacon in a large skillet over medium heat until crisp. Remove to paper towels; drain, reserving 1 tablespoon drippings.

2. In the same skillet, saute Brussels sprouts and onion in reserved drippings until lightly browned. Add water and pepper. Bring to a boil. Reduce heat; cover and simmer for 3-4 minutes or until Brussels sprouts are heated through. Remove from the heat. Stir in bacon and sprinkle with cheese.

BACON-PARMESAN BRUSSELS SPROUTS

CRANBERRY COUSCOUS

FAST FIX ▶
Cranberry Couscous

Here's a fabulous dish to serve alongside chicken, pork chops or even lamb. If you like, toss in some almonds or pistachios at the end for a little crunch.

—*TASTE OF HOME* TEST KITCHEN

START TO FINISH: 15 MIN. • **MAKES:** 6 SERVINGS

- 1 can (14½ ounces) chicken broth
- 1 tablespoon butter
- 1½ cups uncooked couscous
- ¼ cup dried cranberries, chopped
- 3 tablespoons chopped green onions

Bring broth and butter to a boil in a large saucepan. Stir in the couscous, cranberries and onions. Remove from the heat. Cover and let stand for 5 minutes or until broth is absorbed. Fluff with a fork.

New England Butternut Squash

Even the young picky eaters in my house devour this dish. They love the hint of sweetness, and I love that it's good for them. If you don't have maple syrup, try it with a bit of brown sugar.

—LINDA MASSICOTTE-BLACK COVENTRY, CT

START TO FINISH: 30 MIN. • **MAKES:** 5 SERVINGS

- 1 medium butternut squash
- ¼ cup butter, melted
- ¼ cup maple syrup
- ¾ teaspoon ground cinnamon
- ¼ teaspoon ground nutmeg

1. Cut squash in half lengthwise; discard seeds. Place cut side down in a microwave-safe dish; add ½ in. of water. Cover and microwave on high for 15-20 minutes or until very tender; drain.
2. When cool enough to handle, scoop out pulp and mash. Stir in the butter, syrup, cinnamon and nutmeg.

APPLE STUFFING

Gingered Snow Peas

Wow friends and family with quick-cooking, flavorful veggies without ever touching the stove. Ginger makes this dish special. It's one of my favorites.

—SUZANNE KARSTEN WINDERMERE, FL

START TO FINISH: 10 MIN. • **MAKES:** 2 SERVINGS

- ½ pound fresh snow peas, trimmed
- 1 tablespoon water
- 1 tablespoon butter, melted
- ¼ teaspoon ground ginger
- ⅛ teaspoon salt

1. Place peas and water in a 1-qt. microwave-safe dish. Cover and microwave on high for 3-4 minutes or until crisp-tender; drain.
2. Combine the butter, ginger and salt. Drizzle over the peas; toss to coat.

Apple Stuffing

Here's an easy alternative to made-from-scratch stuffing. A few added ingredients lend awesome homemade flavor to stuffing mix.

—TERRI MCKITRICK DELAFIELD, WI

START TO FINISH: 15 MIN. • **MAKES:** 5 SERVINGS

- 1 medium tart apple, chopped
- ½ cup chopped onion
- ¼ cup chopped celery
- 1 tablespoon butter
- 1 package (6 ounces) stuffing mix

In a large skillet, saute the apple, onion and celery in butter until tender. Prepare stuffing mix according to package directions. Stir in apple mixture.

ROASTED CARROTS WITH THYME

FAST FIX

Roasted Carrots with Thyme

Cutting the carrots lengthwise makes this dish extra pretty.

—**DEIRDRE COX** KANSAS CITY, MO

START TO FINISH: 30 MIN.
MAKES: 4 SERVINGS

- 1 **pound medium carrots, halved lengthwise**
- 2 **teaspoons minced fresh thyme or ½ teaspoon dried thyme**
- 2 **teaspoons canola oil**
- 1 **teaspoon honey**
- ¼ **teaspoon salt**

Preheat oven to 400°. Place carrots in a greased 15x10x1-in. baking pan. In a small bowl, mix thyme, oil, honey and salt; brush over carrots. Roast for 20-25 minutes or until tender.

Rosemary Sweet Potato Fries

A local restaurant got me hooked on sweet potato fries. I started experimenting at home, trying to make them taste like theirs, but healthier and baked, not fried. I'm thrilled with this result!

—**JACKIE GREGSTON** HALLSVILLE, TX

PREP: 15 MIN. • **BAKE:** 30 MIN. • **MAKES:** 4 SERVINGS

- 3 **tablespoons olive oil**
- 1 **tablespoon minced fresh rosemary**
- 1 **garlic clove, minced**
- 1 **teaspoon cornstarch**
- ¾ **teaspoon salt**
- ⅛ **teaspoon pepper**
- 3 **large sweet potatoes, peeled and cut into ¼-inch julienned strips (about 2¼ pounds)**

1. Preheat oven to 425°. In a large resealable plastic bag, combine the first six ingredients. Add sweet potatoes; shake to coat.
2. Arrange in a single layer on two 15x10x1-in. baking pans coated with cooking spray. Bake, uncovered, 30-35 minutes or until tender and lightly browned, turning occasionally.

ROSEMARY SWEET POTATO FRIES

CHEDDAR
SPIRALS

Cheddar Spirals

Our kids just love this cheesy pasta and will sample a spoonful right from the slow cooker when they walk by. Sometimes I add cocktail sausages, sliced Polish sausage or cubed ham to turn it into a hearty dinner.
—**HEIDI FERKOVICH** PARK FALLS, WI

PREP: 20 MIN. • **COOK:** 2½ HOURS
MAKES: 15 SERVINGS (¾ CUP EACH)

- 1 package (16 ounces) spiral pasta
- 2 cups half-and-half cream
- 1 can (10¾ ounces) condensed cheddar cheese soup, undiluted
- ½ cup butter, melted
- 4 cups (16 ounces) shredded cheddar cheese

Cook pasta according to package directions; drain. In a 5-qt. slow cooker, combine the cream, soup and butter until smooth; stir in the cheese and pasta. Cover and cook on low for 2½ hours or until cheese is melted.

Crumb-Coated Tomatoes

This recipe brings back many memories of my grandmother. It was her favorite dish for family get-togethers. It's easy to make, takes little time to prepare and is especially tasty with garden-fresh tomatoes.
—**CONNIE SIMON** CLEVELAND, OH

START TO FINISH: 10 MIN. • **MAKES:** 2 SERVINGS

- ½ cup crushed Ritz crackers (about 12)
- ½ teaspoon salt
- ¼ teaspoon pepper
- 1 medium tomato, cut into ¼-inch slices
- 1 egg, beaten
- 2 tablespoons butter

1. In a shallow bowl, combine the cracker crumbs, salt and pepper. Dip tomato slices into egg, then coat with crumb mixture.
2. In a large skillet, cook tomatoes in butter over medium heat for 2-3 minutes on each side or until golden brown. Serve immediately.

Pesto

Homemade pesto always makes a thoughtful hostess gift. Mix things up with the cilantro variation.

—TASTE OF HOME TEST KITCHEN

START TO FINISH: 10 MIN.
MAKES: ¾ CUP

- 1 **cup tightly packed fresh basil or cilantro leaves**
- 1 **cup tightly packed fresh parsley leaves**
- 1 **to 2 garlic cloves**
- ½ **cup olive oil**
- ½ **cup grated Parmesan cheese**
- ¼ **teaspoon salt**

In a food processor, puree all ingredients. Refrigerate for several weeks or freeze in a tightly covered container. Toss a few tablespoons pesto with hot cooked pasta.

Raspberry Butter

This butter will certainly perk up a brunch buffet that includes homemade breads.

—HELEN LAMB SEYMOUR, MO

START TO FINISH: 5 MIN.
MAKES: ABOUT ¾ CUP

- ½ **cup butter, softened**
- ⅓ **cup fresh or frozen raspberries**
- 2 **tablespoons confectioners' sugar**
  Dash lemon juice

In a small bowl, combine all ingredients. Serve immediately. Refrigerate leftovers.

PESTO

Broccoli with Asiago

This is one of the best and simplest ways I've found to serve broccoli. It's also good with Parmesan if you don't have the Asiago cheese

—CJINTEXAS TASTEOFHOME.COM

START TO FINISH: 20 MIN.
MAKES: 4 SERVINGS

- 1 **bunch broccoli, cut into spears**
- 4 **teaspoons minced garlic**
- 2 **tablespoons olive oil**
- ¼ **teaspoon salt**
  Dash pepper
- 1 **cup (4 ounces) shaved Asiago cheese**

1. Place broccoli in a large skillet; cover with water. Bring to a boil. Reduce heat; cover and simmer for 5-7 minutes or until broccoli is tender. Drain well. Remove and keep warm.
2. In the same skillet, saute garlic in oil for 1 minute. Stir in the broccoli, salt and pepper. Top with cheese.

Stir-Fried Zucchini

We love zucchini, and every year it seems our garden plants produce plenty and then some. This is one of my family's favorite ways to put it to good use.

—DEBORAH ELLIOT RIDGE SPRING, SC

START TO FINISH: 10 MIN.
MAKES: 8 SERVINGS

- 2 **pounds sliced zucchini**
- 2 **garlic cloves, minced**
- ¼ **cup olive oil**
- 1 **teaspoon salt**
- ½ **teaspoon Italian seasoning**
- ¼ **teaspoon pepper**

In a large skillet, saute the zucchini and garlic in oil until zucchini is crisp-tender, about 5 minutes. Sprinkle with seasonings. Serve immediately.

Candied Sweet Potatoes

My town is known as the Yam Capital of the United States. This is a simple recipe that goes well with baked ham or roasted turkey.

—ESSIE NEALEY TABOR CITY, NC

PREP: 40 MIN. + COOLING
BAKE: 15 MIN.
MAKES: 8-10 SERVINGS

- 3 **pounds sweet potatoes**
- ½ **cup packed brown sugar**
- 1 **teaspoon ground cinnamon**
- ¼ **cup butter, cubed**
- ¼ **cup corn syrup**

1. Place the sweet potatoes in a Dutch oven and cover with water. Cover and bring to a boil; boil gently 30-45 minutes or until potatoes can be easily pierced with the tip of a sharp knife.
2. While potatoes cool, preheat oven to 375°. When cool enough to handle, peel potatoes and cut into wedges. Place in an ungreased 11x7-in. baking dish. Sprinkle with brown sugar and cinnamon. Dot with butter; drizzle with corn syrup.
3. Bake sweet potatoes, uncovered, for 15-20 minutes or until bubbly, basting with sauce occasionally.

BROCCOLI
WITH ASIAGO

SNAPPY GREEN BEANS

FAST FIX

Snappy Green Beans

The buttery and citrus flavors in this bright side dish go with just about any entree.

—TAMMY NEUBAUER IDA GROVE, IA

START TO FINISH: 15 MIN. • **MAKES:** 6 SERVINGS

- 2 **pounds fresh green beans, trimmed**
- 2 **teaspoons butter, melted**
- 2 **tablespoons minced fresh parsley**
- 2 **teaspoons lemon juice**
- ½ **teaspoon salt**
- ⅛ **teaspoon pepper**

1. Place beans in a large saucepan and cover with water; bring to a boil. Cook, uncovered, for 8-10 minutes or until crisp-tender. Drain well.
2. Remove from the heat. Add the butter, parsley, lemon juice, salt and pepper; toss to coat.

FAST FIX

Creamed Spinach and Mushrooms

Once when my family was snowed in, we had to make do with what was on hand. After looking through the fridge, I came up with this hot, hearty vegetable dish. It's very versatile and takes only 10 minutes from start to finish.

—MICHELLE FERRARIO IJAMSVILLE, MD

START TO FINISH: 10 MIN. • **MAKES:** 2 SERVINGS

- 1½ **cups sliced fresh mushrooms**
- 2 **tablespoons olive oil**
- ½ **teaspoon butter**
- 1 **package (6 ounces) fresh baby spinach**
- 3 **ounces reduced-fat cream cheese, cubed**
- ¼ **teaspoon salt**
- ⅛ **teaspoon pepper**

1. In a small skillet, saute mushrooms in oil and butter until tender. Add spinach; cover and cook for 1 minute or until wilted.
2. Stir in the cream cheese, salt and pepper. Serve immediately.

CREAMED SPINACH AND MUSHROOMS

GARLIC LEMON BUTTER

FAST FIX >

Sesame Asparagus

Lemon juice and sesame seeds turn a nice spring vegetable into an extra-special one. The dish feels fancy with very little work.
—**VIOLET BEARD** MARSHALL, IL

START TO FINISH: 10 MIN. • **MAKES:** 1 SERVING

- 6 **fresh asparagus spears, trimmed**
- ¼ **teaspoon salt, optional**
- 1 **teaspoon butter**
- 1 **teaspoon lemon juice**
- ¾ **teaspoon sesame seeds, toasted**

Place asparagus in a skillet; sprinkle with salt if desired. Add ½ in. of water; bring to a boil. Reduce heat; cover and simmer until crisp-tender, about 4 minutes. Meanwhile, melt butter; add lemon juice and sesame seeds. Drain asparagus; drizzle with the butter mixture.

Garlic-Parmesan Mashed Cauliflower

Here's a skinny alternative to mashed potatoes. With the addition of a little sour cream and Parmesan cheese, this cauliflower is scrumptious.
—**AMY GREEN** CARROLLTON, TX

PREP: 30 MIN. • **BAKE:** 25 MIN. • **MAKES:** 4 SERVINGS

- 1 **medium head cauliflower, broken into florets**
- 2 **garlic cloves, peeled**
- ¼ **cup 2% milk**
- ¼ **cup sour cream**
- ¼ **cup grated Parmesan cheese**
- ¼ **teaspoon salt**
- ¼ **teaspoon pepper**

1. Place 1 in. of water in a large saucepan; add cauliflower and garlic. Bring to a boil. Reduce heat; cover and simmer for 10-12 minutes or until crisp-tender. Drain and cool slightly. Transfer to a blender; add the remaining ingredients. Cover and process until smooth.
2. Spoon into a 1-qt. baking dish coated with cooking spray. Bake, uncovered, at 350° for 25-30 minutes or until heated through and the top is lightly browned.

FAST FIX >

Garlic Lemon Butter

This tangy flavored butter is a nice upgrade from plain. It gives amazing taste to an ear of corn. When I serve this on the side during fresh corn season, everyone wants to know what makes the butter so delicious. It's the garlic!
—**MARGIE WAMPLER** BUTLER, PA

START TO FINISH: 10 MIN. • **MAKES:** ½ CUP

- ½ **cup butter, softened**
- 2 **to 3 teaspoons grated lemon peel**
- 1 **garlic clove, minced**
- 1 **teaspoon minced fresh parsley**
- ¼ **teaspoon salt, optional**
  Pepper to taste

In a small bowl, beat all ingredients until blended. Refrigerate up to 1 week or freeze up to 3 months.

MEGUMI GARCIA'S CRUSTY HOMEMADE BREAD *PAGE 193*

Breads & Rolls

**AMBER MCKINLEY'S
BASIL PARMESAN PUFFS**
PAGE 200

**TORY ROSS' SOUR CREAM
BLUEBERRY MUFFINS** *PAGE 198*

**DAWN HIGGS'
DILL AND CHIVE BREAD**
PAGE 191

Mom's Italian Bread

I think Mom used to bake at least four of these tender loaves at once, and they still never lasted long. She served the bread with every Italian meal. I love it toasted, too.

—LINDA HARRINGTON WINDHAM, NH

PREP: 30 MIN. + RISING
BAKE: 20 MIN. + COOLING
MAKES: 2 LOAVES (12 SLICES EACH)

- 1 package (¼ ounce) active dry yeast
- 2 cups warm water (110° to 115°)
- 1 teaspoon sugar
- 2 teaspoons salt
- 5½ cups all-purpose flour

1. In a large bowl, dissolve yeast in warm water. Add the sugar, salt and 3 cups flour. Beat on medium speed for 3 minutes. Stir in enough remaining flour to form a soft dough.

2. Turn onto a floured surface; knead until smooth and elastic, about 6-8 minutes. Place in a greased bowl, turning once to grease the top. Cover and let rise in a warm place until doubled, about 1 hour.

3. Punch dough down. Turn onto a floured surface; divide in half. Shape each portion into a loaf. Place each loaf seam side down on a greased baking sheet. Cover and let rise until doubled, about 30 minutes.

4. Meanwhile, preheat oven to 400°. With a sharp knife, make four shallow slashes across top of each loaf. Bake 20-25 minutes or until golden brown. Remove from pans to wire racks to cool.

FAST FIX
Rosemary Cheddar Muffins

My stepmother gave me this recipe many years ago, and we've enjoyed these luscious biscuitlike muffins ever since. You might not even need butter!

—BONNIE STALLINGS MARTINSBURG, WV

START TO FINISH: 25 MIN.
MAKES: 1 DOZEN

- 2 cups self-rising flour
- ½ cup shredded sharp cheddar cheese
- 1 tablespoon minced fresh rosemary or 1 teaspoon dried rosemary, crushed
- 1¼ cups 2% milk
- 3 tablespoons mayonnaise

1. Preheat oven to 400°. In a large bowl, combine flour, cheese and rosemary. In another bowl, combine milk and mayonnaise; stir into dry ingredients just until moistened. Spoon into 12 greased muffin cups.

2. Bake 8-10 minutes or until lightly browned and a toothpick inserted in muffin comes out clean. Cool 5 minutes before removing from pan to a wire rack. Serve warm.

ROSEMARY CHEDDAR MUFFINS

Dill and Chive Bread

Chive and onion cream cheese gives yeast bread a tasty punch. I love how easy this flavorful bread is.

—DAWN HIGGS EAST MOLINE, IL

PREP: 15 MIN. • **BAKE:** 3 HOURS
MAKES: 1 LOAF (1½ POUNDS, 16 SLICES)

- ¾ cup water (70° to 80°)
- ½ cup spreadable chive and onion cream cheese
- 2 tablespoons sugar
- 2 teaspoons dill weed
- 1¼ teaspoons salt
- 3 cups all-purpose flour
- 1 package (¼ ounce) active dry yeast

In bread machine pan, place all ingredients in order suggested by manufacturer. Select basic bread setting. Choose crust color and loaf size if available. Bake according to bread machine directions (check dough after 5 minutes of mixing; add 1 to 2 tablespoons of water or flour if needed).

TOP TIP

If you frequently use the same recipe in your bread machine, you can save time by premeasuring all of the dry ingredients needed for one loaf into a resealable plastic bag. With a marker, list on the outside of the bag the liquid ingredients and yeast you'll need to add later.

DILL AND CHIVE BREAD

Bacon Pull-Apart Bread

I made this tender and tasty bread for my husband, and he just loved it! When I'm out of bacon, I use bacon bits.

—**TERRI CHRISTENSEN** MONTAGUE, MI

PREP: 15 MIN. • **BAKE:** 25 MIN. • **MAKES:** 12 SERVINGS

- 12 bacon strips, diced
- 2 tubes (12 ounces each) refrigerated buttermilk biscuits
- 2 cups (8 ounces) shredded part-skim mozzarella cheese
- 1 tablespoon Italian salad dressing mix
- 2 teaspoons olive oil

1. Preheat oven to 375°. In a large skillet, cook bacon over medium heat until cooked but not crisp. Using a slotted spoon, remove to paper towels to drain. Separate biscuits; cut each biscuit into quarters.

2. In a large bowl, combine the cheese, dressing mix, oil and bacon. Place half of the biscuit pieces in a greased 10-in. fluted tube pan; sprinkle with half of the cheese mixture. Top with remaining biscuit pieces and cheese mixture.

3. Bake 25-30 minutes or until golden brown. Cool 5 minutes before inverting onto a serving plate. Serve immediately.

BACON PULL-APART BREAD

Chocolate Biscuit Puffs

I know my favorite snack is fun for kids to make and eat because I dreamed it up at age 9! The puffs are shaped to hide the chocolate inside for a tasty surprise.

—**JOY CLARK** SEABECK, WA

START TO FINISH: 20 MIN. • **MAKES:** 10 SERVINGS

- 1 tube (12 ounces) refrigerated buttermilk biscuits
- 1 milk chocolate candy bar (1.55 ounces)
- 2 teaspoons cinnamon-sugar

1. Preheat oven to 450°. Flatten each biscuit into a 3-in. circle. Break candy bar into 10 pieces; place a piece on each biscuit. Bring up edges to enclose candy and pinch to seal.

2. Place on an ungreased baking sheet. Sprinkle with cinnamon-sugar. Bake 8-10 minutes or until golden brown.

Italian-Style Crescents

This is one of my best easy breads. A touch of pesto and Italian seasoning quickly doctor up refrigerated crescent dough, so you're ready to roll.

—**ANN MARIE BARBER** OAKLAND PARK, FL

START TO FINISH: 25 MIN. • **MAKES:** 8 SERVINGS

- 1 tube (8 ounces) refrigerated crescent rolls
- 8 teaspoons prepared pesto
- 1 egg white, lightly beaten
- 1½ teaspoons Italian seasoning

1. Preheat oven to 375°. Unroll crescent dough; separate into triangles. Spread each with 1 teaspoon pesto. Roll up from the wide end and place pointed side down 2 in. apart on ungreased baking sheets. Curve ends down to form a crescent shape.

2. Brush with egg white; sprinkle with Italian seasoning. Bake 10-13 minutes or until lightly browned.

CRUSTY HOMEMADE BREAD

Crusty Homemade Bread

Crackling homemade bread makes an average day extraordinary. Enjoy this beautiful loaf as is, or stir in a few favorites like cheese, garlic, herbs or dried fruits.

—**MEGUMI GARCIA** MILWAUKEE, WI

PREP: 20 MIN. + RISING • **BAKE:** 50 MIN. + COOLING
MAKES: 1 LOAF (16 SLICES)

- 1½ teaspoons active dry yeast
- 1¾ cups water (70° to 75°)
- 3½ cups plus 1 tablespoon all-purpose flour, divided
- 2 teaspoons salt
- 1 tablespoon cornmeal or additional flour

1. In a small bowl, dissolve yeast in water. In a large bowl, mix 3½ cups flour and salt. Using a rubber spatula, add yeast mixture to flour mixture, stirring until smooth (dough will be sticky). Do not knead. Cover with plastic wrap; let rise at room temperature 1 hour.
2. Punch down dough. Turn onto a lightly floured surface; pat into a 9-in. square. Fold square into thirds, forming a 9x3-in. rectangle. Fold rectangle into thirds, forming a 3-in. square. Turn dough over; place in a greased bowl. Cover with plastic wrap; let rise at room temperature until almost doubled, about 1 hour.

3. Punch down dough and repeat folding process. Return dough to bowl; refrigerate, covered, overnight.
4. Line bottom of a disposable foil roasting pan with parchment paper; dust parchment with cornmeal. Turn dough onto a floured surface. Knead gently 6-8 times; shape into a 6-in. round loaf. Place in prepared pan; dust top with remaining 1 tablespoon flour. Cover pan with plastic wrap; let rise at room temperature until dough expands to a 7½-in.-loaf, about 1¼ hours.
5. Preheat oven to 500°. Using a sharp knife, make a slash (¼ in. deep) across top of loaf. Cover pan tightly with foil. Bake on the lowest oven rack for 25 minutes.
6. Reduce oven setting to 450°. Remove foil; bake bread 25-30 minutes longer or until deep golden brown. Remove loaf to a wire rack to cool.

Parmesan-Ranch Pan Rolls

My mom taught me this simple recipe, which is terrific for feeding a crowd. There's never a crumb left over. Mom made her own bread dough, but using frozen dough is my shortcut.

—**TRISHA KRUSE** EAGLE, ID

PREP: 30 MIN. + RISING • **BAKE:** 20 MIN.
MAKES: 1½ DOZEN

- 2 loaves (1 pound each) frozen bread dough, thawed
- 1 cup grated Parmesan cheese
- ½ cup butter, melted
- 1 envelope buttermilk ranch salad dressing mix
- 1 small onion, finely chopped

1. On a lightly floured surface, divide dough into 18 portions; shape each into a ball. In a small bowl, combine the cheese, butter and ranch dressing mix.
2. Roll balls in cheese mixture; arrange in two greased 9-in.-square baking pans. Sprinkle with onion. Cover and let rise in a warm place until doubled, about 45 minutes.
3. Meanwhile, preheat oven to 350°. Bake rolls for 20-25 minutes or until golden brown. Remove from pans to wire racks.

PROSCIUTTO BREADSTICKS

Oatmeal Molasses Bread

This bread has been our family's favorite for many years, and now I send it to my out-of-town children. It makes wonderful toast! Aniseed gives it a distinctive flavor.

—NITA BAIRD WIBAUX, MT

PREP: 50 MIN. + RISING • **BAKE:** 40 MIN.
MAKES: 2 LOAVES (16 SLICES EACH)

- 2 **cups boiling water**
- 1 **cup old-fashioned oats**
- 2 **packages (¼ ounce each) active dry yeast**
- ⅓ **cup warm water (110° to 115°)**
- ½ **cup molasses**
- 2 **tablespoons butter, softened**
- 1 **tablespoon aniseed, optional**
- 1 **tablespoon salt**
- 5½ **to 6 cups all-purpose flour**

1. In a bowl, pour boiling water over oats; let stand 30 minutes or until mixture has cooled to warm (110°-115°).

2. In a large bowl, dissolve yeast in warm water; let stand 5 minutes. Stir in oat mixture, molasses, butter, anise seed if desired, salt and 2 cups of flour; beat until smooth. Add enough remaining flour to form a soft dough.

3. Turn onto a floured surface; knead until smooth and elastic, about 6-8 minutes. Place dough in a greased bowl, turning once to grease top. Cover and let rise in a warm place until doubled, about 1 hour.

4. Punch dough down; divide in half. Shape into two loaves and place in greased 9x5-in. loaf pans. Cover and let rise until doubled, about 1 hour.

5. Meanwhile, preheat oven to 375°. Bake for 40 minutes or until bread sounds hollow when tapped. Remove from pans to cool on wire racks.

FAST FIX

Prosciutto Breadsticks

Pair these breadsticks with your favorite pasta or egg dish. They're also a tasty brunch substitute for bacon and toast.

—MARIA REGAKIS SAUGUS, MA

START TO FINISH: 30 MIN. • **MAKES:** 1 DOZEN

- 6 **thin slices prosciutto or deli ham**
- 1 **tube (11 ounces) refrigerated breadsticks**
- 1 **egg, lightly beaten**
- ¼ **teaspoon fennel seed, crushed**
- ¼ **teaspoon pepper**

1. Preheat oven to 375°. Cut each slice of prosciutto into four thin strips. Unroll dough; separate into breadsticks. Top each with two strips prosciutto, pressing gently to adhere. Twist each breadstick; place on ungreased baking sheet, pressing ends down firmly. Brush with beaten egg.

2. Combine fennel and pepper; sprinkle over breadsticks. Bake for 10-13 minutes or until golden brown.

DID YOU KNOW?

Molasses is a byproduct of refining cane or beets into sugar. Light and dark molasses are made from the first and second cooking procedures, respectively. Blackstrap, made from the third procedure, is strongest, darkest and most intense. Dark molasses works well in most recipes.

HURRY-UP BISCUITS

Potato Pan Rolls

My family loves these rolls and asks for them often. They don't take long to make because they use quick-rise yeast.

—**CONNIE STORCKMAN** EVANSTON, WY

PREP: 15 MIN. + RISING
BAKE: 20 MIN.
MAKES: 16 ROLLS

- 4½ to 5 cups all-purpose flour
- 3 tablespoons sugar
- 2 packages (¼ ounce each) quick-rise yeast
- 1½ teaspoons salt
- 1¼ cups water
- 3 tablespoons butter
- ½ cup mashed potatoes (without added milk and butter)
   Additional all-purpose flour

1. In a large bowl, combine 2 cups flour, sugar, yeast and salt. In a small saucepan, heat water and butter to 120°-130°. Add to dry ingredients; beat until smooth. Stir in mashed potatoes and enough remaining flour to form a soft dough.

2. Turn onto a floured surface; knead until smooth and elastic, about 6-8 minutes. Cover and let rest for 10 minutes. Divide into 16 pieces. Shape each into a ball. Place in two greased 8-in. or 9-in. round baking pans. Cover and let rise in a warm place until doubled, about 30 minutes.

3. Preheat the oven to 400°. Sprinkle tops of rolls with additional flour. Bake rolls for 18-22 minutes or until golden brown. Remove from pans to wire racks.

FAST FIX ▶
Hurry-Up Biscuits

When I was young, my mom would make these biscuits with fresh cream she got from a local farmer. I don't go to those lengths anymore, but the family recipe is still a real treat.

—**BEVERLY SPRAGUE** BALTIMORE, MD

START TO FINISH: 30 MIN.
MAKES: 1 DOZEN

- 3 cups all-purpose flour
- 4 teaspoons baking powder
- 4 teaspoons sugar
- 1 teaspoon salt
- 2 cups heavy whipping cream

1. Preheat oven to 375°. In a large bowl, whisk flour, baking powder, sugar and salt. Add cream; stir just until moistened.
2. Drop by ¼ cupfuls 1 in. apart onto greased baking sheets. Bake 17-20 minutes or until bottoms are golden brown. Serve warm.

FAST FIX ▶
Cheddar-Parm Loaf

People love the rich and cheesy topping on this garlic bread. It's ready after just a few minutes under the broiler. It goes well with a main-dish salad or soup.

—**TAMMY GRIFFIN** FRANKSTON, TX

START TO FINISH: 10 MIN.
MAKES: 4 SERVINGS

- ½ cup grated Parmesan cheese
- ½ cup shredded cheddar cheese
- ½ cup mayonnaise
- ¼ teaspoon garlic powder
- 1 loaf (8 ounces) French bread, split

In a small bowl, combine the cheeses, mayonnaise and garlic powder. Spread over cut sides of bread. Place on an ungreased baking sheet. Broil 4 in. from the heat for 2-3 minutes or until lightly browned. Cut each piece in half. Serve warm.

Busy-Day Bacon Muffins

Tender and filled with the irresistible flavor of bacon, these simple muffins will disappear in a hurry. Serve them with breakfast, soup or a salad.

—GRACIE SHRADER TRENTON, GA

START TO FINISH: 30 MIN. • **MAKES:** 9 MUFFINS.

- 6 **bacon strips, diced**
- 2 **cups biscuit/baking mix**
- 2 **tablespoons sugar**
- 1 **egg**
- ⅔ **cup milk**

1. Preheat oven to 400°. Cook bacon over medium heat until crisp; drain.

2. Meanwhile, in a large bowl, combine biscuit mix and sugar. In a small bowl, combine egg and milk. Stir into dry ingredients just until moistened. Fold in bacon.

3. Fill greased muffin cups three-fourths full. Bake 13-15 minutes or until a toothpick inserted in the muffin comes out clean. Serve warm.

FREEZE OPTION *Wrap cooled baked muffins in plastic wrap; transfer to a resealable plastic freezer bag. May be frozen up to 3 months. To use, remove plastic wrap. Thaw at room temperature. Warm if desired.*

BUSY-DAY
BACON MUFFINS

RUSTIC
COUNTRY
BREAD

Rustic Country Bread

My husband had a favorite sandwich shop that closed, and after much experimentation, I came close to duplicating their bread's taste and texture.

—DEBRA KEIL OWASSO, OK

PREP: 20 MIN. + RISING • **BAKE:** 20 MIN.
MAKES: 1 LOAF (8 WEDGES)

- 1 **package (¼ ounce) active dry yeast**
- 1½ **teaspoons sugar**
- 1 **cup warm water (110° to 115°)**
- 1 **teaspoon salt**
- 1 **teaspoon balsamic vinegar**
- 2 **cups all-purpose flour**
- 1 **tablespoon olive oil**
   Additional water

1. In a large bowl, dissolve yeast and sugar in warm water. Let stand 5 minutes. Add salt, vinegar and 1½ cups flour. Beat until smooth. Stir in enough of the remaining flour to form a soft dough (dough will be sticky). Do not knead.

2. Transfer to a greased bowl. Cover and let rise in a warm place until doubled, about 50 minutes.

3. Stir dough down. Transfer to a greased 9-in. pie plate. Cover and let rise in a warm place until doubled, about 35 minutes.

4. Preheat oven to 425°. Brush with oil. Bake for 10 minutes. Reduce the heat to 375°; bake bread 10-15 minutes longer or until golden brown, spritzing twice with additional water.

OLD-FASHIONED BROWN BREAD

Old-Fashioned Brown Bread

This chewy, old-fashioned bread boasts a slightly sweet flavor that will transport you back to simpler times.
—**PATRICIA DONNELLY** KINGS LANDING, NB

PREP: 20 MIN. + RISING • **BAKE:** 35 MIN. + COOLING
MAKES: 2 LOAVES (16 SLICES EACH)

- 2⅓ **cups boiling water**
- 1 **cup old-fashioned oats**
- ½ **cup butter, cubed**
- ⅓ **cup molasses**
- 5½ to 6½ **cups all-purpose flour**
- 5 **teaspoons active dry yeast**
- 2 **teaspoons salt**

1. In a large bowl, pour boiling water over oats. Stir in butter and molasses. Let stand until mixture cools to 120°-130°, stirring occasionally.
2. In another bowl, combine 3½ cups flour, yeast and salt. Beat in oat mixture until blended. Stir in enough remaining flour to form a soft dough.
3. Turn onto a floured surface; knead until smooth and elastic, about 6-8 minutes. Place in a greased bowl, turning once to grease the top. Cover and let rise in a warm place until doubled, about 1 hour.
4. Punch dough down. Turn onto a lightly floured surface; divide in half. Shape into loaves. Place in two greased 9x5-in. loaf pans. Cover and let rise until doubled, about 30 minutes.
5. Meanwhile, preheat oven to 375°. Bake 35-40 minutes or until golden brown. Remove from pans to wire racks to cool.

Caramelized Onion Breadsticks

These easy-to-make breadsticks go perfectly with a hearty vegetable beef soup.
—**JENNIFER BERMINGHAM** SHILLINGTON, PA

PREP: 45 MIN. + RISING • **BAKE:** 15 MIN.
MAKES: 1½ DOZEN

- 1 **large sweet onion, halved and thinly sliced**
- 6 **tablespoons butter, divided**
- 1 **teaspoon sugar**
- 1 **loaf (1 pound) frozen bread dough, thawed**

1. In a large skillet over medium-low heat, cook onion in 4 tablespoons butter for 5 minutes or until tender. Add the sugar; cook over low heat for 30-40 minutes longer or until onion is golden brown, stirring frequently.
2. On a lightly floured surface, roll bread dough into an 18x 12-in. rectangle. Spoon onion mixture lengthwise over half of the dough; fold plain half of dough over onion mixture. Cut into eighteen 1-in. strips. Twist each strip twice; pinch ends to seal.
3. Place 2 in. apart on greased baking sheets. Melt the remaining butter; brush over breadsticks. Cover and let rise in a warm place until doubled, about 40 minutes.
4. Meanwhile, preheat the oven to 350°. Bake breadsticks for 12-15 minutes or until lightly browned. Serve warm.

Sour Cream Blueberry Muffins

When we were kids, my mom made these delicious muffins on chilly mornings. Now that I'm all grown up, I enjoy baking them for friends.

—TORY ROSS CINCINNATI, OH

PREP: 15 MIN. • **BAKE:** 20 MIN.
MAKES: 1 DOZEN

- 2 **cups biscuit/baking mix**
- ¾ **cup plus 2 tablespoons sugar, divided**
- 2 **eggs**
- 1 **cup (8 ounces) sour cream**
- 1 **cup fresh or frozen blueberries**

1. Preheat oven to 375°. In a large bowl, combine biscuit mix and ¾ cup sugar. In a small bowl, combine eggs and sour cream; stir into the dry ingredients just until combined. Fold in blueberries.

2. Fill greased muffin cups three-fourths full. Sprinkle with the remaining sugar. Bake for 20-25 minutes or until a toothpick inserted in muffin comes out clean. Cool 5 minutes before removing from pan to a wire rack.

NOTE *If using frozen blueberries, use without thawing to avoid discoloring the batter.*

SOUR CREAM
BLUEBERRY MUFFINS

Virginia Box Bread

When I lived in the South, I was given this melt-in-your-mouth recipe. My family devours these tender rolls as soon as they come out of the oven. Cutting the dough in the pan lets you easily separate them for serving.

—THELMA RICHARDSON LA CROSSE, WI

PREP: 20 MIN. + RISING
BAKE: 20 MIN.
MAKES: 16 SERVINGS

- 1 **package (¼ ounce) active dry yeast**
- ⅔ **cup warm water (110° to 115°)**
- 2 **eggs, lightly beaten**
- 5 **tablespoons butter, melted and cooled**
- 2 **tablespoons sugar**
- 1 **teaspoon salt**
- 3¼ **to 3¾ cups all-purpose flour**

1. In a large bowl, dissolve yeast in warm water. Add eggs, butter, sugar, salt and 2 cups flour; beat until smooth. Add enough remaining flour to form a soft dough.

2. Turn onto a floured surface; knead until smooth and elastic, about 6-8 minutes. Place in a greased bowl, turning once to grease top. Cover and let rise in a warm place until doubled, about 1½ hours.

3. Punch dough down. On a lightly floured surface, roll dough into a 13x9-in. rectangle. Transfer to a greased 13x9-in. baking pan. Using a sharp knife, cut dough into 16 pieces. Cover and let rise until doubled, about 30 minutes.

4. Meanwhile, preheat oven to 375°. Bake 20 minutes or until golden brown. To serve, separate into rolls.

Perfect Dinner Rolls

I loved these rolls as a child, and I'm happy to make them for my kids now. I know I'm giving them the same wonderful memories my mom gave me!

—GAYLEEN GROTE BATTLEVIEW, ND

PREP: 30 MIN. + RISING
BAKE: 15 MIN.
MAKES: 2 DOZEN

- 1 **tablespoon active dry yeast**
- 2¼ **cups warm water (110° to 115°)**
- ⅓ **cup sugar**
- ⅓ **cup shortening**
- ¼ **cup powdered nondairy creamer**
- 2¼ **teaspoons salt**
- 6 **to 7 cups bread flour**

1. In a large bowl, dissolve yeast in warm water. Add the sugar, shortening, creamer, salt and 5 cups flour. Beat until smooth. Stir in enough remaining flour to form a soft dough (dough will be sticky).

2. Turn onto a floured surface; knead until smooth and elastic, about 6-8 minutes. Place in a bowl coated with cooking spray, turning once to coat the top. Cover and let rise in a warm place until doubled, about 1 hour.

3. Punch dough down. Turn onto a lightly floured surface; divide into 24 pieces. Shape each into a roll. Place 2 in. apart on baking sheets coated with cooking spray. Cover and let rise until doubled, about 30 minutes.

4. Meanwhile, preheat oven to 350°. Bake 12-15 minutes or until lightly browned. Remove from pans to wire racks.

VIRGINIA BOX BREAD

FAST FIX

Fresh Herb Flatbread

Since I grow so many herbs, I always look for opportunities to use them in my cooking. This recipe uses two of my favorites, but it's also delicious with other combos. Try thyme and marjoram or oregano and basil.

—**BEV CREDLE** HAMPTON, VA

START TO FINISH: 25 MIN. • **MAKES:** 10 SERVINGS

- 1 tube (8 ounces) refrigerated crescent rolls
- ¼ cup fresh basil leaves, thinly sliced
- 1½ teaspoons minced fresh rosemary
- 1 egg, lightly beaten
- 1 tablespoon grated Parmesan cheese

1. Unroll crescent dough and separate into two rectangles. On a lightly floured surface, roll each into a 10 x 7-in. rectangle, sealing seams and perforations.
2. Place one rectangle on an ungreased baking sheet. Sprinkle basil and rosemary to within ½ in. of edges. Top with remaining dough; pinch edges to seal. Brush with egg; sprinkle with cheese.
3. Bake at 375° for 10-12 minutes or until golden brown. Cut into slices. Serve warm.

BASIL
PARMESAN
PUFFS

Basil Parmesan Puffs

These cute little bites are tasty alongside soup, salad, pasta and so much more! Minced fresh basil lends a burst of flavor.

—**AMBER MCKINLEY** PUNTA GORDA, FL

PREP: 15 MIN. • **BAKE:** 20 MIN./BATCH
MAKES: ABOUT 2 DOZEN

- ¾ cup water
- 6 tablespoons butter, cubed
- ¾ teaspoon salt
- ¾ cup all-purpose flour
- 4 eggs
- 1 cup minced fresh basil
- 1 cup grated Parmesan cheese

1. Preheat oven to 400°. In a large saucepan, bring water, butter and salt to a boil. Add flour all at once and stir until a smooth ball forms. Remove from heat; let stand 5 minutes. Add eggs, one at a time, beating well after each addition. Continue beating until mixture is smooth and shiny. Stir in the basil and cheese.
2. Drop by rounded tablespoonfuls 1 in. apart onto greased baking sheets. Bake 18-20 minutes or until golden brown. Remove to wire racks. Serve warm.

FRESH HERB
FLATBREAD

Easy Yeast Rolls

These tender dinner rolls always disappear in no time. If you've never made homemade yeast bread, this simple dough is the perfect place to start. You can easily cut the recipe in half.

—WILMA HARTER WITTEN, SD

PREP: 45 MIN. + RISING • **BAKE:** 15 MIN. • **MAKES:** 4 DOZEN

- 2 **packages (¼ ounce each) active dry yeast**
- 2 **cups warm water (110° to 115°)**
- ½ **cup sugar**
- 1 **egg**
- ¼ **cup canola oil**
- 2 **teaspoons salt**
- 6 **to 6½ cups all-purpose flour**

1. In a small bowl, dissolve yeast in warm water. In a large bowl, combine sugar, egg, oil, salt, yeast mixture and 4 cups flour; beat on medium speed until smooth. Stir in enough remaining flour to form a stiff dough.

2. Turn dough onto a floured surface; knead until smooth and elastic, about 6-8 minutes. Place in a greased bowl, turning once to grease the top. Cover with plastic wrap and let rise in a warm place until doubled, about 1 hour.

3. Punch down dough. Turn onto a lightly floured surface; divide into four portions. Divide and shape each portion into 12 balls. Roll each ball into an 8-in. rope; tie into a loose knot. Tuck ends under. Place 2 in. apart on greased baking sheets. Cover with kitchen towels; let rise in a warm place until doubled, about 30 minutes. Preheat oven to 350°.

4. Bake 15-20 minutes or until golden brown. Remove from pans to wire racks.

FAST FIX

Orange Coffee Cake Ring

With just three ingredients, this coffee cake couldn't be much easier. It's a great way to dress up sweet rolls.

—TINY DOBBIN WINCHESTER, VA

START TO FINISH: 30 MIN. • **MAKES:** 8 ROLLS

- 1 **tube (13.9 ounces) orange sweet rolls with icing**
- 1 **ounce cream cheese, softened**
- ½ **cup flaked coconut, toasted**

1. Preheat oven to 375°. Set aside icing from sweet rolls. Arrange rolls in a greased 9-in. round baking pan. Bake 18-20 minutes or until golden brown.

2. In a small bowl, combine cream cheese and reserved icing. Spread over rolls. Sprinkle with coconut. Serve warm.

TRISHA KRUSE'S APPLE PIE A LA MODE
PAGE 225

Cakes, Pies & Desserts

**CHRIS NELSON'S
PEANUT BUTTER CUP
TRIFLE** *PAGE 210*

**CLAUDIA YOUMANS' COUNTY
FAIR CHERRY PIE**
PAGE 205

**PAM ANDERSON'S
STRAWBERRY CAKE** *PAGE 206*

STRAWBERRY-HAZELNUT MERINGUE SHORTCAKES

Strawberry-Hazelnut Meringue Shortcakes

In early summer, the strawberry farms in our area open to the public for picking. These shortcakes really show off the big, juicy berries of our harvest.

—BARBARA ESTABROOK RHINELANDER, WI

PREP: 25 MIN. • **BAKE:** 45 MIN. + COOLING
MAKES: 8 SERVINGS

- 2 **egg whites**
- ½ **cup sugar**
- ¼ **cup finely chopped hazelnuts**
- 6 **cups fresh strawberries, hulled and sliced**
- 4 **cups low-fat frozen yogurt**

1. Place egg whites in a small bowl; let stand at room temperature 30 minutes.
2. Preheat oven to 250°. Beat egg whites on medium speed until foamy. Gradually add sugar, 1 tablespoon at a time, beating on high after each addition until sugar is dissolved. Continue beating until stiff glossy peaks form.
3. Drop meringue into eight mounds on a parchment paper-lined baking sheet. With the back of a spoon, shape into 3-in. cups. Sprinkle with hazelnuts. Bake 45-50 minutes or until set and

dry. Turn off oven (do not open oven door); leave in oven 1 hour. Remove from oven; cool completely on baking sheets. Remove meringues from paper.
4. Place 3 cups berries in a large bowl; mash them slightly. Stir in remaining berries. Top meringues with frozen yogurt and strawberries.

HOW TO

MAKE MERINGUE CUPS

❶ Egg whites beaten to stiff peaks will stand up straight and hold a point. Sugar is dissolved when the mixture feels silky-smooth between your fingers.
❷ After spooning meringue onto parchment, make a well in each mound to form a cup. Try to ensure an even thickness: If the meringue is too thin, it will be brittle.

COUNTY FAIR
CHERRY PIE

filling is bubbly. Cover edges during the last 20 minutes to prevent overbrowning.

4. Meanwhile, cut remaining pastry into 12-14 large stars and 16-18 small stars; place on an ungreased baking sheet.

5. Bake at 375° for 8-10 minutes or until golden brown. Remove to wire rack to cool. Sprinkle with confectioners' sugar. Place stars randomly over cooled pie. Sprinkle edges of the pie with confectioners' sugar.

Banana-Chip Mini Cupcakes

These cute little minis are an awesome snack to have ready when the kids come home from school.

—**BEVERLY COYDE** GASPORT, NY

PREP: 30 MIN. • **BAKE:** 15 MIN. + COOLING
MAKES: 3½ DOZEN

- 1 **package (14 ounces) banana quick bread and muffin mix**
- ¾ **cup water**
- ⅓ **cup sour cream**
- 1 **egg**
- 1 **cup miniature semisweet chocolate chips, divided**
- 1 **tablespoon shortening**

1. Preheat oven to 375°. In a large bowl, combine muffin mix, water, sour cream and egg; stir just until moistened. Fold in ½ cup chocolate chips.

2. Fill greased or paper-lined miniature muffin cups two-thirds full. Bake 12-15 minutes or until a toothpick inserted in the center comes out clean. Cool 5 minutes before removing from pans to wire racks to cool completely.

3. For frosting, in a microwave, melt shortening and remaining chocolate chips; stir until smooth. Frost cupcakes.

County Fair Cherry Pie

I'm a teacher and a Navy wife, so simplicity and quickness are both mealtime musts at my house. This cherry pie delivers on both counts.

—**CLAUDIA YOUMANS** VIRGINIA BEACH, VA

PREP: 20 MIN. + STANDING • **BAKE:** 55 MIN. + COOLING
MAKES: 6-8 SERVINGS

- 1¼ **cups sugar**
- 2 **tablespoons cornstarch**
  Dash salt
- 4 **cups pitted tart cherries**
  Pastry for double-crust pie (9 inches)
  Star cookie cutters (½ inch and 2 inches)
  Confectioners' sugar

1. In a large saucepan, combine sugar, cornstarch and salt; stir in cherries. Let stand 30 minutes.

2. Cook and stir cherry mixture over medium heat until mixture boils and starts to thicken.

3. Preheat oven to 375°. Line a 9-in. pie plate with bottom pastry; add filling. Flute edges of the pastry. Bake 45 minutes or until crust is golden brown and

MEXICAN
ICE CREAM

Mexican Ice Cream

I made this ice cream for my grandma and her friends, and they were delighted. This simple, fun dessert is a perfect way to get kids involved in the kitchen.

—**BEN PHIPPS** LIMA, OH

PREP: 20 MIN. + FREEZING
MAKES: 4 SERVINGS

    2 cups vanilla ice cream
    ½ cup frosted cornflakes,
       crushed
    ¼ cup sugar
    1 teaspoon ground cinnamon
    ¼ cup honey

1. Place four ½-cup scoops of ice cream on a waxed paper-lined baking sheet. Freeze for 1 hour or until firm.
2. In a shallow bowl, combine the cornflake crumbs, sugar and cinnamon. Roll the ice cream in crumb mixture to coat. Freeze until serving. Drizzle each serving with 1 tablespoon honey.

Strawberry Cake

Garnish the top with strawberries to hint at the fresh-tasting flavor of this pretty pink cake before you cut it—or let it be a surprise!

—**PAM ANDERSON** BILLINGS, MT

PREP: 25 MIN.
BAKE: 25 MIN. + COOLING
MAKES: 12-16 SERVINGS

    1 package white cake mix
       (regular size)
    1 package (3 ounces)
       strawberry gelatin
    1 cup water
    ½ cup canola oil
    4 egg whites
    ½ cup mashed unsweetened
       strawberries
       Whipped cream or frosting of
       your choice

1. Preheat oven to 350°. In a large bowl, combine dry cake mix, gelatin powder, water and oil. Beat on low speed 1 minute or until moistened; beat on medium 4 minutes.
2. In a small bowl with clean beaters, beat egg whites on high speed until stiff peaks form. Fold egg whites and mashed strawberries into cake batter.
3. Pour into three greased and floured 8-in. round baking pans. Bake 25-30 minutes or until a toothpick comes out clean. Cool for 10 minutes before removing from pans to wire racks to cool completely.
4. Spread whipped cream or frosting between layers and over top and sides of cake. If frosted with whipped cream, store in the refrigerator.

STRAWBERRY
CAKE

Arroz con Leche

Sweet and simple, this creamy dessert is real comfort food in any language. You'll love the warm raisin and cinnamon flavors. It's great served cold, too.

—MARINA CASTLE CANYON COUNTRY, CA

PREP: 5 MIN. • **COOK:** 30 MIN.
MAKES: 4 SERVINGS

- 1½ **cups water**
- ½ **cup uncooked long grain rice**
- 1 **cinnamon stick (3 inches)**
- 1 **cup sweetened condensed milk**
- 3 **tablespoons raisins**

1. In a small saucepan, combine the water, rice and cinnamon. Bring to a boil. Reduce the heat; simmer, uncovered, for 15-20 minutes or until water is absorbed.

2. Stir in milk and raisins. Bring to a boil. Reduce heat; simmer, uncovered, for 10-15 minutes or until thick and creamy, stirring frequently. Discard cinnamon. Serve warm or cold.

DID YOU KNOW?

Sweetened condensed milk is milk with most of the water cooked off, to which sugar (up to 45% by weight) has been added. It's generally used in candy and dessert recipes. Evaporated milk is concentrated in the same way but doesn't contain added sugar. It lends rich texture to foods without the fat of cream.

ARROZ CON LECHE

PINEAPPLE-CARAMEL SPONGE CAKES

Strawberry Pies

I sampled this tasty pie for the first time at our local junior high, where I am a substitute teacher. It's best when strawberries are at their peak.

—**PEGGY KEY** GRANT, AL

PREP: 10 MIN. + CHILLING
MAKES: 2 PIES (8 SERVINGS EACH)

- 1 can (14 ounces) sweetened condensed milk
- ¼ cup lemon juice
- 1 carton (12 ounces) frozen whipped topping, thawed
- 1 quart fresh strawberries, sliced, divided
- 2 graham cracker crusts (9 inches each)

In a large bowl, combine milk and lemon juice. Fold in whipped topping. Set aside ⅓ cup strawberries for garnish; stir remaining strawberries into filling. Spoon into crusts. Refrigerate for at least 4 hours before serving. Garnish with reserved strawberries.

FAST FIX ▶
Pineapple-Caramel Sponge Cakes

Want the flavor of pineapple upside-down cake without the heat and hassle of turning on the oven? Then try this tasty no-bake riff on the classic.

—**LYNN MAHLE** QUINCY, FL

START TO FINISH: 10 MIN. • **MAKES:** 4 SERVINGS

- 1 can (8 ounces) unsweetened crushed pineapple, drained
- ½ cup caramel ice cream topping
- 4 individual round sponge cakes
- 1 cup vanilla ice cream, softened

1. In a small saucepan, combine pineapple and caramel topping. Cook over medium heat for 2-3 minutes or until warmed, stirring occasionally.
2. Place sponge cakes on dessert plates. Top each with a scoop of ice cream and ¼ cup pineapple sauce. Serve immediately.

FAST FIX ▶
Ruby-Red Strawberry Sauce

My best friend, Lynn Young, and I created this recipe for our husbands. We love it on ice cream, and it's splendid served over pancakes and waffles, too.

—**TERRI ZOBEL** RALEIGH, NC

START TO FINISH: 15 MIN. • **MAKES:** 2½ CUPS

- ½ cup sugar
- 4½ teaspoons cornstarch
- ¼ cup orange juice concentrate
- 4 cups sliced fresh strawberries
- ½ teaspoon vanilla extract

In a large saucepan, combine the sugar and cornstarch. Stir in orange juice concentrate until smooth; add strawberries. Bring to a boil; cook and stir for 2 minutes or until thickened. Remove from the heat; stir in vanilla. Cool. Store in the refrigerator.

CHOCOLATE-NUT CARAMEL TART

over medium-low heat until blended, stirring occasionally. Remove from heat; stir in the macadamia nuts. Spread evenly over Nutella.

3. In a microwave, heat reserved Nutella until warmed; drizzle over filling. Refrigerate 1 hour or until firm. If desired, serve with whipped cream.

NOTE *To toast nuts, spread in a 15x10x1-in. baking pan. Bake at 350° for 5-10 minutes or until lightly browned, stirring occasionally. Or, spread in a dry nonstick skillet and heat over low heat until lightly browned, stirring occasionally.*

Peach Almond Dessert

When my dad retired, he took over all the baking in our home. He'd make these and say, "Put on a pot of coffee; let's invite company!" What an effortless way to recall what's most important in life: family and friends.

—**JUSTINE FURMAN-OLSHAN** WILLOW STREET, PA

PREP: 25 MIN. • **BAKE:** 20 MIN. + COOLING
MAKES: 2 DOZEN

- 1 **tube (16½ ounces) refrigerated sugar cookie dough**
- 1 **jar (18 ounces) peach preserves**
- 1½ **cups slivered almonds, divided**
- 4 **egg whites**
- ½ **cup sugar**

1. Preheat oven to 350°. Let dough stand at room temperature 5-10 minutes to soften. Press into an ungreased 13x9-in. baking pan. Bake 12-15 minutes or until golden brown.

2. Spread preserves over crust. Sprinkle with ¾ cup almonds. In a large bowl, beat egg whites on medium speed until soft peaks form. Gradually beat in sugar, 1 tablespoon at a time, on high until stiff glossy peaks form and sugar is dissolved.

3. Spread meringue evenly over almonds. Sprinkle with remaining almonds. Bake 20-25 minutes or until lightly browned. Cool on a wire rack. Store in the refrigerator.

Chocolate-Nut Caramel Tart

With just a few ingredients and in less time than you'd think, this sinfully rich tart is ready to go. It's a good recipe to have up your sleeve.

—**KATHLEEN SPECHT** CLINTON, MT

PREP: 25 MIN. + CHILLING • **MAKES:** 12 SERVINGS

- 1 **sheet refrigerated pie pastry**
- 1 **jar (13 ounces) Nutella, divided**
- 20 **caramels**
- ⅓ **cup heavy whipping cream**
- 1¾ **cups chopped macadamia nuts, toasted**
  Whipped cream, optional

1. Preheat oven to 450°. Unroll pastry into a 9-in. fluted tart pan with removable bottom. Press onto bottom and up sides of pan; trim pastry even with edge (discard or save trimmed pastry for another use). Generously prick bottom of crust with a fork. Bake 9-11 minutes or until golden brown. Cool completely on a wire rack.

2. Reserve 2 tablespoons Nutella for topping; spread remaining Nutella into cooled crust. In a small saucepan, combine caramels and cream; cook

FAST FIX

Peanut Butter Cup Trifle

The billowing layers of the trifle are a nice contrast to the peanut butter cups. You can add a little extra decoration with chocolate jimmies, too.

—**CHRIS NELSON** DECATUR, AR

START TO FINISH: 20 MIN. • **MAKES:** 12 SERVINGS

- 4 **cups cold 2% milk**
- 2 **packages (3.9 ounces each) instant chocolate pudding mix**
- 1 **prepared angel food cake (8 to 10 ounces), cut into 1-inch cubes**
- 1 **carton (12 ounces) frozen whipped topping, thawed**
- 2 **packages (8 ounces each) Reese's mini peanut butter cups**

In a large bowl, whisk milk and pudding mixes 2 minutes. Let stand 2 minutes or until soft-set. In a 3-qt. trifle bowl or glass bowl, layer half of the cake cubes, pudding, whipped topping and peanut butter cups. Repeat layers. Refrigerate until serving.

PEANUT BUTTER CUP TRIFLE

Berries with Vanilla Custard

What a delectable way to enjoy fresh raspberries. This cream sauce also tastes good with other fruit, such as strawberries or peaches.

—**SARAH VASQUES** MILFORD, NH

PREP: 20 MIN. + CHILLING • **MAKES:** 4 SERVINGS

- 1 **cup half-and-half cream**
- 2 **egg yolks**
- 2 **tablespoons sugar**
- 2 **teaspoons vanilla extract**
- 2 **cups fresh raspberries**

In a small saucepan, combine the cream, egg yolks and sugar. Cook and stir over medium heat until mixture reaches 160° and is thick enough to coat the back of a spoon. Transfer to a small bowl; stir in vanilla. Cover and chill until serving. Serve sauce with raspberries.

FAST FIX

Peppermint Stick Sauce

This minty sauce is one of my favorite holiday gifts to give. I place it in a decorative jar and add a package of chopped nuts to sprinkle with it over ice cream, unfrosted brownies or chocolate cake.

—**LINDA GRONEWALLER** HUTCHINSON, KS

START TO FINISH: 15 MIN. • **MAKES:** 3 CUPS

- 1½ **cups finely crushed peppermint candies or candy canes**
- ¾ **cup heavy whipping cream**
- 1 **jar (7 ounces) marshmallow creme**

1. In a large saucepan, combine all ingredients. Cook over medium-low heat until mixture is smooth and candy is melted, stirring occasionally.
2. Pour into small airtight containers. Store in the refrigerator. Serve warm over ice cream or cake.

Shoofly Cupcakes

These old-fashioned molasses cupcakes were my grandmother's specialty. So they wouldn't disappear too quickly, she stored them out of sight. Somehow, we always figured out her hiding places!

—BETH ADAMS JACKSONVILLE, FL

PREP: 15 MIN. • **BAKE:** 20 MIN. + COOLING
MAKES: 2 DOZEN

- 4 **cups all-purpose flour**
- 2 **cups packed brown sugar**
- ¼ **teaspoon salt**
- 1 **cup cold butter, cubed**
- 2 **teaspoons baking soda**
- 2 **cups boiling water**
- 1 **cup molasses**

1. Preheat oven to 350°. In a large bowl, combine flour, brown sugar and salt. Cut in butter until crumbly. Set aside 1 cup for topping. Add baking soda to remaining crumb mixture. Stir in water and molasses.
2. Fill paper-lined muffin cups two-thirds full. Sprinkle with reserved crumb mixture. Bake for 20-25 minutes or until a toothpick inserted near the center comes out clean. Cool 10 minutes before removing from pans to wire racks to cool.
NOTE *This recipe does not use eggs.*

Cherry Marble Cake

I scored this cake recipe from a friend years ago. It's the perfect last-minute treat. Choose any fruit pie filling, such as blueberry, peach or apple. If you use apple, sprinkle a little cinnamon on top.

—TESSA DOWNING DOYLESTOWN, PA

PREP: 15 MIN. • **BAKE:** 30 MIN. • **MAKES:** 16-20 SERVINGS

- 1 **package yellow cake mix (regular size)**
- ¼ **cup canola oil**
- 3 **eggs**
- ½ **cup water**
- 1 **can (21 ounces) cherry pie filling**

1. Preheat the oven to 350°. In a greased 13x9-in. baking pan, combine cake mix and oil. Combine eggs and water; stir into cake mix until blended. Drop tablespoons of pie filling into batter; cut through batter with a knife to swirl.
2. Bake 30-35 minutes or until a toothpick inserted near the center comes out clean (top will have an uneven appearance). Cool on a wire rack.

Rhubarb Fool with Strawberries

A fool is a classic British dessert made with whipped cream and cooked fruit. Try this quick version with rhubarb and berries.

—**CHERYL MILLER** FORT COLLINS, CO

PREP: 30 MIN. + CHILLING
MAKES: 6 SERVINGS

- 3 **cups sliced fresh or frozen rhubarb (1-inch pieces)**
- ⅓ **cup sugar**
- ¼ **cup orange juice**
  Dash salt
- 1 **cup heavy whipping cream**
- 2 **cups fresh strawberries, halved**

1. In a large saucepan, combine rhubarb, sugar, orange juice and salt. Bring to a boil. Reduce heat; simmer, covered, 6-8 minutes or until rhubarb is tender. Cool mixture slightly.

2. Cover and process rhubarb mixture in a blender until smooth. Transfer to a bowl; refrigerate, covered, until cold.

3. Just before serving, in a large bowl, whip cream until soft peaks form. Lightly fold in pureed rhubarb and the strawberries.

RHUBARB FOOL WITH STRAWBERRIES

Poached Pears with Raspberry Sauce

This elegant dessert for two has a wonderful vanilla flavor that is very satisfying. With a simple raspberry sauce adding a dash of bright color, it looks so impressive.

—**DAWN E. BRYANT** THEDFORD, NE

PREP: 20 MIN. + CHILLING
MAKES: 2 SERVINGS

- 1 **cup water**
- ½ **cup sugar**
- ¼ **cup white wine or white cranberry juice**
- 2 **medium pears, peeled and halved**
- 3 **tablespoons seedless raspberry spreadable fruit**
- ½ **teaspoon vanilla extract**
  Fresh raspberries and mint leaves, optional

1. In a small saucepan, bring the water, sugar and wine to a boil. Reduce heat; carefully add pears. Cover and simmer pears for 5-10 minutes or until tender. Remove pears and reserve the cooking liquid.
2. In a small bowl, combine spreadable fruit and vanilla. Stir in enough cooking liquid to form a sauce consistency. Cover and refrigerate sauce and pears separately until chilled.
3. Remove sauce from the refrigerator 15 minutes before serving. Place two pear halves on each dessert plate; top with sauce. Garnish with raspberries and mint if desired.

GOLDEN POUND CAKE

Golden Pound Cake

The surprise ingredient in this cake is a can of Mountain Dew. I sometimes substitute orange cake mix and orange soda for a flavorful variation.

—**VICKI BOYD** MECHANICSVILLE, VA

PREP: 10 MIN.
BAKE: 45 MIN. + COOLING
MAKES: 12 SERVINGS

- 1 **package lemon cake mix (regular size)**
- 1 **package (3.4 ounces) instant vanilla pudding mix**
- 4 **eggs**
- ¾ **cup canola oil**
- 1 **can (12 ounces) Mountain Dew**
  Confectioners' sugar, optional

1. Preheat oven to 350°. In a large bowl, combine cake mix, pudding mix, eggs, oil and soda; beat on low speed 30 seconds. Beat on medium 2 minutes.
2. Pour into a greased and floured 10-in. fluted tube pan. Bake 45-50 minutes or until a toothpick inserted near the center comes out clean. Cool for 10 minutes before removing from pan to a wire rack to cool completely. Dust with some confectioners' sugar if desired.

POACHED PEARS WITH RASPBERRY SAUCE

Dreamy S'more Pie

I love desserts and was looking for a way to use Nutella when I came up with this recipe. I wanted something that could be prepped quickly, too. This cute pie satisfied my craving in no time!

—**KAREN BOWLDEN** BOISE, ID

PREP: 10 MIN. + CHILLING • **BROIL:** 5 MIN.
MAKES: 8 SERVINGS

- 1 package (8 ounces) cream cheese, softened
- 1¼ cups heavy whipping cream
- 1 jar (13 ounces) Nutella
- 1 graham cracker crust (9 inches)
- 3 cups miniature marshmallows

1. In a large bowl, beat cream cheese and cream until thickened. Add Nutella; beat just until combined. Spoon into crust. Cover and refrigerate for at least 3 hours.

2. Just before serving, top with marshmallows; press gently into filling. Broil pie 6 in. from the heat for 1-2 minutes or until the marshmallows are golden brown.

DREAMY S'MORE PIE

MANDARIN TRIFLES

FAST FIX ▶

Mandarin Trifles

This charming tropical dessert comes together in a flash. You will be proud to serve this to a special guest. You'll probably be asked for the recipe!

—***TASTE OF HOME*** TEST KITCHEN

START TO FINISH: 15 MIN. • **MAKES:** 2 SERVINGS

- ½ cup heavy whipping cream
- 2 teaspoons honey
- ¼ cup dried papaya
- 1 can (11 ounces) mandarin oranges, drained

1. In a large bowl, beat cream until it begins to thicken. Add honey; beat until stiff peaks form. Set aside.

2. Place 1 tablespoon dried papaya in each of two cocktail glasses or dessert dishes; layer each with ¼ cup whipped cream. Top with oranges and remaining papaya; dollop with remaining whipped cream. Serve immediately.

TROPICAL RAINBOW DESSERT

Tropical Rainbow Dessert

I like to surprise my nieces and nephews with this amazing layered Jell-O in a rainbow of colors. Cream of coconut mixed into each flavor creates extra layers for more visual excitement.

—DAN KELMENSON WEST BLOOMFIELD, MI

PREP: 30 MIN. + CHILLING • **MAKES:** 12 SERVINGS

- 2 **packages (3 ounces each) strawberry gelatin, divided**
- 5 **cups boiling water, divided**
- 5 **cups cold water, divided**
- 1 **can (15 ounces) cream of coconut, divided**
- 2 **packages (3 ounces each) orange gelatin, divided**
- 2 **packages (3 ounces each) pineapple gelatin, divided**
- 2 **packages (3 ounces each) lime gelatin, divided**

1. In a small bowl, dissolve one package of strawberry gelatin in ¾ cup boiling water. Stir in ¾ cup cold water. Divide among 12 dessert dishes and refrigerate until set, or pour into a 3-qt. gelatin mold coated with cooking spray and refrigerate until set but not firm, 20-25 minutes.

2. In a small bowl, dissolve remaining package of strawberry gelatin in ½ cup boiling water. Add ½ cup cold water and scant ½ cup cream of coconut; stir. Spoon over the first layer. Chill until set but not firm, 20-25 minutes.

3. Repeat six times, alternating plain gelatin layers with creamy gelatin layers. Chill each layer until set but not firm before spooning next layer on top. Refrigerate for 4 hours or overnight. Unmold onto a serving platter.

NOTE *This recipe takes time to prepare since each layer must be set before the next layer is added.*

Lime Tartlets

These sweet-tart treats are perfect for parties. I like to serve them with a tiny slice of melon for color.

—BILLIE MOSS WALNUT CREEK, CA

PREP: 30 MIN. • **BAKE:** 10 MIN./BATCH + COOLING
MAKES: 4 DOZEN

- 2 **packages (15 ounces each) refrigerated pie pastry**
- 1 **package (8 ounces) cream cheese, softened**
- 1 **cup (8 ounces) plain yogurt**
- 3 **tablespoons confectioners' sugar**
- 1 **jar (10 ounces) lime curd, divided**
  Whipped cream, optional

1. Preheat oven to 450°. Roll out each pastry on a lightly floured surface. Using a 2½-in. round cookie cutter, cut out 12 circles from each pastry. Press rounds onto the bottoms and up the sides of greased miniature muffin cups. Prick bottoms with a fork.

2. Bake 8-10 minutes or until golden brown. Cool 5 minutes before removing from pans to wire racks.

3. In a large bowl, beat cream cheese, yogurt and confectioners' sugar until smooth. Stir in ½ cup lime curd. Spoon into tart shells; top with the remaining lime curd. Garnish with whipped cream if desired.

CHOCOLATE
PEANUT BUTTER CAKE

Chocolate Peanut Butter Cake

The addition of marshmallows makes the classic pairing of chocolate and peanut butter even more delectable.

—**BRENDA MELANCON** MCCOMB, MS

PREP: 10 MIN. • **BAKE:** 30 MIN. + COOLING
MAKES: 12-15 SERVINGS

- 2 **cups miniature marshmallows**
- 1 **package chocolate cake mix (regular size)**
- 1¼ **cups water**
- ¾ **cup peanut butter**
- ⅓ **cup canola oil**
- 3 **eggs**
- 1 **cup (6 ounces) semisweet chocolate chips**

1. Preheat oven to 350°. Sprinkle marshmallows into a greased 13x9-in. baking pan. In a large bowl, combine cake mix, water, peanut butter, oil and eggs; beat on low speed 30 seconds. Beat on medium 2 minutes or until smooth. Pour over marshmallows; sprinkle with chocolate chips.
2. Bake for 30-35 minutes or until a toothpick inserted near the center comes out clean. Cool on a wire rack.

Lemon-Berry Ice Cream Pie

I love the combination of fresh strawberries and lemon curd. It's so refreshing, especially in an easy make-ahead dessert like this.

—**ROXANNE CHAN** ALBANY, CA

PREP: 15 MIN. + FREEZING • **MAKES:** 8 SERVINGS

- 1 **pint strawberry ice cream, softened**
- 1 **graham cracker crust (9 inches)**
- 1 **cup lemon curd**
- 2 **cups frozen whipped topping, thawed**
- 1 **pint fresh strawberries, halved**

1. Spoon ice cream into pie crust; freeze 2 hours or until firm.
2. Spread lemon curd over ice cream; top with whipped topping. Freeze, covered, for 4 hours or until firm.
3. Remove from freezer 10 minutes before serving. Serve with strawberries.

Easy Elephant Ears

These cinnamon-sugar bakery favorites are a cinch to make at home. You can't go wrong with just three ingredients and simple assembly.

—**BOB ROSE** WAUKESHA, WI

PREP: 20 MIN. • **BAKE:** 15 MIN./BATCH
MAKES: ABOUT 2½ DOZEN

- 1 **package (17.3 ounces) frozen puff pastry, thawed**
- ½ **cup sugar**
- 2 **teaspoons ground cinnamon**

1. Preheat oven to 375°. On a lightly floured surface, roll one sheet of puff pastry into an 11x8-in. rectangle. Combine the sugar and cinnamon; sprinkle half of mixture over pastry.
2. Working from the short sides, roll up dough jelly-roll style toward the center. With a sharp knife, cut roll into ½-in. slices. Place on parchment paper-lined baking sheets, cut side down. Repeat with the remaining pastry and sugar mixture.
3. Bake 12-15 minutes or until crisp and golden brown. Remove from pans to wire racks.

**LEMON-BERRY
ICE CREAM PIE**

COWABUNGA ROOT
BEER CUPCAKES

Cowabunga Root Beer Cupcakes

I created these especially for my daughter's first birthday party. They're the perfect summertime treat.

—MINDY CARSWELL WALKER, MI

PREP: 10 MIN. • **BAKE:** 15 MIN. + COOLING
MAKES: 24 SERVINGS

- 1 package butter recipe golden cake mix (regular size)
- 4 teaspoons root beer concentrate, divided
- 1 carton (12 ounces) frozen whipped topping, thawed
    Vanilla ice cream

1. Prepare and bake cupcakes according to package directions, adding 2 teaspoons root beer concentrate when mixing batter. Remove to wire racks to cool completely.

2. In a small bowl, mix whipped topping and remaining root beer concentrate until blended; spread over cupcakes. Serve with ice cream.
NOTE *This recipe was tested with McCormick root beer concentrate.*

FAST FIX ▶

Outrageous Peanut Butter Sauce

I developed this thick and creamy sauce in an attempt to re-create a peanut butter topping we had at a restaurant. Served over any kind of ice cream, it's to die for!

—MARY LONG AMHERST, VA

START TO FINISH: 10 MIN. • **MAKES:** 2 CUPS

- 1 cup creamy peanut butter
- ⅔ cup confectioners' sugar
- ½ cup corn syrup
- ¼ cup water
- 1 teaspoon vanilla extract
- ¼ teaspoon salt
- 1 Nutrageous candy bar (3.4 ounces), finely chopped

1. In a large bowl, combine the first six ingredients; fold in candy. Transfer to jars. Cover and store in a cool dark place for up to 4 weeks.

2. To serve, cook and stir in a small saucepan over medium-low heat until heated through. Serve with ice cream.

IRISH CREAM CUSTARDS

3. Bake 20-25 minutes or until a knife inserted near the center comes out clean; centers will still be soft. Immediately remove ramekins from water bath to a wire rack; cool 10 minutes. Refrigerate until cold.

4. To caramelize topping with a kitchen torch, sprinkle custards evenly with remaining sugar. Hold torch flame about 2 in. above custard surface and rotate it slowly until sugar is evenly caramelized. Serve immediately or refrigerate up to 1 hour.

5. To caramelize topping in a broiler, place ramekins on a baking sheet; let stand at room temperature 15 minutes. Preheat broiler. Sprinkle custards evenly with remaining sugar. Broil 3-4 in. from heat 5-7 minutes or until sugar is caramelized. Serve immediately or refrigerate up to 1 hour.

Mocha-Fudge Ice Cream Dessert

This dessert recipe is super-easy but looks and tastes as if it was a lot of work. Best of all, you don't need to heat up the oven.

—CARRIE BURKE CONWAY, MA

PREP: 25 MIN. + FREEZING • **MAKES:** 15 SERVINGS

- 3¾ cups crushed cream-filled chocolate sandwich cookies
- ½ cup butter, melted
- 1 jar (16 ounces) hot fudge ice cream topping, warmed
- ½ gallon coffee ice cream, softened
- 1 carton (8 ounces) frozen whipped topping, thawed
  Chocolate curls or sprinkles, optional

1. Combine cookie crumbs and butter; press onto the bottom and 1 in. up the sides of a 13x9-in. dish. Freeze 1 hour or until firm.

2. Spread hot fudge topping evenly over crust; freeze 30 minutes.

3. Layer with ice cream and whipped topping. Cover and freeze 8 hours or overnight. Garnish with chocolate curls or sprinkles if desired.

Irish Cream Custards

Creme brulee is our favorite dessert and we love Irish cream liqueur, so I decided to put them together for a dinner finale we truly love.

—JOYCE MOYNIHAN LAKEVILLE, MN

PREP: 20 MIN. + CHILLING • **BAKE:** 20 MIN.
MAKES: 6 SERVINGS

- 2 cups heavy whipping cream
- ¼ cup Irish cream liqueur
- 3 eggs
- 2 egg yolks
- ¾ cup plus 2 tablespoons sugar, divided
- 1 teaspoon vanilla extract

1. Preheat oven to 325°. In a saucepan, heat cream and liqueur until bubbles form around sides of pan; remove from heat. In a large bowl, whisk eggs, egg yolks and ¾ cup sugar until blended but not foamy. Slowly stir in hot cream mixture. Stir in vanilla.

2. Place six 6-oz. broiler-safe ramekins in a baking pan large enough to hold them without touching. Pour cream mixture into ramekins. Place pan on oven rack; add very hot water to pan to within ½ in. of top of ramekins.

SURPRISE
SPICE CAKE

Surprise Spice Cake

Canned tomato soup replaces some of the oil in this cake, decreasing the fat, boosting the color and (surprise!) enhancing the taste.

—HANNAH THOMPSON
SCOTTS VALLEY, CA

PREP: 15 MIN.
BAKE: 30 MIN. + COOLING
MAKES: 12 SERVINGS

- 1 package spice cake mix (regular size)
- 1 can (10¾ ounces) condensed tomato soup, undiluted
- 3 eggs
- ½ cup water
- 1 can (16 ounces) cream cheese frosting

1. Preheat oven to 350°. In a large bowl, combine cake mix, soup, eggs and water; beat on low speed 30 seconds. Beat on medium 2 minutes. Pour into a greased 13x9-in. baking dish.
2. Bake 30-33 minutes or until a toothpick inserted near the center comes out clean. Cool on a wire rack. Frost with cream cheese frosting.

Lemon Ladyfinger Dessert

For a special dessert at Easter or any time of year, try this creamy treat. Ladyfingers and lemon curd lend delicate tart flavor to the simple, heavenly creation.

—TASTE OF HOME TEST KITCHEN

PREP: 20 MIN. + CHILLING
MAKES: 12 SERVINGS

- 2 packages (3 ounces each) ladyfingers, split
- 3 cups heavy whipping cream
- 1 package (8 ounces) cream cheese, softened
- ½ cup lemon curd
- ⅔ cup confectioners' sugar

1. Set aside five ladyfingers; line the sides and bottom of a lightly greased 9-in. springform pan with remaining ladyfingers. In a large bowl, beat cream until stiff peaks form; set aside.
2. In another large bowl, beat cream cheese and lemon curd until smooth; add sugar. Beat on medium for 1 minute. Fold in whipped cream. Spread half of cream cheese mixture into prepared pan. Arrange reserved ladyfingers in a spoke pattern over top. Spread with remaining cream cheese mixture. Cover and chill overnight.

LEMON LADYFINGER
DESSERT

Strawberry-Rosemary Yogurt Pops

We planted strawberries a few years ago, and my very favorite treats to make with them are these tangy-sweet frozen yogurt pops! The options are endless: Try using other yogurt flavors like lemon, raspberry or blueberry. You may also replace the rosemary with your favorite herb or simply omit it all together.

—CARMELL CHILDS FERRON, UT

PREP: 20 MIN. + FREEZING
MAKES: 6 POPS

- 1 **cup chopped fresh strawberries**
- 2 **tablespoons balsamic vinegar**
- 2 **tablespoons strawberry preserves**
- 2 **fresh rosemary sprigs**
- 1½ **cups (12 ounces) vanilla yogurt**
- 6 **freezer pop molds or paper cups (3 ounces each) and wooden pop or lollipop sticks**

1. In a small bowl, mix the strawberries, vinegar, preserves and rosemary. Let stand for 30 minutes; discard rosemary.
2. Spoon 2 tablespoons yogurt and 1 tablespoon strawberry mixture into each mold or paper cup. Repeat layers. Top molds with holders. If using cups, top with foil and insert sticks through foil. Freeze until firm.

STRAWBERRY-ROSEMARY YOGURT POPS

ICE CREAM
SANDWICH CAKE

Ice Cream Sandwich Cake

Here's a gooey, chocolaty dessert that guests just can't resist. They'll never guess that you simply dressed up ice cream sandwiches from the store.

—TASTE OF HOME TEST KITCHEN

PREP: 20 MIN. + FREEZING • **MAKES:** 15 SERVINGS

- 19 ice cream sandwiches
- 1 jar (16 ounces) hot fudge ice cream topping
- 1½ cups salted peanuts
- 3 Heath candy bars (1.4 ounces each)
- 1 carton (8 ounces) frozen whipped topping, thawed

1. Cut one ice cream sandwich in half. Place one whole and one half sandwich along a short side of an ungreased 13x9-in. dish. Arrange eight sandwiches in opposite direction in the dish. Remove lid from fudge topping. Microwave for 15-30 seconds to warm; stir. Spread one-half of fudge topping over ice cream sandwiches.

2. In a food processor, combine peanuts and candy bars. Cover and pulse until chopped. Sprinkle one-half of mixture over fudge layer. Repeat layers of ice cream sandwiches and fudge topping. Spread whipped topping over top of cake. Sprinkle with remaining peanut mixture.

3. Cover and freeze for up to 2 months. Remove from the freezer 20 minutes before serving. Cut into squares.

Frozen Hot Chocolate

Chocolate lovers will swoon over this icy treat. Freeze for a full 8 hours for a stiffer consistency. Serve in frosted goblets and top with whipped cream and chocolate syrup for a pretty touch.

—LILY JULOW LAWRENCEVILLE, GA

PREP: 15 MIN. + FREEZING • **MAKES:** 4 SERVINGS

- ¾ cup sugar
- ½ cup baking cocoa
- 2¾ cups 2% milk, divided
- ¼ cup reduced-fat whipped topping
- 4 teaspoons chocolate syrup

1. In a large saucepan, combine sugar and cocoa. Gradually add milk, reserving 2 tablespoons for blending; cook and stir until heated through and sugar is dissolved. Remove from the heat and let cool.

2. Transfer to an 8-in.-square dish. Freeze 2 hours or until edges begin to firm. Stir and return to freezer. Freeze 4 hours longer or until firm.

3. Just before serving, transfer to a food processor; cover and process with the remaining milk until smooth. Garnish with whipped topping and chocolate syrup.

FROZEN HOT
CHOCOLATE

Peppermint Angel Roll

My husband and I love this ice cream angel roll. The angel food cake makes it less heavy than other traditional cake rolls, but it's just as indulgent. Also I love how easy it is, especially during a hectic holiday season!

—**HOLLY DICKE** PLAIN CITY, OH

PREP: 30 MIN. • **BAKE:** 15 MIN. + FREEZING
MAKES: 10 SERVINGS

- 1 **package (16 ounces) angel food cake mix**
- 1 **tablespoon confectioners' sugar**
- ½ **gallon peppermint ice cream, softened**
- 1 **jar (11¾ ounces) hot fudge ice cream topping, warmed**
  Crushed peppermint candies and additional confectioners' sugar, optional

1. Preheat oven to 350°. Prepare cake batter according to package directions. Line a greased 15x10x1-in. baking pan with waxed paper and grease the paper. Spread batter evenly into pan. Bake 15-20 minutes or until cake springs back when lightly touched.
2. Cool 5 minutes. Turn cake onto a kitchen towel dusted with confectioners' sugar. Gently peel off waxed paper. Roll up cake in the towel jelly-roll style, starting with a short side. Cool completely on a wire rack.
3. Unroll cake and spread ice cream over cake to within ½ in. of edges. Roll up again, without towel. Cover and freeze until firm.
4. Cut into slices; drizzle with hot fudge topping. If desired, garnish with crushed candies and dust with confectioners' sugar.

Raspberry Swirled Cheesecake Pie

My dad always said my cheesecake pie was his favorite dessert. He is gone now, but I remember his smile every time I make it. Use this treat to get to a man's heart!

—**PEGGY GRIFFIN** ELBA, NE

PREP: 15 MIN. • **BAKE:** 35 MIN. + CHILLING
MAKES: 8 SERVINGS

- 1 **package (8 ounces) cream cheese, softened**
- ½ **cup sugar**
- 2 **eggs, lightly beaten**

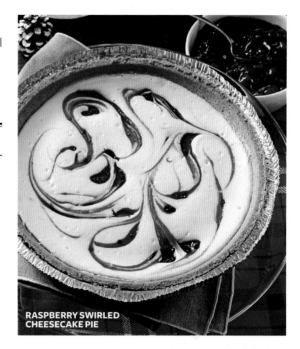

RASPBERRY SWIRLED CHEESECAKE PIE

- 1 **graham cracker crust (9 inches)**
- 1 **can (21 ounces) raspberry pie filling, divided**

1. Preheat oven to 350°. In a large bowl, beat cream cheese and sugar until smooth. Add eggs; beat on low speed just until blended. Pour into crust. Drop ½ cup pie filling by tablespoonfuls over batter. Cut through batter with a knife to swirl.
2. Bake 35-45 minutes or until filling is set. Transfer remaining raspberry filling to a covered container; refrigerate until serving.
3. Cool pie 1 hour on a wire rack. Refrigerate at least 2 hours, covering when completely cooled. Serve with reserved filling.

> ## TOP TIP
>
> Quick, easy, and delicious! I used a chocolate graham cracker crust and would use seedless raspberry jam instead of pie filling next time. Great dessert for company!
> —**GLD2BMOM** TASTEOFHOME.COM

Pots de Creme

Looking for an easy dessert recipe that's still guaranteed to impress? Served in pretty stemmed glasses, this classic chocolate custard really sets the tone.

—**CONNIE DREYFOOS** CINCINNATI, OH

PREP: 15 MIN. + CHILLING • **MAKES:** 5 SERVINGS

- 1 **egg**
- 2 **tablespoons sugar**
  Dash salt
- ¾ **cup half-and-half cream**
- 1 **cup (6 ounces) semisweet chocolate chips**
- 1 **teaspoon vanilla extract**
  Whipped cream, optional

1. In a small saucepan, combine the egg, sugar and salt. Whisk in cream. Cook and stir over medium heat until mixture reaches 160° and coats the back of a spoon.

2. Remove from the heat; whisk in chocolate chips and vanilla until smooth. Pour into small dessert dishes. Cover and refrigerate 8 hours or overnight. Garnish with whipped cream if desired.

POTS DE CREME

FAST FIX

White Chocolate Mousse Tarts

Make each guest feel special with individual white chocolate tarts. If you'd like to use fresh fruit, it looks pretty on top.

—**ANGELA LIVELY** BAXTER, TN

START TO FINISH: 30 MIN. • **MAKES:** 12 SERVINGS

- 6 **ounces white baking chocolate, chopped**
- 1 **can (14 ounces) sweetened condensed milk**
- ¼ **teaspoon vanilla extract**
- 2 **cups heavy whipping cream, whipped**
- 2 **packages (6 count each) individual graham cracker tart shells**
  Assorted fresh fruit, optional

In a microwave, melt chocolate; stir until smooth. Transfer to a large bowl; whisk in milk and vanilla. Fold in whipped cream. Spoon into tart shells. Garnish with fruit if desired. Chill until serving.

Crunchy Amaretto Peach Cobbler

When you finish a meal with this decadent dessert, your guests won't want to leave!

—**DEBRA KEIL** OWASSO, OK

PREP: 10 MIN. • **BAKE:** 30 MIN. • **MAKES:** 12 SERVINGS

- 2 **cans (21 ounces each) peach pie filling**
- ½ **cup amaretto**
- 1 **package (17½ ounces) sugar cookie mix**
- 1 **cup sliced almonds**
- ½ **cup butter, cubed**

1. Preheat oven to 350°. Spread pie filling into an ungreased 13x9-in. baking dish; drizzle with amaretto. Sprinkle cookie mix and almonds over top; dot with butter.

2. Bake 30-35 minutes or until filling is bubbly and topping is golden brown. Serve warm.

Apple Pie a la Mode

I was planning a dinner party, and I wanted a dessert that was sure to dazzle. This caramel apple ice cream pie certainly did the trick. Now it's a family favorite.

—**TRISHA KRUSE** EAGLE, ID

PREP: 15 MIN. + FREEZING • **MAKES:** 8 SERVINGS

- 1 **can (21 ounces) apple pie filling**
- 1 **graham cracker crust (9 inches)**
- 2 **cups butter pecan ice cream, softened if necessary**
- 1 **jar (12 ounces) hot caramel ice cream topping**
- ¼ **cup chopped pecans, toasted**

1. Spread half of the pie filling over crust. Top with half of the ice cream; freeze 30 minutes. Drizzle with half of the caramel topping; layer with remaining pie filling. Freeze 30 minutes. Scoop remaining ice cream over the top. Freeze, covered, until firm.

2. Remove from the freezer 30 minutes before serving. In a microwave, warm remaining caramel topping. Serve pie with warm caramel topping; sprinkle with pecans.

NOTE *To toast nuts, spread in a 15x10x1-in. baking pan. Bake at 350° for 5-10 minutes or until lightly browned, stirring occasionally. Or, spread in a dry nonstick skillet and heat over low heat until lightly browned, stirring occasionally.*

FAST FIX
Hot Fudge Sauce

This fudgy sauce is scrumptious spooned over French vanilla ice cream and sprinkled with toasted pecans. Actually, I could eat the topping all by itself!

—**KAREN WILLOUGHBY** OVIEDO, FL

START TO FINISH: 15 MIN. • **MAKES:** ABOUT 1 CUP

- ½ **cup semisweet chocolate chips**
- 6 **tablespoons evaporated milk**
- 6 **tablespoons light corn syrup**
- ¼ **cup butter, cubed**
- ½ **teaspoon vanilla extract**

1. In a small heavy saucepan, combine the chocolate chips, milk and corn syrup. Cook and stir over low heat until chips are melted and the mixture is smooth.

2. Stir in butter until melted. Cook and stir 5 minutes longer. Remove from heat; stir in vanilla.

Heavenly Angel Food Cake

Dress up angel food cake mix to create this pretty layer cake with luscious chocolate filling. Every soft and airy bite melts in the mouth.

—TERI ROBERTS HILLIARD, OH

PREP: 20 MIN.
BAKE: 35 MIN. + CHILLING
MAKES: 12 SERVINGS

- 1 package (16 ounces) angel food cake mix
- 24 large marshmallows
- 6 milk chocolate candy bars with almonds (1.45 ounces each), chopped
- ⅔ cup milk
- 1 carton (12 ounces) frozen whipped topping, thawed, divided

1. Prepare and bake the cake according to package directions, using an ungreased 10-in. tube pan. Cool.

2. For filling, in a saucepan, combine the marshmallows, candy bars and milk. Cook and stir over low heat until marshmallows are melted. Transfer to a small bowl; cool to room temperature. Fold in ¾ cup whipped topping.

3. Cut cake horizontally into three layers. Place bottom layer on a serving plate; spread with a third of the filling. Repeat layers twice. Refrigerate for at least 1 hour.

4. Frost top and sides of cake with remaining whipped topping.

HEAVENLY ANGEL FOOD CAKE

Minister's Delight

You need only a few pantry ingredients to simmer up this cobbler-like treat. A friend gave me the recipe many years ago, saying that a minister's wife made it every Sunday so she named it accordingly.

—**MARY ANN POTTER** BLUE SPRINGS, MO

PREP: 5 MIN. • **COOK:** 2 HOURS
MAKES: 10-12 SERVINGS

- 1 can (21 ounces) cherry or apple pie filling
- 1 package yellow cake mix (regular size)
- ½ cup butter, melted
- ⅓ cup chopped walnuts, optional

Place pie filling in a 1½-qt. slow cooker. Combine cake mix and butter (mixture will be crumbly); sprinkle over filling. Sprinkle with walnuts if desired. Cover and cook on low for 2-3 hours. Serve in bowls.

TOP TIP

Have made this several times, but I use a 3-quart slow cooker. I like it best with no-added-sugar apple pie filling, spice cake mix and 1 stick unsalted butter. But it's also good with cherry or blueberry pie filling and yellow cake mix. Top with vanilla ice cream or Cool Whip. Yummy!
—**MKOPACZ** TASTEOFHOME.COM

TOFFEE CREAM PIE

Toffee Cream Pie

I came up with this frozen pie by combining several desserts I had enjoyed over the years. I've prepared it with chocolate, vanilla and white chocolate instant pudding, too.

—**TAMMY CAMPBELL** CHESAPEAKE, VA

PREP: 15 MIN. + FREEZING
MAKES: 8 SERVINGS

- 1½ cups half-and-half cream
- 1 package (3.4 ounces) instant vanilla pudding mix
- 6 Heath candy bars (1.4 ounces each), chopped
- 1 carton (8 ounces) frozen whipped topping, thawed, divided
- 1 chocolate crumb crust (9 inches)

1. In a large bowl, whisk cream and pudding mix for 2 minutes. Let stand for 2 minutes or until soft-set. Stir in 1 cup chopped candy. Fold in 2 cups whipped topping. Transfer to crust.
2. Spread remaining whipped topping over top and sprinkle with remaining candy. Cover and freeze pie for at least 4 hours or until firm.

MINISTER'S DELIGHT

**RENEE SCHWEBACH'S
FUDGY MINT COOKIES**
PAGE 238

Cookies, Bars & Candies

**ROBERT SPRENKLE'S
SOFT CHEWY CARAMELS**
PAGE 233

**CHRISTINA SMITH'S
S'MOREOS** *PAGE 236*

**ANNE POWERS' WHITE
CHOCOLATE CEREAL BARS**
PAGE 245

Pecan Roll-Ups

This delectable recipe is sure to become a favorite. Pecans make these goodies rich and satisfying.

—LEE ROBERTS RACINE, WI

PREP: 45 MIN.
BAKE: 15 MIN./BATCH + COOLING
MAKES: 8 DOZEN

- 1 **cup butter, softened**
- 1 **package (8 ounces) cream cheese, softened**
- 2 **cups all-purpose flour**
- ¼ **teaspoon salt**
- 2 **cups pecan halves**
- 1 **cup confectioners' sugar**

1. In a large bowl, beat butter and cream cheese until light and fluffy. Combine flour and salt; gradually add to butter mixture and mix well. Cover and refrigerate for 1-2 hours or until easy to handle.

2. Preheat oven to 350°. Divide dough in half. On a lightly floured surface, roll out one portion into an 18x8-in. rectangle. Cut widthwise into six 3-in. sections; cut each section into 3x1-in. strips. Roll each strip around a pecan half; place 1 in. apart on ungreased baking sheets.

3. Bake 12-15 minutes or until bottoms are lightly browned. Remove cookies to wire racks to cool completely.

4. Roll in confectioners' sugar. Store in an airtight container at room temperature, or freeze for up to 3 months.

Apple Kuchen Bars

This recipe is about tradition, comfort and simplicity. My mom made them, and now I bake them in my own kitchen. I make double batches to pass along the love.

—ELIZABETH MONFORT CELINA, OH

PREP: 35 MIN.
BAKE: 1 HOUR + COOLING
MAKES: 2 DOZEN

- 3 **cups all-purpose flour, divided**
- ¼ **teaspoon salt**
- 1½ **cups cold butter, divided**
- 4 **to 5 tablespoons ice water**
- 8 **cups thinly sliced peeled tart apples (about 8 medium)**
- 2 **cups sugar, divided**
- 2 **teaspoons ground cinnamon**

1. Preheat oven to 350°. Place 2 cups flour and salt in a food processor; pulse until blended. Add 1 cup butter; pulse until butter is the size of peas. While pulsing, add just enough ice water to form moist crumbs. Press mixture onto bottom of a greased 13x9-in. baking pan. Bake for 20-25 minutes or until the edges are lightly browned. Cool on a wire rack.

2. Combine apples, 1 cup sugar and cinnamon; toss to coat. Spoon over the crust. Place remaining flour, butter and sugar in food processor; pulse until coarse crumbs form. Sprinkle over apples. Bake 60-70 minutes or until golden brown and apples are tender. Cool completely on a wire rack. Cut into bars.

APPLE
KUCHEN BARS

Yummy Cracker Snacks

These snacks are always gone before I know it. No matter how many cookies I make, there never seems to be enough.

—D. WEAVER EPHRATA, PA

PREP: 1 HOUR + CHILLING
MAKES: 4 DOZEN

- 96 **Ritz crackers**
- 1 **cup creamy peanut butter**
- 1 **cup marshmallow creme**
- 2 **pounds milk chocolate candy coating, melted**
  Colored sprinkles, optional

1. Spread half of the crackers with peanut butter. Spread remaining crackers with the marshmallow creme; place creme side down over peanut butter crackers, forming a sandwich.

2. Dip sandwiches in melted candy coating, allowing excess to drip off. Place on waxed paper-lined pans; refrigerate for 15 minutes or until set. If desired, drizzle cookies with additional candy coating and decorate with sprinkles. Store in an airtight container.

TOP TIP

I used Club crackers with just p.b. inside. It was like a Butterfinger, in a way. I would do this again. You can customize the decorating for Valentine's or whatever. Fun!

—RAGGAMUFFIN
TASTEOFHOME.COM

YUMMY CRACKER SNACKS

CRANBERRY
PECAN COOKIES

Cranberry Pecan Cookies

Each delightful cookie is loaded with cranberries, nuts and a sweet hint of vanilla. But these little gems start with ready-made cookie dough! Let that be your little secret.
—**LOUISE HAWKINS** LUBBOCK, TX

PREP: 10 MIN. • **BAKE:** 10 MIN./BATCH
MAKES: ABOUT 3½ DOZEN

- 1 tube (16½ ounces) refrigerated sugar cookie dough, softened
- 1 cup chopped pecans
- ⅔ cup white baking chips
- ⅔ cup dried cranberries
- 1 teaspoon vanilla extract

1. Preheat oven to 350°. In a large bowl, combine cookie dough, pecans, chips, cranberries and vanilla. Drop by tablespoonfuls 2 in. apart onto ungreased baking sheets.
2. Bake 10-12 minutes or until lightly browned. Cool 2 minutes before removing from pans to wire racks. Store in an airtight container.

Toffee Candy

This crunchy toffee is covered with milk chocolate and topped off with a generous sprinkling of pecans.
—**JANICE CRANOR** BARTLESVILLE, OK

PREP: 10 MIN. • **COOK:** 30 MIN. + COOLING
MAKES: ABOUT 2½ POUNDS

- 2 teaspoons plus 2 cups butter, divided
- 2 cups sugar
- ¼ cup water
- 1 cup milk chocolate chips
- 1½ cups finely chopped pecans

1. Grease a 15x10x1-in. pan with 2 teaspoons butter; set aside. In a large heavy saucepan, melt remaining butter. Add sugar and water; cook and stir over medium heat until a candy thermometer reads 300° (hard-crack stage).
2. Quickly pour into prepared pan. Immediately sprinkle with chocolate chips. Allow chips to soften for a few minutes, then spread over toffee. Sprinkle with pecans. Let stand until set, about 1 hour. Break into bite-size pieces. Store in an airtight container.

SOFT CHEWY CARAMELS

Soft Chewy Caramels

One of my first experiences with cooking was helping my mother make these caramels for Christmas. We'd make up to 12 batches each year. Today I do almost all of the cooking at home, but my wife does much of the baking.

—ROBERT SPRENKLE HURST, TX

PREP: 5 MIN. • **COOK:** 20 MIN. + COOLING
MAKES: ABOUT 2½ POUNDS

- 1 tablespoon plus 1 cup butter, divided
- 2¼ cups packed brown sugar
- 1 can (14 ounces) sweetened condensed milk
- 1 cup dark corn syrup

1. Line a 15x10x1-in. pan with foil; grease the foil with 1 tablespoon butter. In a heavy saucepan over medium heat, melt remaining butter. Add the brown sugar, milk and corn syrup. Cook and stir mixture until a candy thermometer reads 250° (hard-ball stage).
2. Pour into prepared pan (do not scrape saucepan). Cool completely before cutting.
NOTE *We recommend that you test your candy thermometer before each use by bringing water to a boil; the thermometer should read 212°. Adjust your recipe temperature up or down based on your test.*

Gold Rush Brownies

With six kids to keep an eye on, my mother relied on quick and easy recipes like this. Now my own family, who doesn't usually care for nuts, can't resist these chewy brownies.

—KELLIE ERWIN WESTERVILLE, OH

PREP: 5 MIN. • **BAKE:** 25 MIN. + COOLING
MAKES: 1 DOZEN

- 2 cups graham cracker crumbs
- 1 cup (6 ounces) semisweet chocolate chips
- ½ cup chopped pecans
- 1 can (14 ounces) sweetened condensed milk

1. Preheat oven to 350°. In a bowl, combine crumbs, chocolate chips and pecans. Stir in milk until blended (batter will be stiff). Spread into a greased 8-in.-square baking pan.
2. Bake 25-30 minutes or until a toothpick inserted near the center comes out clean. Cool on a wire rack. Cut into bars.

Pecan Candy Clusters

My grandkids love to help me make (and eat) these yummy four-ingredient treats. What a fun surprise for their parents!

—FLO BURTNETT GAGE, OK

PREP: 30 MIN. + STANDING • **MAKES:** 16 CANDIES

- 2 cups milk chocolate chips, divided
- 64 pecan halves (about 1½ cups)
- 28 caramels
- 2 tablespoons heavy whipping cream

1. Line a baking sheet with waxed paper; set aside. In a microwave, melt 1 cup chocolate chips; stir until smooth. Drop chocolate by tablespoonfuls onto prepared baking sheet. Immediately place four pecans on top of each chocolate drop.
2. Place the caramels in a 1-qt. microwave-safe dish; add cream. Microwave, uncovered, on high for 2 minutes, stirring once. Spoon onto the middle of each cluster.
3. Melt the remaining chocolate chips; stir until smooth. Spread over caramel. Let stand until set.
NOTE *This recipe was tested in a 1,100-watt microwave.*

Go Nuts! Coconut Caramels

I got this recipe from a TV cooking show, but made some adjustments to suit our tastes. We make the candy every Easter, and many more times throughout the year.

—DEANNA POLITO-LAUGHINGHOUSE RALEIGH, NC

PREP: 10 MIN. • **COOK:** 5 MIN. + COOLING
MAKES: ABOUT ¾ POUND

- 1 teaspoon butter
- 24 caramels
- ¾ cup plus 2 tablespoons flaked coconut, divided
- ½ cup white baking chips
- ½ cup salted peanuts

1. Line an 8x4-in. loaf pan with foil and grease the foil with butter; set aside.
2. In a microwave-safe bowl, combine the caramels, ¾ cup coconut, baking chips and peanuts. Microwave on high, uncovered, for 1 minute; stir. Cook, uncovered, 30-60 seconds longer or until caramels are melted; stir to combine. Press into prepared pan. Sprinkle with remaining coconut. Cool.
3. Using foil, lift candy out of pan. Discard foil; cut candy into 1-in. squares.
NOTE *This recipe was tested in a 1,100-watt microwave.*

GO NUTS! COCONUT CARAMELS

Walnut Brownies

Once I ran out of boxed brownie mix and experimented with cake mix instead. The result was so yummy my family thought I'd made brownies from scratch!

—CHARLOTTE BAILLARGEON HINSDALE, MA

PREP: 15 MIN. • **BAKE:** 25 MIN. • **MAKES:** 3 DOZEN

- 1 package chocolate cake mix (regular size)
- 2 eggs
- ¼ cup canola oil
- ¼ cup water
- ½ cup chopped walnuts
- ½ cup semisweet chocolate chips

1. Preheat oven to 325°. In a large bowl, beat cake mix, eggs, oil and water until well blended (batter will be thick). Stir in walnuts and chocolate chips.
2. Spread into a greased 13x9-in. baking pan. Bake 25-33 minutes or until the top springs back when lightly touched in the center. Cool on a wire rack. Cut into bars.

Nutter Butter Truffles

Prepare these truffles 5 to 7 days in advance and store in the refrigerator. They will be easy to serve, with no last-minute prep.

—KATHY CARLAN CANTON, GA

PREP: 1 HOUR + CHILLING • **MAKES:** 4 DOZEN

- 1 package (1 pound) Nutter Butter sandwich cookies
- 1 package (8 ounces) cream cheese, softened
- 8 ounces milk chocolate candy coating, melted
- 8 ounces white candy coating, melted
- 3 ounces bittersweet chocolate, melted

1. Place cookies in a food processor; cover and process until finely crushed. Add cream cheese; process until blended. Roll into 1-in. balls.
2. Dip half of the balls in milk chocolate, allowing excess to drip off. Place on waxed paper. Repeat with remaining balls and white coating. Drizzle bittersweet chocolate over truffles. Let stand until set. Store in an airtight container in the refrigerator.

PINWHEEL MINTS

Pinwheel Mints

Both my grandmother and my mom used to make these eye-catching confections as a replacement for ordinary mints at Christmas. When I offer them at parties, guests tell me the mints are wonderful, and then ask how I create the pretty swirl pattern.

—**MARILOU ROTH** MILFORD, NE

PREP: 45 MIN. + CHILLING • **MAKES:** ABOUT 3 DOZEN

- 1 **package (8 ounces) cream cheese, softened**
- ½ **to 1 teaspoon mint extract**
- 7½ **to 8½ cups confectioners' sugar**
     Red and green food coloring
     Additional confectioners' sugar

1. In a large bowl, beat cream cheese and extract until smooth. Gradually beat in as much confectioners' sugar as possible.
2. Turn onto a work surface dusted with confectioners' sugar; knead in remaining confectioners' sugar until smooth and sugar is absorbed (mixture will be stiff). Divide mixture in half. Using food coloring, tint one portion pink and the other portion light green, kneading until colors are uniform.

Divide each portion in half; shape each half into a 10-in. log to make two pink logs and two green logs. Place one log on a 12-in. piece of waxed paper lightly dusted with confectioners' sugar. Flatten log slightly; cover with a second piece of waxed paper. Roll out candy mixture into a 12x5-in. rectangle. Repeat with remaining logs.
3. Remove top sheet of waxed paper from one pink and one green rectangle. Place one rectangle over the other. Roll up jelly-roll style, starting with a long side. Wrap in waxed paper; twist ends. Repeat with remaining rectangles. Chill overnight.
4. To serve, cut candy into ½-in. slices. Store in an airtight container in the refrigerator for up to 1 week.

Hawaiian Turtle Cups

Because my mother-in-law loves macadamia nuts and my daughter prefers white chocolate, I came up with this twist on classic turtle candy. The dried pineapple plays up the tropical flavors.

—**LARISA SARVER** LA SALLE, IL

PREP: 20 MIN. + CHILLING • **MAKES:** 1 DOZEN

- 1½ **cups white baking chips**
- ½ **cup macadamia nuts, chopped**
- 18 **caramels**
- 2 **teaspoons heavy whipping cream**
- 12 **dried pineapple pieces, chopped**

1. In a microwave, melt white chips; stir until smooth. Pour by teaspoonfuls into greased miniature muffin cups; set aside remaining melted chips. Sprinkle the center of each muffin cup with nuts.
2. In a microwave, melt caramels and cream; stir until smooth. Pour over nuts. Reheat reserved chips if necessary; pour over caramel mixture. Top each with pineapple.
3. Chill for 30 minutes or until set. Carefully run a knife around the edge of each muffin cup to loosen the candy.

DARK CHOCOLATE
RASPBERRY FUDGE

Dark Chocolate Raspberry Fudge

Something about the combination of dark chocolate and raspberry is just so addicting. This fudge makes a heartfelt homemade gift or just a treat that's worth sharing.
—**BARBARA LENTO** HOUSTON, PA

PREP: 15 MIN. + FREEZING • **COOK:** 5 MIN. + CHILLING
MAKES: 3 POUNDS (81 PIECES)

- 1 **package (10 to 12 ounces) white baking chips**
- 1 **teaspoon butter, softened**
- 3 **cups dark chocolate chips**
- 1 **can (14 ounces) sweetened condensed milk**
- ¼ **cup raspberry liqueur**
- ⅛ **teaspoon salt**

1. Place baking chips in a single layer on a small baking sheet. Freeze 30 minutes. Line a 9-in.-square pan with foil; grease foil with butter.
2. In a large microwave-safe bowl, combine dark chocolate chips and milk. Microwave, uncovered, on high for 2 minutes; stir. Microwave in additional 30-second intervals, stirring until smooth. Stir in liqueur and salt. Add white baking chips; stir just until partially melted. Spread into prepared pan. Refrigerate 1 hour or until firm.
3. Using foil, lift fudge out of pan. Remove foil; cut fudge into 1-in. squares. Store in an airtight container in the refrigerator.
NOTE *This recipe was tested in a 1,100-watt microwave.*

S'Moreos

When we were camping, my son introduced us to this twist on classic s'mores. If you have a jar of Nutella around, slather it on the inside of the graham cracker halves before building this one-of-a-kind campfire treat.
—**CHRISTINA SMITH** SANTA ROSA, CA

START TO FINISH: 15 MIN. • **MAKES:** 4 SERVINGS

- 4 **Oreo cookies**
- 3 **tablespoons creamy peanut butter**
- 4 **whole graham crackers, halved**
- 1 **milk chocolate candy bar (1.55 ounces), quartered**
- 4 **large marshmallows**

1. Spread both sides of each Oreo cookie with peanut butter; place over half of the halved graham crackers. Top with chocolate.
2. Using a long metal skewer or long-handled fork, toast marshmallows 6 in. from medium-hot heat until golden brown, turning occasionally. Place on chocolate; cover with remaining graham crackers. Serve immediately.

Tumbleweeds

With melted butterscotch chips and peanut butter, these surprisingly easy clusters are guaranteed to delight. Crispy potato sticks and crunchy peanuts make the sweet-salty treats so satisfying.
—**PEGGY GRAY** SAVANNAH, TN

PREP: 25 MIN. + CHILLING • **MAKES:** 5 DOZEN

- 1 **package (11 ounces) butterscotch chips**
- 2 **tablespoons creamy peanut butter**
- 1 **jar (12 ounces) dry roasted peanuts**
- 1 **can (4 ounces) potato sticks**

1. In a microwave-safe bowl, melt butterscotch chips and peanut butter; stir until smooth. Stir in peanuts and potato sticks.
2. Drop by tablespoonfuls onto waxed paper-lined pans. Refrigerate until set. Store in an airtight container.

S'MOREOS

Fudgy Mint Cookies

Chocolate lovers will get a double dose with this tender, cakelike cookie with its chocolaty mint-flavored middle.

—RENEE SCHWEBACH DUMONT, MN

PREP: 15 MIN. • **BAKE:** 10 MIN./BATCH
MAKES: ABOUT 3 DOZEN

- 1 **package devil's food cake mix (regular size)**
- ½ **cup butter, softened**
- 2 **eggs**
- 1 **tablespoon water**
- 2 **tablespoons confectioners' sugar**
- 2 **packages (5 ounces each) chocolate-covered thin mints**

1. Preheat oven to 375°. In a large bowl, mix cake mix, butter, eggs and water to form a soft dough. Shape dough into 1-in. balls; roll in confectioners' sugar. Place 2 in. apart on ungreased baking sheets.
2. Bake 8-10 minutes or until set. Immediately press a mint into center of each cookie. Cool on pans 2 minutes. Remove from pans to wire racks to cool.

HOW TO

SHAPE COOKIE DOUGH

Roll the cookie dough between your palms until it forms a ball. A 1-in. ball will use about 2 teaspoons of dough. If dough is sticky, you can chill it until easy to handle, lightly flour your hands, or spritz hands with cooking spray.

FUDGY MINT COOKIES

Coconut Brownies

Brownies are always an easy treat, and no one seems to tire of them. Served warm with ice cream, these goodies thrill the sweet tooth.

—**BARBARA CARLUCCI** ORANGE PARK, FL

PREP: 10 MIN.
BAKE: 30 MIN. + COOLING
MAKES: 2 DOZEN

- 1 **package fudge brownie mix (13x9-inch pan size)**
- 1 **cup (8 ounces) sour cream**
- 1 **cup coconut-pecan frosting**
- 2 **eggs**
- ¼ **cup water**
- 1 **cup (6 ounces) semisweet chocolate chips**

1. Preheat oven to 350°. In a large bowl, combine brownie mix, sour cream, frosting, eggs and water just until moistened.
2. Pour into a 13x9-in. baking dish coated with cooking spray. Bake 30-35 minutes or until center is set (do not overbake). Sprinkle with chocolate chips; let stand 5 minutes. Spread chips over brownies.

Jelly Bean Bark

Homemade Easter candy really doesn't get simpler than this. All you need are three ingredients, a microwave and a pan.

—**MAVIS DEMENT** MARCUS, IA

PREP: 15 MIN. + STANDING
MAKES: 2 POUNDS

- 1 **tablespoon butter**
- 1¼ **pounds white candy coating, coarsely chopped**
- 2 **cups small jelly beans**

1. Line a 15x10x1-in. pan with foil; grease foil with butter. In a microwave, melt candy coating; stir until smooth. Spread into prepared pan. Top with jelly beans, pressing to adhere. Let stand until set.
2. Cut or break bark into pieces. Store in an airtight container.

Raspberry Oatmeal Bars

Cake mix makes the prep work a snap for these tasty bars. The raspberry jam adds a pop of color and sweetness, and oats lend a homey touch.

—**TRISH BOSMAN-GOLATA** ROCK HILL, SC

PREP: 20 MIN.
BAKE: 35 MIN. + COOLING
MAKES: 2 DOZEN

- 1 **package yellow cake mix (regular size)**
- 2½ **cups quick-cooking oats**
- ¾ **cup butter, melted**
- 1 **jar (12 ounces) seedless raspberry preserves**
- 1 **tablespoon water**

1. Preheat oven to 350°. In a large bowl, combine cake mix, oats and butter until crumbly. Press 3 cups of the crumb mixture into a greased 13x9-in. baking pan. Bake 10 minutes. Cool pan on a wire rack for 5 minutes.
2. In a small bowl, stir preserves and water until blended. Spread over crust. Sprinkle with the remaining crumb mixture. Bake 25-28 minutes or until lightly browned. Cool completely on a wire rack. Cut into bars.

COCONUT BROWNIES

Pecan Sandies Cookies

Whenever Mother made these cookies, there never seemed to be enough! Even now when I make them, they disappear quickly. These melt-in-your-mouth treats are great with a cold glass of milk or a steaming mug of hot chocolate.

—DEBBIE CARLSON SAN DIEGO, CA

PREP: 20 MIN. • **BAKE:** 20 MIN./BATCH + COOLING
MAKES: ABOUT 5 DOZEN

- 2 **cups butter, softened**
- 1 **cup confectioners' sugar**
- 2 **tablespoons water**
- 4 **teaspoons vanilla extract**
- 4 **cups all-purpose flour**
- 2 **cups chopped pecans**
  Additional confectioners' sugar

1. Preheat oven to 300°. In a large bowl, cream butter and sugar. Add water and vanilla; mix well. Gradually add flour; fold in pecans.
2. Roll dough into 1-in. balls. Place on ungreased baking sheets and flatten with fingers.
3. Bake 20-25 minutes or until bottom edges are golden brown. Cool on a wire rack. When cool, dust with confectioners' sugar.

POLKA-DOT MACAROONS

PECAN SANDIES COOKIES

Polka-Dot Macaroons

You can mix up these macaroons studded with M&M's in a hurry—and they'll disappear about as quickly as you make them.

—JANICE LASS DORR, MI

PREP: 15 MIN. • **BAKE:** 10 MIN./BATCH + COOLING
MAKES: ABOUT 4½ DOZEN

- 5 **cups flaked coconut**
- 1 **can (14 ounces) sweetened condensed milk**
- ½ **cup all-purpose flour**
- 1½ **cups M&M's Minis**

1. Preheat oven to 350°. In a large bowl, combine coconut, milk and flour; mix well. Stir in M&M's.
2. Drop by rounded tablespoonfuls 2 in. apart onto greased baking sheets. Bake 8-10 minutes or until edges are lightly browned. Remove from pans to wire racks to cool.
FREEZE OPTION *Freeze cookies, layered between waxed paper, in freezer containers. To use, thaw before serving.*

CARAMEL CASHEW CLUSTERS

Caramel Cashew Clusters

Several years ago, a co-worker came across candies like these in a store and asked if I could make them. After some trial and error, I came up with a winning recipe.

—**KAREN DANIELS** JEFFERSON CITY, MO

PREP: 25 MIN. + STANDING • **MAKES:** 2½ DOZEN

- 2 **teaspoons butter**
- 2 **pounds milk chocolate candy coating, coarsely chopped, divided**
- 1 **cup salted cashew halves**
- 28 **caramels**
- 2 **tablespoons heavy whipping cream**

1. Line baking sheets with waxed paper and butter the paper; set aside.

2. In a microwave, melt 1 pound of candy coating; stir until smooth. Drop by scant tablespoonfuls onto prepared pans. Let stand until partially set, about 3 minutes. Top each with six or seven cashew halves. Let stand until completely set.

3. In a small heavy saucepan, combine caramels and cream. Cook and stir over low heat until melted; stir until smooth. Spoon over cashews. Reheat caramel over low heat if it thickens. Melt remaining candy coating; spoon over caramel. Let stand until set.

Chewy Caramel Bars

There are requests for this recipe everywhere it goes! The Rolo candies make these bars extra gooey and good.

—**DEBRA DAVIDSON-CREGEUR** HARBOR BEACH, MI

PREP: 10 MIN. • **BAKE:** 40 MIN. + COOLING
MAKES: 2 DOZEN

- 1 **package yellow cake mix (regular size)**
- 1 **can (5 ounces) evaporated milk**
- ¼ **cup butter, melted**
- ½ **cup chopped nuts**
- 36 **Rolo candies, halved**

1. Preheat oven to 350°. In a large bowl, beat the cake mix, milk and butter until blended (batter will be thick). Stir in nuts. Press half of mixture into a greased 13x9-in. baking pan. Bake 10-12 minutes or until set.

2. Place candies, cut side down, over crust. Drop remaining batter by tablespoonfuls over the top. Bake 25-30 minutes longer or until golden brown. Cool on a wire rack. Cut into bars.

SCOTCH
SHORTBREAD
COOKIES

Scotch Shortbread Cookies

This simple three-ingredient recipe makes wonderfully rich, tender cookies. Serve them with fresh berries of the season for a light dessert. You'll get miles of smiles when you provide these for afternoon tea or at a bridal or baby shower.

—**MARLENE HELLICKSON** BIG BEAR CITY, CA

PREP: 15 MIN. • **BAKE:** 25 MIN. • **MAKES:** 4 DOZEN

- 4 **cups all-purpose flour**
- 1 **cup sugar**
- 1 **pound cold butter, cubed**

1. Preheat oven to 325°. In a large bowl, combine flour and sugar. Cut in butter until the mixture resembles fine crumbs. Knead dough until smooth, about 6-10 times. Pat dough into an ungreased 15x10x1-in. baking pan. Pierce with a fork.

2. Bake 25-30 minutes or until lightly browned. Cut into squares while warm. Cool on a wire rack.

NOTE *This recipe makes a dense, crisp bar, so it does not call for baking powder or soda.*

Toffee Meringue Drops

The original recipe called for mini chocolate chips and crushed peppermint candy. I didn't have those ingredients on hand, so I substituted toffee bits. Everyone loved the tasty results!

—**BETTE RICHARDS** CALEDONIA, ON

PREP: 25 MIN. • **BAKE:** 25 MIN. + STANDING
MAKES: 3 DOZEN

- 2 **egg whites**
- ⅛ **teaspoon cream of tartar**
- ½ **cup sugar**
- ½ **cup milk chocolate English toffee bits**
- ½ **cup finely chopped pecans**

1. Preheat oven to 250°. In a large bowl, beat the egg whites and cream of tartar on medium speed until soft peaks form. Gradually add sugar, 1 tablespoon at a time, beating on high until stiff glossy peaks form and sugar is dissolved, about 6 minutes. Fold in toffee bits and pecans.

2. Drop by tablespoonfuls 2 in. apart onto parchment paper-lined baking sheets. Bake 25-30 minutes or until set and dry. Turn oven off; leave cookies in oven 1 hour.

3. Cool completely on pans on wire racks. Store in an airtight container.

TOFFEE
MERINGUE
DROPS

DARK CHOCOLATE ORANGE TRUFFLES

Crunchy Chocolate Mint Balls

My mom made these for us every year when we were growing up. We'd always have an ice cream container full of them in the freezer. I now make them every year for my family. For a special touch, I like to place my truffles in mini cupcake holders.

—**AMANDA TRIFF** DARTMOUTH, NS

PREP: 50 MIN. + FREEZING • **MAKES:** 4½ DOZEN

- 1 **package (10 ounces) mint chocolate chips**
- ¼ **cup butter, softened**
- 1 **can (14 ounces) sweetened condensed milk**
- 1¼ **cups chocolate wafer crumbs (about 22 wafers)**
  White jimmies

1. In a double boiler or metal bowl over hot water, melt chips and butter; stir until smooth. Stir in milk. Add wafer crumbs; mix to coat. Refrigerate for 1 hour or until easy to handle.

2. Roll into 1-in. balls; roll in jimmies. Place on a waxed paper-lined 15x10x1-in. baking pan; freeze until firm. Transfer to a resealable plastic freezer bag. May be frozen for up to 1 month.

TO USE FROZEN BALLS *Thaw at room temperature.*

Dark Chocolate Orange Truffles

I love chocolate truffles, so you can imagine my delight when I came across the recipe for these dark and decadent confections. The hint of orange makes them deliciously different from other candies.

—**THERESA YOUNG** MCHENRY, IL

PREP: 15 MIN. + CHILLING • **MAKES:** 2½ DOZEN

- 1 **package (12 ounces) dark chocolate chips**
- ¾ **cup heavy whipping cream**
- 1 **teaspoon orange extract**
- ⅓ **cup sugar**

In a microwave, melt chocolate; stir until smooth. Gradually stir in cream until blended. Stir in extract. Cool to room temperature, stirring occasionally. Refrigerate until firm. Shape into ¾-in. balls. Roll in sugar.

Magic Wands

You don't have to be a magician to conjure up these cute and colorful treats. Customize the colors to match your party's theme.

—**RENEE SCHWEBACH** DUMONT, MN

PREP: 40 MIN. + STANDING • **MAKES:** 2 DOZEN

- 1½ **cups white baking chips**
- 1 **package (10 ounces) pretzel rods**
  Colored candy stars or sprinkles
  Colored sugar or edible glitter

In a microwave, melt chips; stir until smooth. Dip each pretzel rod halfway into melted chips; allow excess to drip off. Sprinkle with candy stars and colored sugar. Place on waxed paper; let stand until dry. Store in an airtight container.

NOTE *Edible glitter is available from Wilton Industries. Call 800-794-5866 or visit wilton.com.*

Chocolate Peanut Treats

When I was in high school, I took these sweet and crunchy squares to bake sales—and they were the first to sell out. I still make them for family and friends who love the classic combination of chocolate and peanut butter.

—CHRISTY ASHER
COLORADO SPRINGS, CO

PREP: 20 MIN. + CHILLING
MAKES: ABOUT 2 DOZEN

- ¾ cup graham cracker crumbs
- ½ cup butter, melted
- 2 cups confectioners' sugar
- ½ cup chunky peanut butter
- 1 cup (6 ounces) semisweet chocolate chips

1. In a bowl, combine cracker crumbs and butter. Stir in sugar and peanut butter. Press into a greased 8-in.-square pan.

2. In a microwave or double boiler, melt the chocolate chips; stir until smooth. Spread over the peanut butter layer. Chill for 30 minutes; cut into squares. Chill until firm, about 30 minutes longer. Store in the refrigerator.

DID YOU KNOW?

Unless otherwise specified, *Taste of Home* recipes are tested with lightly salted butter. Unsalted (or sweet) butter is sometimes used to achieve a buttery flavor, such as in shortbread cookies or buttercream frosting. In these recipes, added salt would detract from the buttery taste.

CHOCOLATE
PEANUT TREATS

White Chocolate Cereal Bars

A friend gave me the recipe for this fresh take on traditional crispy treats. They're so quick to make, you can prepare them during a TV commercial and you won't miss much of your program.

—ANNE POWERS MUNFORD, AL

START TO FINISH: 15 MIN.
MAKES: ABOUT 3 DOZEN

- 4 **cups miniature marshmallows**
- 8 **ounces white baking chips (about 1⅓ cups)**
- ¼ **cup butter, cubed**
- 6 **cups Rice Krispies**

1. In a Dutch oven, combine marshmallows, baking chips and butter. Cook and stir over medium-low heat until melted. Remove from heat. Add Rice Krispies; stir to coat.

2. Transfer to a greased 13x9-in. pan; gently press mixture evenly into pan. Cut into bars.

Ice Cream Kolachkes

These sweet pastries have Polish and Czech roots and can also be spelled "kolaches." They are usually filled with poppy seeds, nuts, jam or a mashed fruit mixture. The ice cream is a unique twist on traditional kolachkes, and it's simplest to use a square cookie cutter to cut the dough.

—DIANE TURNER BRUNSWICK, OH

PREP: 1 HOUR + CHILLING
BAKE: 15 MIN./BATCH
MAKES: 10 DOZEN

- 2 **cups butter, softened**
- 1 **pint vanilla ice cream, softened**
- 4 **cups all-purpose flour**
- 2 **tablespoons sugar**
- 2 **cans (12 ounces each) apricot and/or raspberry cake and pastry filling**
- 1 **to 2 tablespoons confectioners' sugar, optional**

1. In the bowl of a heavy-duty stand mixer, beat butter and ice cream until blended (mixture will appear curdled). Add flour and sugar; mix well. Divide dough into four portions; cover and refrigerate 2 hours or until easy to handle.

2. Preheat oven to 350°. On a lightly floured surface, roll one portion of dough into a 12x10–in. rectangle; cut into 2-in. squares. Place a teaspoonful of filling in the center of each square. Overlap two opposite corners of dough over filling; pinch tightly to seal. Place 2 in. apart on ungreased baking sheets. Repeat with remaining dough and filling.

3. Bake 11-14 minutes or until bottoms are lightly browned. Cool 1 minute before removing from pans to wire racks. Sprinkle with the confectioners' sugar if desired.

NOTE *This recipe was tested with Solo brand cake and pastry filling. Look for it in the baking aisle.*

WHITE CHOCOLATE CEREAL BARS

Indexes

General Index

APPETIZERS

DIPS & SPREADS

Amaretto-Peach Cheese Spread 32
Broccoli Cheddar Spread.............. 31
Green Onion Bagel Dip................ 35
Pina Colada Fruit Dip................. 32
Homemade Guacamole............... 38
Lemon Garlic Hummus 27

NUTS & SNACKS

Candied Pecans...................... 37
Fun-on-the-Run Snack Mix 44
Party Pretzels 47
Peanut Butter Chocolate Pretzels 43
Sweet & Salty Popcorn 33

OTHER APPETIZERS

Baked Crab Rangoon 27
Balsamic-Glazed Chicken Wings 36
Caramel Apple and Brie Skewers 29
Cheese Straws 32
Cheese-Stuffed Meatball Sliders 35
Chocolate Mint Apple Fondue......... 44
Chocolate-Covered Bacon 26
Chutney-Topped Brie 30
Deep-Fried Cheese Bites 34
Dunked Strawberries................. 31
Effortless Egg Rolls................... 42
Foolproof Mushrooms................ 36
Garlic Toast Pizzas 46
Grilled Shrimp with Spicy-Sweet Sauce . 40
Ham & Pickle Wraps 47
Italian Meatball Buns 29
Marmalade Meatballs 39
Mini Phyllo Tacos..................... 30
Mozzarella Sticks.................... 31
Pepper Shooters..................... 34
Polenta Parmigiana................... 44
Savory Stuffed Figs................... 47
White Chocolate Brie Cups 42

APPLES & APPLESAUCE

All-Day Apple Butter 179
Apple Kuchen Bars 230
Apple Sausage Puffs 12
Apple Stuffing 181
Apple Yogurt Parfaits 20
Applesauce-Raspberry Gelatin Mold 153
Baked Pork Chops with Apple Slices 90
Caramel Apple and Brie Skewers 29
Chocolate Mint Apple Fondue 44

ARTICHOKES

Artichoke Blue Cheese Fettuccine 142
Broiled Tomatoes with Artichokes 170
Spinach-Artichoke Rigatoni............ 145

ASPARAGUS

Asparagus Souffle 146
Bow Ties with Asparagus and
  Prosciutto.......................... 93
Sesame Asparagus 187

AVOCADOS

Homemade Guacamole 38
No-Fuss Avocado Onion Salad.......... 161
Tomato & Avocado Sandwiches 58

BACON

Bacon Honey Walleye 138
Bacon-Parmesan Brussels Sprouts...... 180
Bacon Pull-Apart Bread 192
Bacon-Swiss Pork Chops 96
BLT Salad with Pasta.................. 156
Busy-Day Bacon Muffins 196
Chicken with Shallot Sauce 115
Chipotle BLT Wraps 61
Chocolate-Covered Bacon.............. 26
Easy Beans & Potatoes with Bacon 176
Glazed Bacon 18
Ham and Swiss Stromboli 59
Hawaiian Barbecue Beans 166
Loaded Breakfast Potatoes 17
Pesto Tortellini Salad 159
Potato Chowder...................... 56
Ravioli Carbonara.................... 99
Roasted Cauliflower & Brussels
  Sprouts 164
Savory Stuffed Figs................... 47

BANANAS

Banana Chip Pancakes................. 12
Banana Split Fruit Salad............... 159
Nutty Waffle Sandwiches.............. 22
Peanut Butter Banana Oatmeal 14

BARS

White Chocolate Cereal Bars 245
Raspberry Oatmeal Bars............... 239
Chewy Caramel Bars 241
Apple Kuchen Bars 230
Chocolate Peanut Treats.............. 244

BEANS

Black Bean and Beef Tostadas 85
Easy Black Bean Salsa................. 39
Hawaiian Barbecue Beans 166
Hot Dog Bean Soup 59
Lemon Garlic Hummus 27
Southern Skillet Chops 101
Southwest Chicken.................... 122
Spanish Omelets 19
Spicy Pumpkin & Corn Soup........... 60
Sweet Potato & Bean Quesadillas....... 146

BEEF

(also see Corned Beef; Ground Beef)

Blue Cheese-Stuffed Steaks for Two 82
Brisket with Cranberry Gravy 76
Easy Stuffed Shells 78
Grilled Flank Steak................... 80
Java Roast Beef 76
Marinated Chuck Roast................ 73
Peppered Beef Tenderloin 86
Sirloin with Mushroom Sauce........... 83
Slow Cooker Beef au Jus 75
Slow-Cooked Swiss Steak.............. 78
Southwest Steak 84
Spicy French Dip 50
Spinach Steak Pinwheels.............. 85
Tex-Mex Shredded Beef Sandwiches 66

BEER

Deep-Fried Cheese Bites 34
Grilled Seasoned Bratwurst............. 52
Shredded Turkey Sandwiches........... 56

BEVERAGES

After-Dinner White Chocolate Mocha ... 26
Berry Berry Lemonade 37
Honey Cinnamon Milk................. 40
Lemony Cooler....................... 28
Luscious Lime Slush 34
Mom's Tangerine Iced Tea 38
Raspberry-Swirled Lemon Milk Shakes ... 45
Strawberry Lemonade Smoothie 43

BISCUIT/BAKING MIX

Banana Chip Pancakes................. 12
Busy-Day Bacon Muffins............... 196
Sour Cream Blueberry Muffins.......... 198

BLUEBERRIES

Berry Berry Lemonade 37
Berry Yogurt Cups..................... 23
Blueberry Oatmeal 18
Kids' Favorite Blueberry Muffins 18
Sour Cream Blueberry Muffins.......... 198

BREADS & ROLLS

(also see Breakfast Recipes; Frozen Bread
Dough; Refrigerated Biscuits; Refrigerated
Crescent Rolls)

Bacon Pull-Apart Bread................ 192
Basil Parmesan Puffs 200
Busy-Day Bacon Muffins............... 196
Caramelized Onion Breadsticks......... 197
Cheddar-Parm Loaf 195
Chocolate Biscuit Puffs................ 192
Crusty Homemade Bread.............. 193
Dill and Chive Bread 191
Easy Yeast Rolls..................... 201
Fresh Herb Flatbread................. 200
Hurry-Up Biscuits 195

Italian-Style Crescents 192
Mom's Italian Bread 190
Oatmeal Molasses Bread 194
Old-Fashioned Brown Bread 197
Orange Coffee Cake Ring 201
Parmesan-Ranch Pan Rolls 193
Perfect Dinner Rolls 199
Potato Pan Rolls 195
Prosciutto Breadsticks 194
Rosemary Cheddar Muffins 190
Rustic Country Bread 196
Sour Cream Blueberry Muffins 198
Virginia Box Bread 199

BREAKFAST RECIPES
BREADS
Apple Sausage Puffs 12
Cappuccino Chip Muffins 16
Chocolate-Orange Scones 19
Fluffy Biscuit Muffins 22
Ham 'n' Swiss Rolls 16
Kids' Favorite Blueberry Muffins 18
Pull-Apart Caramel Coffee Cake 8
Sausage Cheese Biscuits 10
Scrambled Egg Poppers 8
EGG MAIN DISHES
Breakfast Bread Bowls 23
Cheddar Broccoli Quiche 16
Cheese Souffles 20
Corned Beef 'n' Cheese Strata 20
Green 'n' Gold Egg Bake 13
Meal in a Muffin Pan 9
Scrambled Egg Poppers 8
Spanish Omelets 19
Weekend Breakfast Bake 14
MEATS
Apple Sausage Puffs 12
Glazed Bacon 18
Maple-Glazed Sausages 14
Spicy Sausage Patties 17
OATS
Blueberry Oatmeal 18
Peanut Butter Banana Oatmeal 14
OTHER MAIN DISH
Sausage Hash Skillet 13
PANCAKES, WAFFLES
& FRENCH TOAST
Banana Chip Pancakes 12
Jam 'n' Cream French Toast 10
Marmalade French Toast Sandwiches . . . 15
Nutty Waffle Sandwiches 22
SIDE DISHES
Creamy Peaches 9
Loaded Breakfast Potatoes 17
YOGURT
Apple Yogurt Parfaits 20
Berry Yogurt Cups 23
Cherry Yogurt 10

BROCCOLI
Broccoli Casserole 169
Broccoli Cheddar Spread 31
Broccoli Saute 165
Broccoli with Asiago 185

Greek Deli Kabobs 40
Ham & Broccoli Pasta 98
Ramen Broccoli Soup 53

BROWNIES
Coconut Brownies 239
Gold Rush Brownies 233
Walnut Brownies 234

BRUSSELS SPROUTS
Bacon-Parmesan Brussels Sprouts 180
Roasted Cauliflower & Brussels
   Sprouts 164

CAKE MIX
Cherry Marble Cake 211
Chewy Caramel Bars 241
Chocolate Peanut Butter Cake 216
Cowabunga Root Beer Cupcakes 218
Fudgy Mint Cookies 238
Golden Pound Cake 213
Heavenly Angel Food Cake 226
Minister's Delight 227
Peppermint Angel Roll 223
Raspberry Oatmeal Bars 239
Surprise Spice Cake 220
Walnut Brownies 234

CAKES, TORTES & CUPCAKES
Banana-Chip Mini Cupcakes 205
Cherry Marble Cake 211
Chocolate Peanut Butter Cake 216
Cowabunga Root Beer Cupcakes 218
Golden Pound Cake 213
Heavenly Angel Food Cake 226
Lemon Ladyfinger Dessert 220
Pineapple-Caramel Sponge Cakes 208
Shoofly Cupcakes 211
Strawberry Cake 206
Surprise Spice Cake 220
Peppermint Angel Roll 223

CANDIES
Caramel Cashew Clusters 241
Crunchy Chocolate Mint Balls 243
Dark Chocolate Orange Truffles 243
Dark Chocolate Raspberry Fudge 236
Go Nuts! Coconut Caramels 234
Hawaiian Turtle Cups 235
Jelly Bean Bark 239
Magic Wands 243
Nutter Butter Truffles 234
Pecan Candy Clusters 233
Pinwheel Mints 235
Soft Chewy Caramels 233
Toffee Candy 232
Tumbleweeds 236

CANDY COATING
Chocolate-Covered Bacon 26
Jelly Bean Bark 239
Nutter Butter Truffles 234
Sweet & Salty Popcorn 33
Yummy Cracker Snacks 231

CARAMEL
Apple Pie a La Mode 225
Caramel Apple and Brie Skewers 29
Caramel Cashew Clusters 241
Chewy Caramel Bars 241
Chocolate-Nut Caramel Tart 209
Go Nuts! Coconut Caramels 234
Hawaiian Turtle Cups 235
Pecan Candy Clusters 233
Pineapple-Caramel Sponge Cakes 208
Pull-Apart Caramel Coffee Cake 8
Soft Chewy Caramels 233

CARROTS
Chive Buttered Carrots 166
Roasted Carrots with Thyme 182

CAULIFLOWER
Garlic-Parmesan Mashed
   Cauliflower 187
Roasted Cauliflower & Brussels
   Sprouts 164
Three-Vegetable Pasta Sauce 147

CHEESE
(also see Cream Cheese)
APPETIZERS
Broccoli Cheddar Spread 31
Caramel Apple and Brie Skewers 29
Cheese Straws 32
Cheese-Stuffed Meatball Sliders 35
Chutney-Topped Brie 30
Deep-Fried Cheese Bites 34
Foolproof Mushrooms 36
Garlic Toast Pizzas 46
Greek Deli Kabobs 40
Mini Phyllo Tacos 30
Mozzarella Sticks 31
Polenta Parmigiana 44
White Chocolate Brie Cups 42
BREADS
Bacon Pull-Apart Bread 192
Basil Parmesan Puffs 200
Cheddar-Parm Loaf 195
Parmesan-Ranch Pan Rolls 193
Rosemary Cheddar Muffins 190
BREAKFAST RECIPES
Cheddar Broccoli Quiche 16
Cheese Souffles 20
Corned Beef 'n' Cheese Strata 20
Green 'n' Gold Egg Bake 13
Ham 'n' Swiss Rolls 16
Sausage Cheese Biscuits 10
Spanish Omelets 19
Weekend Breakfast Bake 14
MAIN DISHES
Artichoke Blue Cheese Fettuccine 142
Bacon-Swiss Pork Chops 96
Baked Parmesan Flounder 127
Blue Cheese-Stuffed Steaks for Two 82
Chicken Caesar Florentine 114
Chicken Enchilada Bake 119
Greek Grilled Catfish 130
Ham & Sun-Dried Tomato Alfredo 103

CHEESE
MAIN DISHES *(continued)*
Jazzy Mac 'n' Cheese 145
Lasagna Rolls 74
Mashed Potato Hot Dish 87
Mediterranean Stuffed Chicken Breasts 118
Personal Margherita Pizzas 144
Polenta Lasagna. 142
Ravioli Casserole 146
Spinach Pizza 147
Spinach-Artichoke Rigatoni. 145
Tomato Spinach Spirals 143

SALADS & SALAD DRESSINGS
Balsamic Asiago Salad. 158
Chunky Blue Cheese Dressing 156
Dilled Potatoes with Feta. 157
Fresh Mozzarella Tomato Salad. 158
Pesto Tortellini Salad 159

SANDWICHES
Chicken Parmesan Patty Melts 54
Ham and Swiss Stromboli 59
Mozzarella Ham Stromboli 57
Mushroom Swiss Burgers 53
Pesto Grilled Cheese Sandwiches. 60

SIDE DISHES
Broccoli with Asiago 185
Cheddar Spirals 183
Garlic-Parmesan Mashed Cauliflower . . 187

CHERRIES
Cherry Yogurt. 10
County Fair Cherry Pie 205

CHICKEN
(also see Cornish Hens)
African Chicken & Sweet Potatoes. 110
Balsamic Chicken with Roasted
    Tomatoes 108
Balsamic-Glazed Chicken Wings 36
BBQ & Ranch Chicken Pizza 116
Cheesy Bow Tie Chicken. 121
Chicken & Vegetable Kabobs 113
Chicken Caesar Florentine. 114
Chicken Enchilada Bake. 119
Chicken Parmesan Patty Melts. 54
Chicken Tortellini Skillet 109
Chicken with Shallot Sauce 115
Crispy Baked Chicken. 112
Crispy Buffalo Chicken Roll-Ups
    for Two 121
Greek Lemon Chicken. 117
Grilled Brown Sugar-Mustard Chicken . . 117
Honey Hoisin Chicken & Potatoes 115
Mango Chutney Chicken Curry 123
Mediterranean Stuffed Chicken Breasts. 118
No-Fuss Chicken 110
Oregano Roasting Chicken 114
Pesto-Olive Chicken 123
Pretzel-Crusted Chicken. 109
Quick Ravioli & Spinach Soup. 69
Raspberry Chicken 113
Simple Chicken Soup 57
Smoky Gouda & Chicken Sandwiches. . . . 55

Southwest Chicken. 122
Tender Barbecued Chicken 112
Zesty Chicken Soft Tacos 111

CHOCOLATE
(also see Candy Coating; White Chocolate)
Banana-Chip Mini Cupcakes 205
Chocolate Biscuit Puffs 192
Chocolate-Covered Bacon. 26
Chocolate Mint Apple Fondue 44
Chocolate-Orange Scones. 19
Chocolate Peanut Butter Cake. 216
Chocolate Peanut Treats. 244
Coconut Brownies 239
Crunchy Chocolate Mint Balls. 243
Dark Chocolate Orange Truffles 243
Dark Chocolate Raspberry Fudge 236
Frozen Hot Chocolate 222
Fudgy Mint Cookies 238
Gold Rush Brownies 233
Heavenly Angel Food Cake 226
Hot Fudge Sauce 225
Ice Cream Sandwich Cake 222
Mocha-Fudge Ice Cream Dessert 219
Peanut Butter Chocolate Pretzels. 43
Pecan Candy Clusters 233
Peppermint Angel Roll. 223
Pots de Creme 224
S'Moreos. 236
Toffee Candy. 232

CHUTNEY
African Chicken & Sweet Potatoes. 110
Chutney-Topped Brie. 30
Mango Chutney Chicken Curry 123

COCONUT & COCONUT MILK
Go Nuts! Coconut Caramels 234
Orange Coffee Cake Ring. 201
Pina Colada Fruit Dip 32
Polka-Dot Macaroons 240
Thai Shrimp Pasta 129
Tropical Rainbow Dessert. 215

COFFEE
Cappuccino Chip Muffins. 16
Java Roast Beef 76
Mocha-Fudge Ice Cream Dessert 219

COLESLAW MIX
Easy Caesar Coleslaw. 153
Poppy Seed Slaw 154

CONDENSED SOUP
Broccoli Casserole. 169
Cheddar Broccoli Quiche. 16
Cheddar Spirals 183
Easy Skillet Supper 72
Hot Dog Bean Soup 59
Mashed Potato Hot Dish 87
Potato Chowder. 56
Quick Clam Chowder. 63
Quick Tater Tot Bake 81
Save a Penny Casserole. 87

Simple Chicken Soup 57
Simple Shepherd's Pie 78
Surprise Spice Cake 220
Tex-Mex Pasta 82
Weekend Breakfast Bake 14

CONDIMENTS
All-Day Apple Butter. 179
Creamy Herb Spread 171
Freezer Raspberry Sauce 171
Garlic Lemon Butter. 187
Maple-Honey Cranberry Sauce 169
Pesto 184
Quick & Easy Honey Mustard. 167
Raspberry Butter 184
Spicy Olive Relish. 176

COOKIES
Cranberry Pecan Cookies. 232
Fudgy Mint Cookies 238
Ice Cream Kolachkes 245
Pecan Roll-Ups 230
Pecan Sandies Cookies 240
Polka-Dot Macaroons 240
S'Moreos. 236
Scotch Shortbread Cookies. 242
Toffee Meringue Drops. 242
Yummy Cracker Snacks. 231

CORN
Cheddar Creamed Corn 173
Easy Skillet Supper 72
Fiesta Corn Chip Salad. 161
Sauteed Corn with Tomatoes & Basil . . . 174
Southwest Chicken. 122
Southwestern Corn Salad. 152

CORNED BEEF
Corned Beef 'n' Cheese Strata 20
Meal in a Muffin Pan. 9

CORNISH HENS
Glazed Cornish Hens 118

CORNMEAL & CORN BREAD MIX
(also see Polenta)
Meal in a Muffin Pan. 9
Polenta Chili Casserole 144

CRANBERRIES
Brisket with Cranberry Gravy 76
Cranberry Couscous 180
Cranberry Pecan Cookies. 232
Cranberry Turkey Breast with Gravy . . . 119
Cranberry-Apricot Pork Tenderloins . . . 100
Fun-on-the-Run Snack Mix. 44
Maple-Honey Cranberry Sauce 169
Poppy Seed Slaw 154
Roasted Turkey with Maple Cranberry
    Glaze. 120
Turkey-Cranberry Bagels 68

CREAM CHEESE

Amaretto-Peach Cheese Spread 32
Baked Crab Rangoon 27
Dreamy S'more Pie 214
Green Onion Bagel Dip 35
Jam 'n' Cream French Toast 10
Lime Tartlets 215
Marmalade French Toast Sandwiches 15
Nutter Butter Truffles 234
Pecan Roll-Ups 230
Pina Colada Fruit Dip 32
Pinwheel Mints 235
Raspberry Swirled Cheesecake Pie 223

DESSERT SAUCES

Freezer Raspberry Sauce 171
Hot Fudge Sauce 225
Peppermint Stick Sauce 210
Ruby-Red Strawberry Sauce 208

DESSERTS

(also see Bars; Brownies; Cakes, Tortes &
Cupcakes; Candies; Cookies; Dessert Sauces;
Frozen Desserts; Pies & Tarts)
Arroz con Leche 207
Berries with Vanilla Custard 210
Crunchy Amaretto Peach Cobbler 224
Easy Elephant Ears 216
Irish Cream Custards 219
Mandarin Trifles 214
Minister's Delight 227
Outrageous Peanut Butter Sauce 218
Peach Almond Dessert 209
Peanut Butter Cup Trifle 210
Poached Pears with Raspberry Sauce . . . 213
Pots de Creme 224
Rhubarb Fool with Strawberries 212
Strawberry-Hazelnut Meringue
  Shortcakes 204
Tropical Rainbow Dessert 215

EGGS

Berries with Vanilla Custard 210
Breakfast Bread Bowls 23
Cheddar Broccoli Quiche 16
Cheese Souffles 20
Corned Beef 'n' Cheese Strata 20
Green 'n' Gold Egg Bake 13
Irish Cream Custards 219
Marmalade French Toast Sandwiches 15
Meal in a Muffin Pan 9
Peach Almond Dessert 209
Scrambled Egg Poppers 8
Simple Lettuce Salad 157
Spaetzle Dumplings 168
Spanish Omelets 19
Strawberry-Hazelnut Meringue
  Shortcakes 204
Toffee Meringue Drops 242
Weekend Breakfast Bake 14
Zucchini-Parmesan Bake 148

FISH

(also see Seafood)
Bacon Honey Walleye 138
Baked Italian Tilapia 138
Baked Parmesan Flounder 127
Creole Baked Tilapia 131
Crumb-Coated Red Snapper 130
Flounder Florentine 135
Greek Grilled Catfish 130
Grilled Tuna Steaks 135
Lemon-Garlic Salmon Steaks 127
Orange-Pecan Salmon 136
Pesto Halibut 136
Pistachio Baked Salmon 139
Salmon with Lemon-Dill Butter 129
Tarragon Flounder 132
Tasty Maple-Glazed Salmon 133
Teriyaki Mahi Mahi 126
Thai Barbecued Salmon 131
Tomato Salmon Bake 134
Tuna Alfredo 133

FRENCH FRIES

Cheesy Chili Fries 143
Garlic-Chive Baked Fries 168
Rosemary Sweet Potato Fries 182

FROZEN BREAD DOUGH

Caramelized Onion Breadsticks 197
Italian Meatball Buns 29
Parmesan-Ranch Pan Rolls 193
Scrambled Egg Poppers 8
Frozen Desserts
Apple Pie a La Mode 225
Dreamy S'more Pie 214
Frozen Hot Chocolate 222
Ice Cream Sandwich Cake 222
Lemon-Berry Ice Cream Pie 216
Mexican Ice Cream 206
Mocha-Fudge Ice Cream Dessert 219
Peppermint Angel Roll 223
Strawberry-Rosemary Yogurt Pops 221
Toffee Cream Pie 227

FROZEN DESSERTS

Apple Pie a La Mode 225
Dreamy S'more Pie 214
Frozen Hot Chocolate 222
Ice Cream Sandwich Cake 222
Lemon-Berry Ice Cream Pie 216
Mexican Ice Cream 206
Mocha-Fudge Ice Cream Dessert 219
Peppermint Angel Roll 223
Strawberry-Rosemary Yogurt Pops 221
Toffee Cream Pie 227

FROZEN MEATBALLS

Easy Stuffed Shells 78
Italian Meatball Buns 29
Marmalade Meatballs 39
Vegetable Meatball Soup 66

FRUIT

(also see specific listings; Fruit Curd)
Arroz con Leche 207
Cranberry-Apricot Pork Tenderloins 100
Mandarin Trifles 214
Mom's Tangerine Iced Tea 38
Savory Stuffed Figs 47

FRUIT CURD

Lemon Ladyfinger Dessert 220
Lemon-Berry Ice Cream Pie 216
Lime Tartlets 215

GELATIN

Applesauce-Raspberry Gelatin Mold 153
Green Flop Jell-O 159
Rhubarb Pear Gelatin 156
Tropical Rainbow Dessert 215

GREEN BEANS

Easy Beans & Potatoes with Bacon 176
Kielbasa Skillet 94
Mashed Potato Hot Dish 87
Snappy Green Beans 186
Zesty Garlic Green Beans 178

GREEN ONIONS

Baked Crab Rangoon 27
Green Onion Bagel Dip 35

GRILLED RECIPES

Bacon Honey Walleye 138
BBQ Hot Dog & Potato Packs 98
Burger Americana 64
Buttery Grilled Shrimp 132
Chicken & Vegetable Kabobs 113
Chipotle-Raspberry Pork Chops 101
Greek Grilled Catfish 130
Greek Lemon Chicken 117
Grilled Brown Sugar-Mustard Chicken . . . 117
Grilled Flank Steak 80
Grilled Jerk Chops 93
Grilled Lobster Tails 128
Grilled Seasoned Bratwurst 52
Grilled Shrimp with Spicy-Sweet Sauce . . . 40
Grilled Tuna Steaks 135
Herbed Potato Packs 165
Marinated Pork Medallions 91
Orange-Glazed Ham Steaks 90
Rosemary Pork Tenderloin 103
Savory Stuffed Figs 47
Southwest Steak 84
Spicy Grilled Eggplant 178

GROUND BEEF

Black Bean and Beef Tostadas 85
Burger Americana 64
Cheeseburger Pockets 72
Easy Skillet Supper 72
Fast Beef and Rice 87
Lasagna Rolls 74
Louisiana-Style Taco Soup 50
Mashed Potato Hot Dish 87

GROUND BEEF
(continued)
Mexican Stuffed Peppers 73
Mini Phyllo Tacos 30
Mom's Sloppy Tacos 77
Mushroom Swiss Burgers 53
Pepper Jack Meat Loaf 83
Pizza Crescent Bake 77
Potato Leek Skillet 81
Quick Tater Tot Bake 81
Save a Penny Casserole 87
Simple Shepherd's Pie 78
Southwest Beef Pie 74
Spicy Meat Loaf 86
Tex-Mex Pasta 82
Veggie Beef Patties 81

HAM
(also see Prosciutto)
Ham & Broccoli Pasta 98
Ham & Noodles with Veggies 105
Ham & Pickle Wraps 47
Ham & Spinach Couscous 96
Ham & Sun-Dried Tomato Alfredo 103
Ham & Sweet Potato Packets 102
Ham 'n' Swiss Rolls 16
Ham and Swiss Stromboli 59
Ham with Ruby-Red Glaze 92
Holiday Baked Ham 99
Honey-Glazed Spiral Ham 91
Loaded Breakfast Potatoes 17
Maple-Peach Glazed Ham 94
Mozzarella Ham Stromboli 57
Orange-Glazed Ham Steaks 90
Pineapple Ham Steaks 104
Pretzel-Crusted Chicken 109

HONEY
Bacon Honey Walleye 138
Honey-Apple Turkey Breast 109
Honey Cinnamon Milk 40
Honey-Glazed Spiral Ham 91
Honey Hoisin Chicken & Potatoes 115
Honey Lemon Schnitzel 104
Honey-Spice Acorn Squash 173
Lime-Marinated Fish 134
Maple-Honey Cranberry Sauce 169
Mexican Ice Cream 206
Quick & Easy Honey Mustard 167

HOT DOGS
BBQ Hot Dog & Potato Packs 98
Hot Dog Bean Soup 59
Pigs in a Blanket 67

JAM, JELLY, MARMALADE & PRESERVES
Amaretto-Peach Cheese Spread 32
Baked Pork Chops with Apple Slices 90
Berry Vinaigrette 153
Chipotle Pomegranate Pulled Pork 69
Chipotle-Raspberry Pork Chops 101
Grilled PBJ Sandwiches 63
Jam 'n' Cream French Toast 10

Maple-Peach Glazed Ham 94
Marmalade French Toast Sandwiches 15
Marmalade Meatballs 39
No-Fuss Chicken 110
Orange-Glazed Ham Steaks 90
Orange-Pecan Salmon 136
Orange Turkey Croissants 55
Peach Almond Dessert 209
Poached Pears with Raspberry Sauce . . . 213
Pork Chops with Apricot Sauce 105
Raspberry Chicken 113
Raspberry Oatmeal Bars 239
Strawberry-Rosemary Yogurt Pops 221
Turkey & Apricot Wraps 51

KALE
Kale Salad 152
Turkey Sausage Butternut & Kale Soup . . 62

LEMON
Berry Berry Lemonade 37
Garlic Lemon Butter 187
Greek Lemon Chicken 117
Honey Lemon Schnitzel 104
Lemon Dijon Dressing 154
Lemon Garlic Hummus 27
Lemon-Garlic Salmon Steaks 127
Lemon Ladyfinger Dessert 220
Lemony Cooler 28
Pistachio Baked Salmon 139
Salmon with Lemon-Dill Butter 129
Strawberry Lemonade Smoothie 43

LETTUCE
Balsamic Asiago Salad 158
BLT Salad with Pasta 156
Chipotle BLT Wraps 61
Simple Lettuce Salad 157

LIME
Grilled Jerk Chops 93
Lime-Marinated Fish 134
Luscious Lime Slush .34
Southwest Steak 84

LIQUEUR & LIQUOR
Amaretto-Peach Cheese Spread 32
Crunchy Amaretto Peach Cobbler 224
Dark Chocolate Raspberry Fudge 236
Irish Cream Custards 219
Luscious Lime Slush 34
Raspberry-Swirled Lemon Milk Shakes . . . 45

MAPLE
Maple-Glazed Sausages 14
Maple-Honey Cranberry Sauce 169
Maple-Peach Glazed Ham 94
New England Butternut Squash 181
Roasted Turkey with Maple Cranberry
    Glaze 120
Tasty Maple-Glazed Salmon 133

MARSHMALLOWS & MARSHMALLOW CREME
Chocolate Peanut Butter Cake 216
Dreamy S'more Pie 214
Heavenly Angel Food Cake 226
Peppermint Stick Sauce 210
Pina Colada Fruit Dip 32
Rhubarb Pear Gelatin 156
S'Moreos 236
White Chocolate Cereal Bars 245
Yummy Cracker Snacks 231

MEAT LOAF & MEATBALLS
Cheese-Stuffed Meatball Sliders 35
Easy Stuffed Shells 78
Italian Meatball Buns 29
Marmalade Meatballs 39
Pepper Jack Meat Loaf 83
Spicy Meat Loaf 86
Vegetable Meatball Soup 66

MEATLESS
Artichoke Blue Cheese Fettuccine 142
Asparagus Souffle 146
Cheddar Broccoli Quiche 16
Cheese Souffles 20
Cheesy Chili Fries 143
Grilled PBJ Sandwiches 63
Jazzy Mac 'n' Cheese 145
Marmalade French Toast Sandwiches 15
Nutty Cheese Tortellini 145
Nutty Waffle Sandwiches 22
Peppered Portobello Penne 143
Personal Margherita Pizzas 144
Pesto Grilled Cheese Sandwiches 60
Pesto Portobello Pizzas 149
Polenta Chili Casserole 144
Polenta Lasagna 142
Ravioli Casserole 146
Sage & Browned Butter Ravioli 149
Simply Elegant Tomato Soup 64
Spinach-Artichoke Rigatoni 145
Spinach Pizza 147
Sweet Potato & Bean Quesadillas 146
Three-Vegetable Pasta Sauce 147
Tomato & Avocado Sandwiches 58
Tomato Spinach Spirals 143
Zucchini-Parmesan Bake 148

MINT
Chocolate Mint Apple Fondue 44
Crunchy Chocolate Mint Balls 243
Fudgy Mint Cookies 238
Minty Watermelon-Cucumber Salad 155
Peppermint Angel Roll 223
Peppermint Stick Sauce 210
Pinwheel Mints 235

MOLASSES
Oatmeal Molasses Bread 194
Old-Fashioned Brown Bread 197
Shoofly Cupcakes 211

MUSHROOMS

Creamed Spinach and Mushrooms 186
Foolproof Mushrooms 36
Mushroom & Peas Rice Pilaf............ 174
Mushroom Swiss Burgers............... 53
Pesto-Olive Chicken 123
Peppered Portobello Penne 143
Pesto Portobello Pizzas................. 149
Sausage Hash Skillet.................. 13
Sauteed Garlic Mushrooms............. 176
Sirloin with Mushroom Sauce........... 83
Wild Rice and Mushroom Soup......... 67

NOODLES

Asian Shrimp Soup 51
Ham & Noodles with Veggies.......... 105
Ramen Broccoli Soup 53
Thai Shrimp Pasta 129

NUTELLA

Chocolate-Nut Caramel Tart............ 209
Dreamy S'more Pie 214
Nutty Waffle Sandwiches............... 22

NUTS

(also see Nutella; Peanuts & Peanut Butter)

Candied Pecans 37
Caramel Cashew Clusters............... 241
Chewy Caramel Bars 241
Chocolate-Nut Caramel Tart............ 209
Cranberry Pecan Cookies.............. 232
Crunchy Amaretto Peach Cobbler 224
Dilled Peas with Walnuts............... 164
Hawaiian Turtle Cups................... 235
Italian Meatball Buns................... 29
Nutty Cheese Tortellini 145
Orange-Pecan Salmon.................. 136
Orange Turkey Croissants 55
Peach Almond Dessert 209
Pecan Candy Clusters 233
Pecan Roll-Ups 230
Pecan Sandies Cookies 240
Pistachio Baked Salmon 139
Poppy Seed Slaw 154
Savory Stuffed Figs.....................47
Strawberry-Hazelnut Meringue
  Shortcakes........................... 204
Toffee Candy.......................... 232
Toffee Meringue Drops................. 242
Walnut Brownies...................... 234

OATS

Blueberry Oatmeal 18
Oatmeal Molasses Bread 194
Old-Fashioned Brown Bread........... 197
Peanut Butter Banana Oatmeal 14
Raspberry Oatmeal Bars............... 239

OLIVES

Pesto-Olive Chicken 123
Spicy Olive Relish..................... 176

ONIONS

(also see Green Onions)

Caramelized Onion Breadsticks......... 197
Mediterranean Orange Salad 158
No-Fuss Avocado Onion Salad......... 161
Pickled Sweet Onions 175
Sausage Hash Skillet....................13

ORANGE

Chocolate-Orange Scones............... 19
Dark Chocolate Orange Truffles 243
Mandarin Pork and Wild Rice 97
Mandarin Trifles 214
Mediterranean Orange Salad 158

OREO COOKIES

Mocha-Fudge Ice Cream Dessert 219
S'Moreos.............................. 236

PANCAKE MIX

Chocolate-Orange Scones............... 19
Kids' Favorite Blueberry Muffins 18

PASTA

(also see Noodles)

Artichoke Blue Cheese Fettuccine 142
BLT Salad with Pasta.................. 156
Bow Ties with Asparagus and
  Prosciutto............................ 93
Cheddar Spirals 183
Cheesy Bow Tie Chicken............... 121
Chicken Tortellini Skillet 109
Cranberry Couscous 180
Easy Stuffed Shells 78
Ham & Broccoli Pasta 98
Ham & Spinach Couscous 96
Ham & Sun-Dried Tomato Alfredo...... 103
Jazzy Mac 'n' Cheese 145
Lasagna Rolls.......................... 74
Nutty Cheese Tortellini 145
Peppered Portobello Penne 143
Pesto Tortellini Salad 159
Quick Ravioli & Spinach Soup........... 69
Ranch Turkey Pasta Dinner 108
Ravioli Carbonara...................... 99
Ravioli Casserole 146
Sage & Browned Butter Ravioli 149
Shrimp Pasta Alfredo 137
Spaghetti with Creamy White Clam
  Sauce.............................. 132
Spinach-Artichoke Rigatoni 145
Tex-Mex Pasta......................... 82
Tomato Spinach Spirals................ 143

PEACHES

Creamy Peaches......................... 9
Ham & Sweet Potato Packets........... 102
Smoky Gouda & Chicken Sandwiches.... 55

PEANUTS & PEANUT BUTTER

African Chicken & Sweet Potatoes...... 110
Chocolate Peanut Butter Cake.......... 216
Chocolate Peanut Treats.............. 244
Fun-on-the-Run Snack Mix.............. 44

Go Nuts! Coconut Caramels 234
Grilled PBJ Sandwiches................. 63
Ice Cream Sandwich Cake 222
Nutty Waffle Sandwiches............... 22
Outrageous Peanut Butter Sauce 218
Peanut Butter Banana Oatmeal 14
Peanut Butter Chocolate Pretzels....... 43
S'Moreos.............................. 236
Tumbleweeds 236
Yummy Cracker Snacks................. 231

PEARS

Poached Pears with Raspberry Sauce ... 213
Rhubarb Pear Gelatin 156

PEAS

Dilled Peas with Walnuts............... 164
Gingered Snow Peas.................... 181
Mushroom & Peas Rice Pilaf........... 174
Shrimp Pasta Alfredo 137

PEPPERS

Chipotle-Raspberry Pork Chops 101
Easy Black Bean Salsa................. 39
Mexican Stuffed Peppers 73
Pepper Shooters 34
Southwestern Corn Salad.............. 152
Spicy French Dip 50
Spicy Olive Relish..................... 176

PESTO

Cheese-Stuffed Meatball Sliders 35
Italian-Style Crescents 192
Pepper Shooters 34
Pesto................................ 184
Pesto Grilled Cheese Sandwiches 60
Pesto Halibut......................... 136
Pesto-Olive Chicken 123
Pesto Portobello Pizzas................. 149
Pesto Tortellini Salad 159

PICKLES

Crisp Sweet Pickles..................... 173
Ham & Pickle Wraps 47
Pickled Sweet Onions 175

PIE FILLING

Apple Pie a La Mode................... 225
Cherry Marble Cake 211
Crunchy Amaretto Peach Cobbler 224
Minister's Delight..................... 227
Raspberry Swirled Cheesecake Pie...... 223

PIES & TARTS

Chocolate-Nut Caramel Tart............ 209
County Fair Cherry Pie 205
Lime Tartlets 215
Strawberry Pies 208
White Chocolate Mousse Tarts 224
Raspberry Swirled Cheesecake Pie...... 223

PINEAPPLE
Grilled Jerk Chops. 93
Hawaiian Barbecue Beans 166
Hawaiian Turtle Cups 235
Pineapple-Caramel Sponge Cakes. 208
Pineapple Ham Steaks. 104

PIZZA SAUCE
Garlic Toast Pizzas. 46
Personal Margherita Pizzas 144
Pizza Crescent Bake 77

POLENTA
Polenta Lasagna. 142
Polenta Parmigiana 44

PORK
(also see Bacon; Ham; Hot Dogs;
Prosciutto; Sausage)
Bacon-Swiss Pork Chops 96
Baked Pork Chops with Apple Slices 90
Carnitas Tacos. 92
Chipotle Pomegranate Pulled Pork. 69
Chipotle-Raspberry Pork Chops 101
Cranberry-Apricot Pork Tenderloins 100
Grilled Jerk Chops. 93
Honey Lemon Schnitzel 104
Mandarin Pork and Wild Rice 97
Marinated Pork Medallions 91
Pork Chops with Apricot Sauce 105
Root Beer Pulled Pork Sandwiches. 58
Rosemary Pork Tenderloin. 103
Slow-Cooked Ribs 102
Slow Cooker Spareribs 94
Southern Skillet Chops 101
Tender Teriyaki Pork. 97

POTATOES
BBQ Hot Dog & Potato Packs 98
Browned Butter Red Potatoes 172
Dilled Potatoes with Feta 157
Easy Beans & Potatoes with Bacon 176
Easy Skillet Supper 72
Garlic-Chive Baked Fries 168
Herbed Potato Packs. 165
Honey Hoisin Chicken & Potatoes 115
Loaded Breakfast Potatoes 17
Mashed Potato Hot Dish 87
Potato Chowder. 56
Potato Gnocchi 175
Potato Leek Skillet. 81
Potato Pan Rolls. 195
Ranch Potato Cubes. 169
Sausage Hash Skillet. 13
Scalloped Shrimp and Potatoes. 139

PROSCIUTTO
Bow Ties with Asparagus and Prosciutto . . 93
Prosciutto Breadsticks. 194

PUDDING MIX
Golden Pound Cake 213
Peanut Butter Cup Trifle. 210
Toffee Cream Pie. 227

RASPBERRIES
Banana Split Fruit Salad. 159
Berries with Vanilla Custard. 210
Freezer Raspberry Sauce 171
Raspberry Butter 184
Raspberry-Swirled Lemon Milk Shakes 45

REFRIGERATED BISCUITS
Bacon Pull-Apart Bread. 192
Cheeseburger Pockets. 72
Chocolate Biscuit Puffs 192
Pull-Apart Caramel Coffee Cake 8
Sausage Cheese Biscuits. 10

REFRIGERATED CRESCENT ROLLS
Apple Sausage Puffs 12
BBQ & Ranch Chicken Pizza 116
Fresh Herb Flatbread. 200
Ham 'n' Swiss Rolls 16
Italian-Style Crescents 192
Pigs in a Blanket 67
Pizza Crescent Bake 77

RHUBARB
Rhubarb Fool with Strawberries 212
Rhubarb Pear Gelatin. 156

RICE
Arroz con Leche. 207
Gumbo in a Jiffy. 56
Kielbasa Skillet. 94
Louisiana-Style Taco Soup 50
Mandarin Pork and Wild Rice 97
Mushroom & Peas Rice Pilaf 174
No-Fuss Chicken 110
Simple Spanish Rice 170
Wild Rice and Mushroom Soup 67

SALADS & SALAD DRESSINGS
Applesauce-Raspberry Gelatin Mold 153
Balsamic Arugula Salad 160
Balsamic Asiago Salad 158
Banana Split Fruit Salad. 159
Berry Vinaigrette 153
BLT Salad with Pasta. 156
Buttermilk Salad Dressing 154
Chunky Blue Cheese Dressing 156
Dilled Potatoes with Feta 157
Easy Caesar Coleslaw. 153
Fiesta Corn Chip Salad. 161
Fresh Mozzarella Tomato Salad 158
Green Flop Jell-O. 159
Kale Salad 152
Lemon Dijon Dressing 154
Low-Fat Tangy Tomato Dressing. 160
Mediterranean Orange Salad 158
Minty Watermelon-Cucumber Salad 155
No-Fuss Avocado Onion Salad. 161
Pesto Tortellini Salad 159
Poppy Seed Slaw 154
Rhubarb Pear Gelatin. 156
Simple Lettuce Salad 157

SOUTHWESTERN (partial)
Southwestern Corn Salad. 152
Super Spinach Salad. 161

SALSA
Easy Black Bean Salsa. 39
Southwest Chicken 122
Tex-Mex Pasta 82

SANDWICHES
Burger Americana. 64
Chicken Parmesan Patty Melts. 54
Chipotle BLT Wraps 61
Chipotle Pomegranate Pulled Pork. 69
Grilled PBJ Sandwiches 63
Grilled Seasoned Bratwurst. 52
Ham and Swiss Stromboli 59
Mozzarella Ham Stromboli. 57
Mushroom Swiss Burgers. 53
Orange Turkey Croissants 55
Pesto Grilled Cheese Sandwiches 60
Pigs in a Blanket 67
Root Beer Pulled Pork Sandwiches. 58
Sausage & Spinach Calzones. 62
Shredded Turkey Sandwiches. 56
Smoky Gouda & Chicken Sandwiches. . . . 55
Spicy French Dip 50
Tex-Mex Shredded Beef Sandwiches 66
Tomato & Avocado Sandwiches 58
Turkey & Apricot Wraps. 51
Turkey-Cranberry Bagels 68

SAUSAGE
Apple Sausage Puffs 12
Cheese-Stuffed Meatball Sliders 35
Effortless Egg Rolls 42
Garlic Toast Pizzas. 46
Greek Deli Kabobs. 40
Grilled Seasoned Bratwurst. 52
Gumbo in a Jiffy. 56
Homemade Italian Turkey Sausage. 122
Kielbasa Skillet. 94
Maple-Glazed Sausages. 14
Sausage & Spinach Calzones. 62
Sausage Cheese Biscuits. 10
Sausage Hash Skillet. 13
Spicy Sausage Patties. 17
Spinach Sausage Soup. 54
Turkey Sausage Butternut & Kale Soup . . 62
Weekend Breakfast Bake 14

SEAFOOD
(also see Fish)
Asian Shrimp Soup 51
Baked Crab Rangoon 27
Buttery Grilled Shrimp. 132
Grilled Lobster Tails 128
Grilled Shrimp with Spicy-Sweet Sauce. . . 40
Quick Clam Chowder. 63
Scalloped Shrimp and Potatoes. 139
Scallops in Sage Cream 126
Shrimp Pasta Alfredo. 137
Spaghetti with Creamy White Clam
   Sauce 132
Thai Shrimp Pasta 129

SIDE DISHES

BEANS
Hawaiian Barbecue Beans 166

DUMPLINGS
Potato Gnocchi 175
Spaetzle Dumplings 168

PASTA
Cheddar Spirals 183
Cranberry Couscous 180

POTATOES
Browned Butter Red Potatoes 172
Garlic-Chive Baked Fries 168
Herbed Potato Packs 165
Potato Gnocchi 175
Ranch Potato Cubes 169

RICE
Mushroom & Peas Rice Pilaf 174
Simple Spanish Rice 170

STUFFING
Apple Stuffing 181

VEGETABLES
Bacon-Parmesan Brussels Sprouts 180
Broccoli Casserole 169
Broccoli Saute 165
Broccoli with Asiago 185
Broiled Tomatoes with Artichokes 170
Candied Sweet Potatoes 185
Cheddar Creamed Corn 173
Chinese-Style Zucchini 167
Chive Buttered Carrots 166
Creamed Spinach and Mushrooms 186
Crumb-Coated Tomatoes 183
Dilled Peas with Walnuts 164
Easy Beans & Potatoes with Bacon 176
Garlic-Parmesan Mashed Cauliflower . . 174
Gingered Snow Peas 181
Honey-Spice Acorn Squash 173
New England Butternut Squash 181
Roasted Carrots with Thyme 182
Roasted Cauliflower & Brussels Sprouts 164
Rosemary Sweet Potato Fries 182
Sauteed Corn with Tomatoes & Basil . . 174
Sauteed Garlic Mushrooms 176
Sesame Asparagus 187
Snappy Green Beans 186
Spicy Grilled Eggplant 178
Stir-Fried Zucchini 185
Zesty Garlic Green Beans 178

SLOW COOKER RECIPES

All-Day Apple Butter 179
Brisket with Cranberry Gravy 76
Carnitas Tacos 92
Cheddar Creamed Corn 173
Cheddar Spirals 183
Chipotle Pomegranate Pulled Pork 69
Cranberry Turkey Breast with Gravy 119
Easy Beans & Potatoes with Bacon 176
Hawaiian Barbecue Beans 166
Java Roast Beef 76
Marmalade Meatballs 39
Minister's Delight 227
Potato Chowder 56
Root Beer Pulled Pork Sandwiches 58

Shredded Turkey Sandwiches 56
Slow-Cooked Ribs 102
Slow-Cooked Swiss Steak 78
Slow Cooker Beef au Jus 75
Slow Cooker Spareribs 94
Southwest Chicken 122
Spicy French Dip 50
Tender Teriyaki Pork 97
Tex-Mex Shredded Beef Sandwiches 66

SOUPS
(also see Condensed Soup)

Asian Shrimp Soup 51
Egg Drop Soup 64
Gumbo in a Jiffy 56
Hot Dog Bean Soup .59 Louisiana-Style Taco
Soup 50
Potato Chowder 56
Quick Clam Chowder 63
Quick Ravioli & Spinach Soup 69
Ramen Broccoli Soup 53
Simple Chicken Soup 57
Simply Elegant Tomato Soup 64
Spicy Pumpkin & Corn Soup 60
Spinach Sausage Soup 54
Springtime Strawberry Soup 50
Turkey Sausage Butternut & Kale Soup . . 62
Vegetable Meatball Soup 66
Wild Rice and Mushroom Soup 67

SPAGHETTI SAUCE

Cheese-Stuffed Meatball Sliders 35
Chicken Tortellini Skillet 109
Easy Stuffed Shells 78
Lasagna Rolls 74
Polenta Parmigiana 44
Ravioli Casserole 146

SPINACH

Creamed Spinach and Mushrooms 186
Flounder Florentine 135
Green 'n' Gold Egg Bake 13
Quick Ravioli & Spinach Soup 69
Sausage & Spinach Calzones 62
Scalloped Shrimp and Potatoes 139
Spinach-Artichoke Rigatoni 145
Spinach Pizza 147
Spinach Sausage Soup 54
Spinach Steak Pinwheels 85
Super Spinach Salad 161
Three-Vegetable Pasta Sauce 147
Tomato Spinach Spirals 143

SQUASH
(see Winter Squash; Zucchini)

STRAWBERRIES

Berry Yogurt Cups 23
Dunked Strawberries 31
Lemon-Berry Ice Cream Pie 216
Nutty Waffle Sandwiches 22
Rhubarb Fool with Strawberries 212
Ruby-Red Strawberry Sauce 208
Springtime Strawberry Soup 50
Strawberry Cake 206
Strawberry-Hazelnut Meringue
Shortcakes 204
Strawberry Lemonade Smoothie 43
Strawberry Pies 208
Strawberry-Rosemary Yogurt Pops 221

SWEET POTATOES

African Chicken & Sweet Potatoes 110
Candied Sweet Potatoes 185
Ham & Sweet Potato Packets 102
Rosemary Sweet Potato Fries 182
Sweet Potato & Bean Quesadillas 146

TOMATOES

Baked Italian Tilapia 138
Balsamic Asiago Salad 158
Balsamic Chicken with Roasted
Tomatoes 108
Black Bean and Beef Tostadas 85
BLT Salad with Pasta 156
Blue Cheese-Stuffed Steaks for Two 82
Broiled Tomatoes with Artichokes 170
Chipotle BLT Wraps 61
Crumb-Coated Tomatoes 183
Easy Black Bean Salsa 39
Fresh Mozzarella Tomato Salad 158
Gumbo in a Jiffy 56
Ham & Sun-Dried Tomato Alfredo 103
Jazzy Mac 'n' Cheese 145
Low-Fat Tangy Tomato Dressing 160
Mediterranean Stuffed Chicken Breasts . 118
Pesto Grilled Cheese Sandwiches 60
Sauteed Corn with Tomatoes & Basil . . . 174
Simple Spanish Rice 170
Simply Elegant Tomato Soup 64
Southern Skillet Chops 101
Spinach Pizza 147
Three-Vegetable Pasta Sauce 147
Tomato & Avocado Sandwiches 58
Tomato Salmon Bake 134
Tomato Spinach Spirals 143
Vegetable Meatball Soup 66

TORTILLAS

Carnitas Tacos 92
Chicken Enchilada Bake 119
Chipotle BLT Wraps 61
Sweet Potato & Bean Quesadillas 146
Turkey & Apricot Wraps 51

TURKEY
(also see Sausage)

Breaded Turkey Slices 116
Cranberry Turkey Breast with Gravy 119
Homemade Italian Turkey Sausage 122

TURKEY
(continued)
Honey-Apple Turkey Breast............. 109
Orange Turkey Croissants 55
Ranch Turkey Pasta Dinner 108
Roasted Turkey with Maple Cranberry
Glaze..................................... 120
Shredded Turkey Sandwiches........... 56
Turkey & Apricot Wraps................. 51
Turkey-Cranberry Bagels 68

VEGETABLES
(also see specific listings)
Baked Italian Tilapia 138
Balsamic Arugula Salad 160
Chicken & Vegetable Kabobs 113
Effortless Egg Rolls 42
Ham & Noodles with Veggies........... 105
Minty Watermelon-Cucumber Salad 155
Simple Chicken Soup 57

Simple Shepherd's Pie 78
Spicy Grilled Eggplant 178
Spicy Pumpkin & Corn Soup............. 60
Tender Barbecued Chicken............. 112

WATERMELON
Banana Split Fruit Salad................. 159
Minty Watermelon-Cucumber Salad 155

WHITE CHOCOLATE
(also see Candy Coating; White Chocolate)
After-Dinner White Chocolate Mocha ... 26
Cappuccino Chip Muffins................. 16
Cranberry Pecan Cookies 232
Dark Chocolate Raspberry Fudge 236
Go Nuts! Coconut Caramels 234
Hawaiian Turtle Cups 235
Magic Wands............................. 243
White Chocolate Brie Cups............. 42
White Chocolate Cereal Bars 245

White Chocolate Mousse Tarts 224

WINTER SQUASH
Honey-Spice Acorn Squash............. 173
New England Butternut Squash........ 181
Turkey Sausage Butternut & Kale Soup .. 62

YOGURT
Apple Yogurt Parfaits.................... 20
Banana Split Fruit Salad................. 159
Berry Yogurt Cups....................... 23
Cherry Yogurt........................... 10
Lime Tartlets 215
Springtime Strawberry Soup........... 50
Strawberry-Rosemary Yogurt Pops 221

ZUCCHINI
Chinese-Style Zucchini.................. 167
Stir-Fried Zucchini....................... 185
Zucchini-Parmesan Bake............... 148

Alphabetical Index

A
African Chicken & Sweet Potatoes...... 110
After-Dinner White Chocolate Mocha ... 26
All-Day Apple Butter..................... 179
Amaretto-Peach Cheese Spread 32
Apple Kuchen Bars 230
Apple Pie a La Mode..................... 225
Apple Sausage Puffs 12
Apple Stuffing........................... 181
Apple Yogurt Parfaits.................... 20
Applesauce-Raspberry Gelatin Mold 153
Arroz con Leche.......................... 207
Artichoke Blue Cheese Fettuccine 142
Asian Shrimp Soup 51
Asparagus Souffle 146

B
Bacon Honey Walleye 138
Bacon-Parmesan Brussels Sprouts...... 180
Bacon Pull-Apart Bread.................. 192
Bacon-Swiss Pork Chops 96
Baked Crab Rangoon 27
Baked Italian Tilapia 138
Baked Parmesan Flounder............... 127
Baked Pork Chops with Apple Slices 90
Balsamic Arugula Salad 160
Balsamic Asiago Salad 158
Balsamic Chicken with Roasted
Tomatoes 108
Balsamic-Glazed Chicken Wings 36
Banana-Chip Mini Cupcakes 205
Banana Chip Pancakes................... 12
Banana Split Fruit Salad................. 159
Basil Parmesan Puffs 200
BBQ & Ranch Chicken Pizza 116

BBQ Hot Dog & Potato Packs 98
Berries with Vanilla Custard............. 210
Berry Berry Lemonade 37
Berry Vinaigrette 153
Berry Yogurt Cups....................... 23
Black Bean and Beef Tostadas 85
BLT Salad with Pasta.................... 156
Blue Cheese-Stuffed Steaks for Two 82
Blueberry Oatmeal 18
Bow Ties with Asparagus and
Prosciutto............................ 93
Breaded Turkey Slices 116
Breakfast Bread Bowls................... 23
Brisket with Cranberry Gravy 76
Broccoli Casserole....................... 169
Broccoli Cheddar Spread 31
Broccoli Saute........................... 165
Broccoli with Asiago..................... 185
Broiled Tomatoes with Artichokes 170
Browned Butter Red Potatoes 172
Burger Americana....................... 64
Busy-Day Bacon Muffins................ 196
Buttermilk Salad Dressing 154
Buttery Grilled Shrimp.................. 132

C
Candied Pecans 37
Candied Sweet Potatoes................. 185
Cappuccino Chip Muffins................. 16
Caramel Apple and Brie Skewers........ 29
Caramel Cashew Clusters............... 241
Caramelized Onion Breadsticks......... 197
Carnitas Tacos........................... 92
Cheddar Broccoli Quiche................. 16
Cheddar Creamed Corn 173
Cheddar-Parm Loaf 195
Cheddar Spirals 183
Cheese Souffles 20
Cheese Straws 32
Cheese-Stuffed Meatball Sliders 35

Cheeseburger Pockets................... 72
Cheesy Bow Tie Chicken................. 121
Cheesy Chili Fries....................... 143
Cherry Marble Cake 211
Cherry Yogurt........................... 10
Chewy Caramel Bars 241
Chicken & Vegetable Kabobs 113
Chicken Caesar Florentine............... 114
Chicken Enchilada Bake................. 119
Chicken Parmesan Patty Melts.......... 54
Chicken Tortellini Skillet 109
Chicken with Shallot Sauce............. 115
Chinese-Style Zucchini.................. 167
Chipotle BLT Wraps 61
Chipotle Pomegranate Pulled Pork...... 69
Chipotle-Raspberry Pork Chops 101
Chive Buttered Carrots.................. 166
Chocolate Biscuit Puffs.................. 192
Chocolate-Covered Bacon............... 26
Chocolate Mint Apple Fondue 44
Chocolate-Nut Caramel Tart............ 209
Chocolate-Orange Scones............... 19
Chocolate Peanut Butter Cake.......... 216
Chocolate Peanut Treats................ 244
Chunky Blue Cheese Dressing 156
Chutney-Topped Brie.................... 30
Coconut Brownies 239
Corned Beef 'n' Cheese Strata 20
County Fair Cherry Pie 205
Cowabunga Root Beer Cupcakes 218
Cranberry-Apricot Pork Tenderloins 100
Cranberry Couscous 180
Cranberry Pecan Cookies................ 232
Cranberry Turkey Breast with Gravy 119
Creamed Spinach and Mushrooms 186
Creamy Herb Spread 171
Creamy Peaches......................... 9
Creole Baked Tilapia 131
Crisp Sweet Pickles...................... 173
Crispy Baked Chicken.................... 112

Crispy Buffalo Chicken Roll-Ups
for Two 121
Crumb-Coated Red Snapper. 130
Crumb-Coated Tomatoes 183
Crunchy Amaretto Peach Cobbler 224
Crunchy Chocolate Mint Balls. 243
Crusty Homemade Bread. 193

D

Dark Chocolate Orange Truffles 243
Dark Chocolate Raspberry Fudge 236
Deep-Fried Cheese Bites 34
Dill and Chive Bread 191
Dilled Peas with Walnuts. 164
Dilled Potatoes with Feta 157
Dreamy S'more Pie 214
Dunked Strawberries 31

E

Easy Beans & Potatoes with Bacon 176
Easy Black Bean Salsa. 39
Easy Caesar Coleslaw. 153
Easy Elephant Ears 216
Easy Skillet Supper 72
Easy Stuffed Shells 78
Easy Yeast Rolls. 201
Effortless Egg Rolls. 42
Egg Drop Soup. 64

F

Fast Beef and Rice. 87
Fiesta Corn Chip Salad. 161
Flounder Florentine 135
Fluffy Biscuit Muffins 22
Foolproof Mushrooms 36
Freezer Raspberry Sauce 171
Fresh Herb Flatbread. 200
Fresh Mozzarella Tomato Salad 158
Fried Chicken Tenders. 116
Frozen Hot Chocolate 222
Fudgy Mint Cookies 238
Fun-on-the-Run Snack Mix. 44

G

Garlic-Chive Baked Fries 168
Garlic Lemon Butter. 187
Garlic-Parmesan Mashed
Cauliflower. 187
Garlic Toast Pizzas. 46
Gingered Snow Peas. 181
Glazed Bacon 18
Glazed Cornish Hens 118
Go Nuts! Coconut Caramels 234
Gold Rush Brownies 233
Golden Pound Cake 213
Greek Deli Kabobs. 40
Greek Grilled Catfish. 130
Greek Lemon Chicken. 117
Green 'n' Gold Egg Bake 13
Green Flop Jell-O. 159
Green Onion Bagel Dip 35
Grilled Brown Sugar-Mustard
Chicken 117
Grilled Flank Steak. 80

Grilled Jerk Chops. 93
Grilled Lobster Tails 128
Grilled PBJ Sandwiches. 63
Grilled Seasoned Bratwurst. 52
Grilled Shrimp with Spicy-Sweet
Sauce 40
Grilled Tuna Steaks 135
Gumbo in a Jiffy. 56

H

Ham & Broccoli Pasta 98
Ham & Noodles with Veggies 105
Ham & Pickle Wraps 47
Ham & Spinach Couscous 96
Ham & Sun-Dried Tomato Alfredo. 103
Ham & Sweet Potato Packets. 102
Ham 'n' Swiss Rolls 16
Ham and Swiss Stromboli 59
Ham with Ruby-Red Glaze 92
Hawaiian Barbecue Beans 166
Hawaiian Turtle Cups 235
Heavenly Angel Food Cake 226
Herbed Potato Packs. 165
Holiday Baked Ham 99
Homemade Guacamole 38
Homemade Italian Turkey Sausage. 122
Honey-Apple Turkey Breast. 109
Honey Cinnamon Milk. 40
Honey-Glazed Spiral Ham 91
Honey Hoisin Chicken & Potatoes 115
Honey Lemon Schnitzel 104
Honey-Spice Acorn Squash. 173
Hot Dog Bean Soup 59
Hot Fudge Sauce 225
Hurry-Up Biscuits 195

I

Ice Cream Kolachkes 245
Ice Cream Sandwich Cake 222
Irish Cream Custards 219
Italian Meatball Buns. 29
Italian-Style Crescents 192

J

Jam 'n' Cream French Toast 10
Java Roast Beef 76
Jazzy Mac 'n' Cheese 145
Jelly Bean Bark 239

K

Kale Salad 152
Kids' Favorite Blueberry Muffins 18
Kielbasa Skillet. 94

L

Lasagna Rolls. 74
Lemon-Berry Ice Cream Pie 216
Lemon Dijon Dressing 154
Lemon Garlic Hummus. 27
Lemon Ladyfinger Dessert. 220
Lemon-Garlic Salmon Steaks 127
Lemony Cooler. 28
Lime-Marinated Fish. 134
Lime Tartlets 215

Loaded Breakfast Potatoes 17
Louisiana-Style Taco Soup 50
Low-Fat Tangy Tomato Dressing. 160
Luscious Lime Slush. 34

M

Magic Wands. 243
Mandarin Pork and Wild Rice 97
Mandarin Trifles 214
Mango Chutney Chicken Curry 123
Maple-Glazed Sausages. 14
Maple-Honey Cranberry Sauce 169
Maple-Peach Glazed Ham. 94
Marinated Chuck Roast. 73
Marinated Pork Medallions 91
Marmalade French Toast Sandwiches. . . . 15
Marmalade Meatballs. 39
Mashed Potato Hot Dish 87
Meal in a Muffin Pan. 9
Mediterranean Orange Salad 158
Mediterranean Stuffed Chicken
Breasts. 118
Mexican Ice Cream 206
Mexican Stuffed Peppers 73
Mini Phyllo Tacos. 30
Minister's Delight. 227
Minty Watermelon-Cucumber Salad 155
Mocha-Fudge Ice Cream Dessert 219
Mom's Italian Bread 190
Mom's Sloppy Tacos. 77
Mom's Tangerine Iced Tea 38
Mozzarella Ham Stromboli. 57
Mozzarella Sticks 31
Mushroom & Peas Rice Pilaf 174
Mushroom Swiss Burgers. 53

N

New England Butternut Squash. 181
No-Fuss Avocado Onion Salad. 161
No-Fuss Chicken 110
Nutter Butter Truffles 234
Nutty Cheese Tortellini 145
Nutty Waffle Sandwiches. 22

O

Oatmeal Molasses Bread 194
Old-Fashioned Brown Bread. 197
Orange Coffee Cake Ring. 201
Orange-Glazed Ham Steaks. 90
Orange-Pecan Salmon. 136
Orange Turkey Croissants 55
Oregano Roasting Chicken 114
Outrageous Peanut Butter Sauce 218

P

Parmesan-Ranch Pan Rolls. 193
Party Pretzels 47
Peach Almond Dessert 209
Peanut Butter Banana Oatmeal 14
Peanut Butter Chocolate Pretzels. 43
Peanut Butter Cup Trifle. 210
Pecan Candy Clusters 233
Pecan Roll-Ups 230
Pecan Sandies Cookies 240

Pepper Jack Meat Loaf 83
Pepper Shooters 34
Peppered Beef Tenderloin 86
Peppered Portobello Penne 143
Peppermint Angel Roll 223
Peppermint Stick Sauce 210
Perfect Dinner Rolls 199
Personal Margherita Pizzas 144
Pesto 184
Pesto Grilled Cheese Sandwiches 60
Pesto Halibut 136
Pesto-Olive Chicken 123
Pesto Portobello Pizzas 149
Pesto Tortellini Salad 159
Pickled Sweet Onions 175
Pigs in a Blanket 67
Pina Colada Fruit Dip 32
Pineapple-Caramel Sponge Cakes 208
Pineapple Ham Steaks 104
Pinwheel Mints 235
Pistachio Baked Salmon 139
Pizza Crescent Bake 77
Poached Pears with Raspberry Sauce . . . 213
Polenta Chili Casserole 144
Polenta Lasagna 142
Polenta Parmigiana 44
Polka-Dot Macaroons 240
Poppy Seed Slaw 154
Pork Chops with Apricot Sauce 105
Potato Chowder 56
Potato Gnocchi 175
Potato Leek Skillet 81
Potato Pan Rolls 195
Pots de Creme 224
Pretzel-Crusted Chicken 109
Prosciutto Breadsticks 194
Pull-Apart Caramel Coffee Cake 8

Q

Quick & Easy Honey Mustard 167
Quick Clam Chowder 63
Quick Ravioli & Spinach Soup 69
Quick Tater Tot Bake 81

R

Ramen Broccoli Soup 53
Ranch Potato Cubes 169
Ranch Turkey Pasta Dinner 108
Raspberry Butter 184
Raspberry Chicken 113
Raspberry Oatmeal Bars 239
Raspberry Swirled Cheesecake Pie 223
Raspberry-Swirled Lemon Milk Shakes . . . 45
Ravioli Carbonara 99
Ravioli Casserole 146
Rhubarb Fool with Strawberries 212
Rhubarb Pear Gelatin 156
Roasted Carrots with Thyme 182
Roasted Cauliflower & Brussels
  Sprouts 164

Roasted Turkey with Maple Cranberry
  Glaze 120
Root Beer Pulled Pork Sandwiches 58
Rosemary Cheddar Muffins 190
Rosemary Pork Tenderloin 103
Rosemary Sweet Potato Fries 182
Ruby-Red Strawberry Sauce 208
Rustic Country Bread 196

S

Sage & Browned Butter Ravioli 149
Salmon with Lemon-Dill Butter 129
Sausage & Spinach Calzones 62
Sausage Cheese Biscuits 10
Sausage Hash Skillet 13
Sauteed Corn with Tomatoes & Basil . . . 174
Sauteed Garlic Mushrooms 176
Save a Penny Casserole 87
Savory Stuffed Figs 47
Scalloped Shrimp and Potatoes 139
Scallops in Sage Cream 126
Scotch Shortbread Cookies 242
Scrambled Egg Poppers 8
Sesame Asparagus 187
Shoofly Cupcakes 211
Shredded Turkey Sandwiches 56
Shrimp Pasta Alfredo 137
Simple Chicken Soup 57
Simple Lettuce Salad 157
Simple Shepherd's Pie 78
Simple Spanish Rice 170
Simply Elegant Tomato Soup 64
Sirloin with Mushroom Sauce 83
Slow-Cooked Ribs 102
Slow-Cooked Swiss Steak 78
Slow Cooker Beef au Jus 75
Slow Cooker Spareribs 94
Smoky Gouda & Chicken Sandwiches 55
S'Moreos 236
Snappy Green Beans 186
Soft Chewy Caramels 233
Sour Cream Blueberry Muffins 198
Southern Skillet Chops 101
Southwest Beef Pie 74
Southwest Chicken 122
Southwest Steak 84
Southwestern Corn Salad 152
Spaetzle Dumplings 168
Spaghetti with Creamy White Clam
  Sauce 132
Spanish Omelets 19
Spicy French Dip 50
Spicy Grilled Eggplant 178
Spicy Meat Loaf 86
Spicy Olive Relish 176
Spicy Pumpkin & Corn Soup 60
Spicy Sausage Patties 17
Spinach-Artichoke Rigatoni 145
Spinach Pizza 147
Spinach Sausage Soup 54

Spinach Steak Pinwheels 85
Springtime Strawberry Soup 50
Stir-Fried Zucchini 185
Strawberry Cake 206
Strawberry-Hazelnut Meringue
  Shortcakes 204
Strawberry Lemonade Smoothie 43
Strawberry Pies 208
Strawberry-Rosemary Yogurt Pops 221
Super Spinach Salad 161
Surprise Spice Cake 220
Sweet & Salty Popcorn 33
Sweet Potato & Bean Quesadillas 146

T

Tarragon Flounder 132
Tasty Maple-Glazed Salmon 133
Tender Barbecued Chicken 112
Tender Teriyaki Pork 97
Teriyaki Mahi Mahi 126
Tex-Mex Pasta 82
Tex-Mex Shredded Beef Sandwiches 66
Thai Barbecued Salmon 131
Thai Shrimp Pasta 129
Three-Vegetable Pasta Sauce 147
Toffee Candy 232
Toffee Cream Pie 227
Toffee Meringue Drops 242
Tomato & Avocado Sandwiches 58
Tomato Salmon Bake 134
Tomato Spinach Spirals 143
Tropical Rainbow Dessert 215
Tumbleweeds 236
Tuna Alfredo 133
Turkey & Apricot Wraps 51
Turkey-Cranberry Bagels 68
Turkey Sausage Butternut & Kale Soup . . 62

V

Vegetable Meatball Soup 66
Veggie Beef Patties 81
Virginia Box Bread 199

W

Walnut Brownies 234
Weekend Breakfast Bake 14
White Chocolate Brie Cups 42
White Chocolate Cereal Bars 245
White Chocolate Mousse Tarts 224
Wild Rice and Mushroom Soup 67

Y

Yummy Cracker Snacks 231

Z

Zesty Chicken Soft Tacos 111
Zesty Garlic Green Beans 178
Zucchini-Parmesan Bake 148